MW00331430

CONFESSIONS OF A
PHANTOM
PILOT

CONFESSIONS OF A
PHANTOM PILOT

MEMORIES OF FLYING THE PHANTOM FGR2

TUG WILSON

FONTHILL

Fonthill Media Language Policy

Fonthill Media publishes in the international English language market. One language edition is published worldwide. As there are minor differences in spelling and presentation, especially with regard to American English and British English, a policy is necessary to define which form of English to use. The Fonthill Policy is to use the form of English native to the author. Tug Wilson was born and educated in Thirsk, North Yorkshire; therefore, British English has been adopted in this publication.

Fonthill Media Limited
Fonthill Media LLC
www.fonthillmedia.com
office@fonthillmedia.com

First published in the United Kingdom and the United States of America 2021
Reprinted 2022

British Library Cataloguing in Publication Data:
A catalogue record for this book is available from the British Library

ISBN 978-1-78155-850-8

Typeset in 10.5pt on 13pt Sabon
Printed and bound in England

Contents

92 Squadron Battle Flight, RAF Wildenrath, West Germany (22 April 1990)

Scramble!

I pulled on my flying helmet just as the scramble message came through.

'Mike-Lima 72. Vector 090. Angels 30. Gate. Two high fast flyers inbound. Scramble, scramble, scramble. Acknowledge!'

'72 Scrambling!' called my navigator and I knew this was it—not a practice—this was my first live Battle Flight scramble, and I was bricking it!

About two minutes earlier, I had been fast asleep on one of the sofas in the battle flight 'shed', which was a couple of Portakabins next to the hardened aircraft shelter (HAS) housing my Phantom FGR2. The 'hooter', which was just above my head, had gone off and I went from fast asleep to supersonic in a heartbeat. I ran out of the shed to see the HAS doors opening automatically and was dimly aware of the three ground crew bursting out of the other door beside me. I scooped up my life jacket, which was standing up on the floor just inside the big HAS doors, and flung it on just as I reached the steps to the aircraft. Having jumped up into the cockpit, I plugged my life jacket into the connector on the left side of my ejection seat for oxygen and communications and then pulled my helmet on. As soon as the comms cord from my helmet was connected, I heard the scramble message and all hell broke loose.

I could hear the Houchin external power cart start up, providing external AC power so I could start the jet, and my hands were a blur as they flicked around switches and throttles to bring the lumbering bastard of a jet to life. I remembered to hold the generator switches on as the Houchin was disconnected by the ground crew (they had a tendency to flick off and abort the start sequence), and then I am pretty sure I had an out of body experience. I pictured myself strapping in as the engines wound up, giving hand signals to the ground crew. My heart was pounding the inside of my chest, straining against the life jacket. I was a force of nature—a beam of pure light—and I was really living for the first time in my life. How dare those Russian bastards threaten to violate our airspace? Well not today! You've got me to contend with and I am mightily pissed off!

In no time at all, we were taxiing out of the HAS. The Houchin was disconnected and the safety pins were removed from our weapons, canopies down, ejection seat pins and canopy pin out. Flaps went to take-off setting, and afterburners came in as soon as we entered the runway. Airborne in an instant, we were ready to fight. Our wheels-off time was given later as two minutes forty-three seconds from the hooter going off—cool!

The keyword in the scramble message was 'Gate'. This means we were cleared to go supersonic. So, there we were at 28,000 feet going about 1.2 Mach somewhere near Düsseldorf with a moment to catch our breath. At about this point, my nav said, 'Something feels a bit weird, Tug'. I was glad he mentioned it because I was feeling a bit odd myself. I looked around the cockpit and saw that we were not pressurised. I had forgotten to put the vent knob in. The vent knob was a long stick coming out of the left-hand console with a flat button about the size of a £2 coin on the top. When the canopies were down, I was supposed to push it in to pressurise the cockpit. In the melee of the scramble, I had forgotten.

Unfortunately, you cannot ease it in, so I warned my nav and then slammed it home. We instantly pressurised to about 8,000 feet, which pushed our eardrums so far back into our heads they almost met in the middle. My nav felt better and got down to searching for the targets on the radar, but I felt a bit worse. As I shook my fuzzy head, I noticed that my oxygen mask was not connected to my life jacket. Basically, I had climbed to the top of Everest (in only a couple of minutes) without any oxygen and was going hypoxic. So, I connected that up with a shake of my head and got down to business.

I would like to say we got them on the radar, threatened them over the radio, and they turned for home, but that would be bullshit. They had approached the inner German border and then turned for home before we even got there—just checking our reaction times as usual. I didn't care though. I was no longer a Battle Flight virgin. I was finally a real fighter pilot, after years of training and practice. This was what I dreamed of as a kid.

Actually, I dreamed of being an astronaut. My earliest memory is watching Neil Armstrong walk on the moon on a small black and white television with my parents and older brother. When anyone asked me what I wanted to be when I grew up, I would say, 'I want to be an astronaut'. However, I grew up in North Yorkshire in the 1970s, where the astronaut programme was fairly thin on the ground. After a brief flirtation with wanting to be a vet (James Herriot, the famous author, was our town vet), until I discovered you had to get arms deep in a cow's arse, I decided on the closest thing to space travel that I could get—flying fighters in the Royal Air Force—and in that aircraft, I was living that dream.

With no targets to shoot at, we patrolled up and down the border for half an hour, looking hard, with all the Russian radars in East Germany sniffing at us, then made our way back to Wildenrath. I was absolutely elated when we landed. As we taxied in though, I was brought back to earth with a bump. Once we were clear of the runway, we put our seat and canopy safety pins back in and popped the canopies up. It was an unwritten rule that fighter pilots taxied with the canopy up, even if it was pissing down outside. Nothing was to get in the way of looking cool—trust me on that.

Anyway, as I unstrapped from my ejection seat, I found that my right-hand shoulder strap had not been connected into the QRF (quick release fitting—think of a four-point harness used in a racing car, except this has five points as it includes a negative 'G' strap at the bottom). If I had ejected on this trip, I would have fallen out of my harness. Do you know what? In those ninety minutes, I had never lived as much in my life before. I had also never turned in such piss poor performance on safety-critical checks, either before or since. What a buzz though!

228 Phantom Operational Conversion Unit, RAF Leuchars, Scotland (3 April 1989)

This Aeroplane Is Trying to Kill Me!

My love affair with the Phantom did not start well. The first take-off scared the living shit out of me as I was pretty convinced the jet was trying to kill me. The way you got the Phantom airborne was to hold it on the brakes and power up the engines to 80 per cent (the brakes couldn't hold any more power than that) then release the brakes with the stick hard back in your guts. As you start to roll, push the throttles forward to full dry power against the stop (no afterburner yet—this is called mil power). Then you 'rock the throttles outboard', which lights the burner, and push them up to the end of their range of travel. You now have full afterburner and you are really accelerating following a kick in your arse from the extra thrust. As the end of the runway approaches at an alarming rate, the jet decides it might as well get airborne after all and lurches into the sky. You then have to check forwards on the stick to hold the aircraft at 10 degrees nose up, to gracefully climb away as you raise the landing gear and flaps.

It all sounds easy when I look back on it. However, at the time, I was twenty-three years old and still didn't know my arse from my elbow when it came to 'proper' flying. Sure, I had my RAF wings and was on the last stage of a comprehensive three-year flying training programme, but this was something else. I had flown the Chipmunk, the Jet Provost, and the Hawk. I had even dropped practice bombs and shot a gun in the Hawk, but none of these aircraft were trying to kill me, I think. This one, though, felt different.

First off, when I climbed into it, I thought the steps were never going to end—I've never seen a jet so tall. I was almost on oxygen by the time I made it into the cockpit. Then the noise! Starting the APU and the engines filled the air with a brutal ear-piercing roar. I couldn't believe I was actually in charge of it all (up to a point, that is). Then the take-off almost did me in. The kick from the burner was a shock, but watching the instrument panel rattle up and down all the way down the runway made me think it hadn't been bolted in properly. I could barely read anything that the instruments were trying to tell me.

Also, the instructors casually used to say that once you were airborne, if you didn't check forwards to that 10 degrees nose up, the jet would flip onto its back, crash into the ground and kill you. Apparently, when the first Phantom was delivered, the crew suffered a double hydraulic failure in the powered controls and the stabilator stuck in the stick hard back position, basically looping the aircraft onto the ground after take-off. This was all on my mind during my first trip, and we haven't even spoken about flying circuits and landing yet.

Once we were airborne and not dead, I calmed down a bit. We have a couple of phrases in aviation that are apt here. The first is 'maxed out'. This is where we are working at the very limits of our mental capacity or sometimes beyond. The second phrase is 'being behind the aircraft'. It is a similar thing in that we are not able to think ahead of the aircraft and have become purely reactive rather than proactive—in essence, we are just along for the ride. I will be honest with you and say that as we climbed away on that first trip, I was so maxed out, I was barely hanging on to the tailplane by my fingertips. It was absolutely exhilarating though.

Looking out of the top of the canopy into the bright blue was almost a euphoric moment. For the past year and a bit, I had been flying the Hawk trainer and my view out of the top of the canopy had been obscured by a zigzag of miniature detonating cord (MDC). If I were to eject from a Hawk, the MDC would explode and shatter the canopy so the ejection seat could rise gracefully through it without too much damage to the pilot. On ejection in a Phantom, the canopy is completely blown off behind the aircraft before the seats rise out of the cockpit, so there is no need for MDC and my view is unobstructed. The view of the clouds and the sky was just beautiful. It was these simple pleasures—a moment of pure gold—that convince you that you truly love flying. These golden moments can be few and far between in the high-speed, sweaty, hyperventilating environment of flying training, so they are to be treasured.

Enough of that, though. It is back to business as I had a lot to learn on this and every other trip. I was flying with Coops, who was one of the flight commanders on the squadron and a qualified flying instructor (QFI). He was a nice older chap who smoked a pipe—a bit old school. He seemed nice enough on the ground but transformed into a bit of a bastard in the air. I was to find out this happened a lot with instructors on the OCU.

So, Coops started teaching me how to handle the F4. We looked at a few aerobatics, use of afterburner, energy management, and stalling. This bit was in preparation for teaching me how to fly a circuit and land later on in the trip. I still had very little clue as to what I was doing, but trying my best nonetheless. This was what happened at the start of any flying training course—you are unfamiliar with a lot of what is happening; the learning curve is horrifically steep; there is a very uncomfortable feeling with lots of stress; and you feel like you are playing catch up the whole time, not to mention the constant threat of the 'chop'. The chop was the thing we most dreaded—the end of our dream—suspension from fast jet training. Sounds miserable, doesn't it? See why the golden moments are so important to us now?

What Can You See? My Face

All too quickly, we were out of gas and it was time to go home and have a go at landing. As I turned for Leuchars, Coops was trying to demonstrate something on the radar. He was 'painting' a picture of the Scottish coastline on the scope to show how the radar could be used as a navigation aid as well as for its primary task of finding enemy aircraft. At the top of the instrument panel, there was a repeater scope with a round glass screen right in front of my eyes. It showed the picture that the back-seater has on his radar scope, and in the future, I would need that picture to be able to fire my weapons effectively.

Now, the radar only began transmitting once we were airborne. This was a safety feature as we did not want it to irradiate on the ground as it would be harmful to our ground crew. Therefore, there was a weight-off wheels microswitch in the landing gear that signalled to the radar when we were airborne and it could switch on. In order to see the picture in the front, I had to push the 'Op/Erase' button just to the right of my scope to bring my picture to life. This was one of the after take-off checks that I forgot, of course, because I was so maxed-out by the take-off.

Coops was obviously pleased with himself that he had managed to paint the coastline (he was a pilot remember and not a navigator so not used to using the radar), and he told me to look into my scope and tell him what I saw. Without thinking, I just said, 'My face,' because it was just a piece of glass. This was one of those moments where I instantly knew I had made a dick of myself. 'Push the Op/Erase button you idiot!' he helpfully replied.

'Ah, okay,' and I pushed the button. There now followed two minutes of uncomfortable silence as my scope warmed up and the picture came alive. I told him I could see the coastline of Fife, but I knew the moment for Coops had passed and we were setting up for the recovery.

Coops took control of the aircraft using the stick and throttles in the back. Dual check rides like this were conducted in a twin-stick aeroplane. The rear cockpit could be configured to take a control column and a pair of throttles so QFIs could demonstrate various manoeuvres. Although Coops had control, he asked me to 'follow him through' on the flying controls. This is a teaching technique flying instructors use to give student pilots the feel of what is happening on the controls as they demonstrate a flying technique. The instructor flies the aircraft from the back and the student lightly holds the throttles and control column as it happens. By the way, in my experience, 'follow me through' is generally a waste of time.

We broke into the circuit at about 3–4G in order to scrub off speed and rolled out on the downwind heading. Set the power at about 87 per cent on each engine and let the speed settle. Coops called 'Downwind to roll' to Air Traffic Control (ATC) and we went through our pre-landing checks. As the landing gear went down, the hydraulic utilities caption lit up on the emergency warning panel and I had to cancel the flashing attention-getter light on the right console just below the panel. This meant changing hands on the stick so that I could use my right hand to push the button. Once I put the flaps to half, there was another hydraulic caption with the attention-getter and some sort of bleed air caption that needs cancelling also. Crikey—it looked like the whole thing was falling to pieces!

We got to the end of downwind and Coops called 'Finals gear down'. ATC cleared us to roll, and Coops taught me how to fly around the final turn. He directed my eyes to the angle of attack (AOA) gauge just to the left of my repeater scope. AOA is the angle of the airflow to the chord line of the wing (think leading edge for ease). Without going into basic aerodynamics here, it is the reference we use to fly fast jet aircraft. The slower you are, the higher the AOA required to generate the lift you need to keep you airborne. If you have too much AOA, and it keeps increasing, the airflow will disconnect from the upper surface of the wing, and the usual sequence of events is flick, stall, spin, crash, burn, die—another amusing saying the instructors used.

The AOA we use to fly around finals in the Phantom is 19.2 units. These units are an arbitrary figure but are indicated on the AOA gauge and also by some helpful indicator lights up on the right canopy strut in front of me. There was a circle called the doughnut that lit up if you were at the correct 'on speed'. Below it was an inverted V telling you that you were not pulling enough units if it lit up and were therefore too fast. More worrying was the V on top of the doughnut. If this was lit, it meant you had too much AOA and were therefore too slow—keep pulling here, and flick, stall, spin, crash, burn, die.

Of course, Coops' circuit was right on the doughnut, maybe with a bit of lower V lit from time to time, and he gracefully put the jet down on the numbers at the start of the runway, just beyond the piano keys, before pushing the throttles to full mil power to get us airborne again. Gear up, flaps up, and it was my go. I rolled us out downwind and Coops pointed out that I was 100 feet low on rollout. I mentally patted myself on the back that this was a good day for me if I was only 100 feet away from the circuit height, but I thought Coops expected more from me, so I sorted it out. Into the routine of the call to ATC, the pre-landers and the full flap were down as I turned finals, cancelling the cautions throughout it all. My final turn was an ugly fight between the doughnut and the Vs as well as the picture outside and involved me sawing the throttles back and forth until Coops coached me into 'walking the throttles' gently back and forth, one at a time, so my left hand made a little zigzagging motion that smoothed out my speed control. I say he coached me.

'Stop sawing the bloody throttles and walk them like I told you to in the brief!' he shouted in the cockpit. It seemed to work, and I did two more circuits that didn't kill us, and I landed off the second one. As soon as we landed, I pulled the drag chute handle, and a parachute deployed from the rear of the jet just above the jet pipes. We came down to a slow taxi speed. I released the chute as we left the runway and taxied back to the line. I was desperately trying to remember the shutdown checks, but my brain had turned to mush. However, I needn't have worried, as there was plenty of time to recall them while Coops zeroed the inertial navigation system (the INAS) back to the latitude and longitude of our parking slot. It was so inaccurate that it had buggered off to China in the hour and a half we had been airborne, and it took Coops ages to bring it back, as I stumbled through the shutdown.

I felt so maxed out; my head was still airborne somewhere over the North Sea, still trying to catch up with the aeroplane. Despite all of that, my feet hit the tarmac at the bottom of the steps and I couldn't stop smiling. Coops looked as miserable as he did when he climbed in the jet, but I guess he had seen it all before. I had now flown the Phantom and they would never be able to take that away from me. However, there was still the debrief to get through.

Ah yes—debriefing. Just when you thought the trip was over, you had to sit through/survive the instructor debriefing you. Now, the holy trinity of military aviation is planning, briefing, and debriefing. We do all three of these things for every trip that we fly. The most important of these is debriefing as this is where we do most of our learning. A lot of the time in the air, we are too maxed out to take in exactly what is going on, so we use the debrief to reconstruct the sortie and bring out the learning points. This then helps us to put right any mistakes we have made on future trips that we fly. The further through flying training I got, the more adversarial the debriefing seemed to become, with students actually failing trips sometimes purely on their performance in the debrief.

You could also pass a poor trip with a good account of yourself in the debrief, but that was usually harder than splitting the atom. The basic approach to debriefing in those days was that if you did something right, then that was your bloody job so we didn't mention it. If you did something wrong though, they would flay the skin from your back until you got it right. I exaggerate a bit here of course, but it wasn't a million miles away, believe me.

Debriefing on the OCU was tough, but nowhere near as bad as the previous flying training school we had been through prior to Leuchars. The tactical weapons unit (TWU) school at RAF Chivenor can only be described as a bloodbath. Tac Weapons was supposed to take newly qualified pilots and turn them into tactical pilots. We had gained our RAF wings flying the Hawk in the supportive school at RAF Valley and were posted to Chivenor where they would teach us how to fight in the Hawk. Air combat, live strafing and bombing, simulated attack profiles were all extremely demanding exercises in their own right. They were made harder by the brutal debriefing sessions afterwards, given by the instructors, and in particular the qualified weapons instructors (QWIs). On the whole, these guys were utter bastards. 'Why instruct when you can destruct?' must have been their motto. I bloody hate QWIs.

I remember our arrival brief by the Boss of the squadron. 'Right you lot. You've got your wings so sort it out! We don't spoon feed you here. In fact, the fire hose is on. Get with the programme or fuck off and fly Hercules or some shit like that! Welcome to Chivenor!' They chopped six out of eight guys on the course behind us before they were halfway through the programme—like I said, utter bastards and some of the worst instruction I have ever had. The idea was obviously to put us through the 'hard school' they had been through because that would make men out of us. It was like a survival course for us students, so whatever they threw at us at Leuchars, it was nothing compared to what we had just seen. Anyway, I survived the debrief with Coops and went for a celebratory beer with my coursemates in the officers' mess bar.

There were eleven of us on the course, and we were a bit of a wide mix—four *ab initio* pilots including me, two *ab initio* navigators, three retreads (previous F4 experience coming back to the jet after ground tours), one of whom was a pilot, and one nav who were going back to the front line as flight commanders. The other pilot was a wing commander and was going to be OC Ops Wing at RAF Wattisham in Suffolk. We also had a Jaguar pilot who was going on an exchange tour to fly Recce Phantoms with the German Air Force, and a German Air Force nav who was coming on exchange with the RAF.

The baby pilots were me, Ivan, Joel, and Willy. I had been on the previous course at Chivenor with Ivan, but nearly every course through training with Willy (so-called because he was a bit of a knob). The baby navs were Andy and Les. OC Ops was a wing commander and the future flight commanders were both squadron leader rank so 'Sir' to me. We didn't really have much to do with the Jag guy, and the German was *Hauptman* Odo Larger. Odo was absolutely brilliant and turned out to be a huge help to us new guys on the course with all his previous experience.

Every course in flying training begins with the traditional 'meet and greet'. This should mean that all the instructors and students get together in the bar after work one day early in the course and get to know each other over a couple of barrels of beer. Well, that was the theory anyway. What usually happened was that all the instructor staff stayed on one side of the room and talked to each other, with all the students on the other side—a bit like the worst school disco you ever went to. The staff didn't really want to be there as they all had families to go home to and the students didn't want to talk to the staff as we were worried we would make fools of ourselves or come across as too cocky. It is a well-known fact that you can't pass the course at the meet and greet, but you can go a bloody long way to failing it by making the wrong impression. The stakes are high!

Eventually, a couple of the staff come over to break the ice. These were the guys who proved themselves to be the most likeable throughout the course and I was lucky enough to fly a fair bit with them. That then led to a general mixing between students and instructors, and the beer began to flow to lubricate the chat. We were happy to drink away as we were in ground school so no flying for a while.

Towards the end of the meet and greet, I was standing with Ivan and we saw the Boss coming towards us. This is one of those defining moments when you meet the Boss for the first time. Both of us stood a little straighter as he came over. We had only heard good things about him. The previous Phantom instructors at Tac Weapons couldn't tell us enough about what a great man he was, and it seemed that the staff loved him. He made a little strained small talk and some awful banter that Ivan and I laughed at rather too loudly, fuelled by the beer and our desperate need to be accepted.

As we got into it though, I had this nagging feeling that the Boss was a bit of a cock. I thought it must be my mistake as he had a great reputation, but with every word and phrase, it just became a bit more uncomfortable. While I was wrestling with this mentally, out of nowhere, while we were forcing our laughter out again, Ivan just let go of his pint of lager. I watched in slow motion as his glass fell. He had a look of horror on his face, but he was still forcing out a laugh at the Boss's latest terrible joke. The glass crashed on the floor, shattered, and splattered beer all over the Boss's suede brogues. There was a moment of silence as everyone looked over at us. Then the Boss looked Ivan straight in the eyes and said, 'That is a criminal waste of beer young man,' and strode off.

'What the hell are you doing Ivan?!' I hissed.

'Shit! I am chopped!' he said.

'Yeah—and me too!' I replied.

We cleaned up the glass and had a final beer for Ivan to cry into before turning in for the night. Chatting to our fellow students, it was apparent that everyone had thought the same thing about the Boss as me. However, they hadn't spilled beer on his nice shoes, so I figured Ivan and I were worst placed with him. Right then, I had no idea how poorly placed we were.

Ground School and Stuff

Our lives settled down into about three to four weeks' worth of technical lectures and simulator sorties. My usual approach to ground school was the same as the majority of students—learn, exam, dump, and go flying. There just seemed to be so much to learn on previous aircraft we had flown, such as the Hawk and the Jet Provost, but this was on another scale. I really did try my best to absorb all of the tech on the Phantom, but it was mostly beyond me. Engines now had afterburners; three or four hydraulic systems; AC and DC electrics; weapons systems; fuel system; primary and secondary flying controls; the radar; and boundary layer control. As soon as I heard in flying controls about the 'walking beam bell crank', I was completely lost. The only shining light was that most of my course mates were equally flummoxed, so we came to the conclusion that this jet was held up by magic, or something like that.

So, we took all of our lack of knowledge and tried to apply it in the simulator. The simulators were run by a mix of older and very experienced staff pilots and navigators that were towards the end of their careers, but still flying on the OCU. They were bolstered by a couple of younger guys who were being punished for a bit of flying indiscipline involving getting caught doing a very low unauthorised flypast over Broughty Ferry. This only made them cooler in our eyes of course! All of the sim guys were brilliant. They took us from zero knowledge and limited ability, moulding us into a group who just about knew their arses from their elbows—just enough not to kill ourselves on the first few trips.

The first sim rides were predominantly teaching all of the checks and procedures to help us get the aircraft started, airborne, guff around the sky for a bit, and then land from an instrument approach. The sim had no visuals so was pretty much an instrument trainer for the pilots. It looked real enough from the outside though and the cockpit was just like the aircraft. While us baby pilots practised all our checks including pre-start, post-start, pre-take-off, post-take-off, recovery, pre-landing, post-landing, and shut down, the baby navs got to grips with the nav kit (INAS), radar, and various challenge and response checks. This was the first time the pilots had worked together with someone else in the cockpit as our whole flying training programme up to then had been geared around us doing everything for ourselves (with greater or lesser success).

The whole thing was to get to the end of Tac Weapons with a 'single-seat recommendation'. This meant you were good enough to fly a single-seat aircraft such as the Harrier or Jaguar. These were both ground attack aircraft and I wanted to fly a fighter. Our only single-seat fighter was the Lightning (shit-hot fast rocket ship), but they stopped taking students to it about four months before I left Tac Weapons. Therefore, the only fighters were the Phantom and the Tornado F3.

The Tornado fighter was a sack of shit with a rubbish radar in those days, and the Phantom was a hero's aeroplane—it was no contest really. Oh, and I was fortunate enough to be quite average through training so was never going to worry the single-seat world—lucky me! So, with all of that, I settled in to letting the navs do all the radar work, help with navigation, and do all the admin stuff that seems trivial until you try and do it all yourself one day and truly appreciate the value of flying with another professional. With the nav picking up all that workload I could then relax in the front. Yeah, right! Even in the sim, I would sweat buckets. The Phantom was a nightmare for a young pilot to get to grips with, and of course, a few of the staff used it as an instrument of torture. Yet, despite how difficult the course was, and how tricky the jet was to fly, I was absolutely smitten by it.

My First Love

It was nothing to look at mind you. They do say you should always go out with an ugly girl then no one else will steal her away from you. I am absolutely sure girls say the same about guys, and boy was the Phantom ugly! There is a legendary story about the US Air Force asking

McDonnel Douglas if they had delivered it upside down due to the anhedral tail and its overall odd shape. It was bulky too. The RAF even put bigger Rolls-Royce Spey engines in the aeroplane, which bowed out the fuselage, giving you the impression she had let herself go a bit. They were all filthy with oil and soot stains, particularly around the jet pipes. It was the sort of aircraft where you felt unclean just sitting in it. Then there was the big black arm with a hook on it under the rear end—half a ton of metal to take a cable on a carrier or at an airfield if you had some sort of emergency. Being a carrier aircraft, it had a really chunky undercarriage that should withstand even the heaviest of student landings—handy given how shit we were. Even with that though, the Phantom that was the gate guard, just inside the main gate at Leuchars had been the victim of a heavy landing, so obviously, it wasn't indestructible.

The cockpit wasn't any prettier either. It was functional and manly—not a sniff of any digital glass displays, just old school steam-driven instruments and controls with very little thought given to ergonomic cockpit design. Cockpits these days are designed from the pilot outwards, delivering data in easily digestible formats. This helps the pilot build a picture of what is going on in the world. I got the impression when the first Phantoms rolled off the production line in St Louis, the McDonnel Douglas guys patted themselves on the back that they had built a world-beater—ugly bastard, but a world-beater nonetheless. Then, somebody spoiled the party by looking in the cockpit and announcing, 'Guys! We forgot to put stuff in it!' They then must have superglued the cockpit and thrown in a bag of random instruments and kit into it—so much for cockpit design! Hence, I spent the first few sims just trying to work out where the hell everything was. Funny thing though, it didn't matter. None of it mattered. Just about everyone that I knew who flew the Phantom loved it. I still do.

Once it dragged its sorry arse airborne (generally with full afterburner and most of the runway), it was beautiful. Walking back to the mess after work in the dark and seeing the jet get airborne over my head—two blue flame trails roaring—actually gave me goosebumps. I was so lucky to be in this position, even with all the drama we were going through in flying training. Late at night in the mess, we would regularly hear the roar as a Phantom got airborne, followed by a station tannoy that said, 'Northern QRA has been launched on an operational mission'. I was beside myself when I heard that. To think that in about six months to a year that could be me sitting on quick reaction alert and getting launched to intercept a Russian Bear was an awesome thought. I had a lot more sorties and test rides to get through before I got to a front-line squadron though.

Supersonic

The next few flying trips came thick and fast and were interspersed with further technical and operational briefings. One of them was the air-to-air refuelling (AAR) brief and was given by a tanker navigator from the RAF Brize Norton Tristar squadron. He wandered in carrying about 6 feet of heavy-duty fuel hose, a refuelling basket, and the end of a refuelling probe that looked disturbingly like a steel cock. With those props, he couldn't fail and it looked like this was going to be the most interesting brief in ground school—unfortunately not. He took four and a half hours to tell us how to 'crash' our Phantom into the basket and then allow highly volatile liquid to be pumped at high pressure through the probe into the aircraft.

The man had a gift for sucking the interest out of a subject and the enthusiasm out of his audience, and by the time he pushed the steel cock into the basket, none of us could muster the effort to make even the cheapest and easiest of jokes. About an hour in, he had lost us. That, allied with the fact that AAR was not something we did as students on the OCU (it was taught on the squadron), meant we took no notice of him at all. As usual, this was going to catch me out later on—you would think I would have learnt these lessons by then, but alas, no.

My next two trips were with a kindly soul called Gibby. It was a bit like flying with your Dad, which was a welcome change from Coops. Our first trip together included going supersonic and finished by engaging the approach end cable on the runway (a bit like a carrier landing). We blasted airborne out of Leuchars and pressed far enough out over the sea so that our sonic boom didn't blow out any windows back on land. I rocked the throttles outboard and pushed over into a gentle dive. I was channelling a bit of Chuck Yeager, and expecting everything to rattle and shake—maybe even a couple of the instrument glasses would shatter as we went through the Mach? The next thing I know, none of this has happened, and we are supersonic.

Lots of people describe their first experience of going supersonic as being a bit disappointing—just a number on the dial, etc. Not me though—I was going utterly crazy in the cockpit, I was so excited. Poor Gibby must have thought he was flying with a lunatic, but he took it well, while I whooped my way around the sky. He was able to calm me down enough at the end of the trip to get me back to Leuchars for a few circuits before we took the cable.

Each fast jet airfield and suitable military diversion airfield had cables strung across each end of the runway a few hundred feet past the threshold. There were a couple of different types around the bazaars, but Leuchars had the standard RHAG (rotary hydraulic arrestor gear). We called on the radio for the approach end cable to be rigged for us. Normally, it would lay flat on the runway so it could be trampled easily, so had to be raised on lots of rubber grommets so that the hook could capture it. The overrun end cable was always rigged in case of an aborted take-off. Once the approach end was ready, I went through the pre-landers with Gibby and lowered the gear, flap, and, for the first time, the hook. Gibby got me to tighten my straps and we set up on finals to take the cable. I felt the hook thunk a bit as it hit the ground before us and we rolled over the cable. Nothing seemed to happen, then I was thrown forwards in my seat as the cable stopped us from about 160 knots to zero in not very many feet (the exact figures were taught in ground school, but learn, exam, dump...).

As soon as we stopped, I applied power to stretch the cable out and then back to idle to let it drag us backwards. It was an odd feeling going backwards in an aircraft I can tell you, but it meant that the hook came out of the cable and we could raise it up again on a signal from the ground crew who were there in anticipation of our cable engagement. After that, we gracefully taxied away and another big event was ticked off on my 'must do list for flying fighters'. The debrief with Gibby was a breeze, and I was pleased to see he was taking me up again the next day. The plan on the next trip was to shut one of the engines down and show how easy it is to relight again in flight following a flameout. I wasn't sure this was such a good idea (having only flown single-engined aircraft before) but Gibby convinced me it would be okay.

It was an odd feeling taking the right-hand throttle off in the air and seeing the RPM go below flight idle, but Gibby was sure it was okay. We got out our flight reference cards (FRCs), and he took me through the relighting drill—of course, it didn't work. So, we tried again and it still wouldn't relight. 'Ok we'll try it once more Tug and then take it back if it doesn't come up'. He was a cool as a cucumber while I was muttering about what a stupid idea it was to turn the engine off in the first place. It finally relit the third time, which pleased Gibby no end, but did nothing for my confidence, I can tell you. We finished the trip with a practice diversion to Edinburgh airport as that was our closest and usual diversion airfield, and then back on deck at Leuchars. All told, I was feeling a bit more comfortable with the jet and was gaining a little bit of confidence.

First Solo

Next up was my pre-solo check with Coops. After this trip, if all went well, I would be flying with one of the staff navigators in the back—a huge responsibility given that I would have the grand total of six hours in the jet. I can't imagine what the staff navs were thinking as they climbed into the cockpit behind someone like me on that 'solo' ride—no wonder most of them insisted on doing this trip in a twin-sticker (stick and throttles in the back).

I don't mind admitting I was bricking it as I walked out with my very first navigator to the aeroplane. Uncle Tony was one of the best-liked navs on the squadron, and I was lucky to have him in the boot for this important trip. He was just what I needed—nice, relaxed, and obviously enjoying the mere act of going flying. We went supersonic (without me whooping this time) then I flew some ropey looking aerobatics, which Uncle Tony tolerated with a grace that defied belief and made me like him even more.

But then it was down to the serious stuff. Back to Leuchars for the dreaded circuits and practice landings. I threw away the first circuit as I didn't get the pull on soon enough round finals and flew through the centreline. If Uncle Tony was worried, he didn't show it. In fact, he must have sensed my disappointment as he said with a chuckle. 'Nice try Tug, we almost got in off that one'. Just enough banter to lighten the mood followed by a bit of advice. 'Next time all you need to do is pull it straight to 19 units and you've got it cracked'. That is just what I did on the next few circuits, finally culminating in a relatively smooth landing. After shutting down, Uncle Tony shook my hand and said, 'Well done Tug. Nice and smooth'. I felt 10 feet tall. Ivan, Joel, and Willy all did their first solos on the same day, so it was definitely time for a celebratory beer or two.

Mess Life

The officers' mess at Leuchars was a nice mix of traditional and modern. A new block had been built on the side, with the most up-to-date rooms and shower/toilet blocks I had ever seen in the RAF. My room was clean and functional with nice smart built-in wardrobes and a sink unit. A single bed, desk, and chair were pretty much all I needed. Traditional came in the form of the usual mess public rooms in the main structure such as anterooms, dining rooms, and bars. All RAF messes were built on the same design way back, such that you should have been able to fly into any airbase, warn in (check in to the mess), and feel right at home due to its familiar layout.

Leuchars had two bars—the main one and the 'Scruff's Bar'. Basically, you could wear uniform or flying suits in the main bar up to 6 p.m. (except on Fridays, when happy hour started). Then you had to de-camp to the Scruff's or go and change into jacket and tie. The irony was that the Scruff's at Leuchars was way smarter and modern than the main bar. Other Scruff's bars that I had been in were little more than broom cupboards with a serving hatch to the bar.

We didn't care where we drank though. We were proper Phantom pilots now—well at least up until the next trip where we could fail and be chopped. We had lived our whole lives in flying training with the threat and fear of the chop hanging over our heads. The general feeling was that the further you got and the closer to the front line, the lower the chance of the chop as they had already weeded out most of those that weren't going to make it. They had also spent a shitload of cash on us by this stage, so surely it made no sense to chop us now? Pity those bastards at Chivenor hadn't had the brief. That night then, we upheld the age-old tradition of celebrating our minor success with major amounts of alcohol, then retired hurt early doors. Solo in a Phantom—they can't take that away from me whatever happened next.

We had a couple more trips to get through that week before our first weekend on the town as Phantom drivers. My next sortie was with the loveliest guy on the squadron, Cliff Parsley, who was going to put me through my paces on instrument flying in the Phantom. I had always had a bit of a knack for IF in the past, so this one went quite well for me.

When flying, the idea is that you look out of the window and fly at an attitude relative to the visual horizon. The accuracy of heading height and speed comes from regular reference to the flight instruments on the panel. Traditionally, when learning to fly, the temptation is to get fixated on those instruments and then chase the needles for accuracy, completely forgetting to look out. IF gave us the opportunity to chase all we liked, hence I was comfortable doing that without having the worry of looking out—one less thing to do as far as I was concerned.

We guffed around the sky doing departures and approaches of varying types—some using full ATC talkdown and others using internal sources such as ILS, radar, and INAS. Cliff was a dream to fly with, and once again, I felt my confidence grow a little. This was a good thing as my last trip of the week was with Les, one of the baby navs on the course. This 'crew solo' was almost a rite of passage on the course and would be the very first time I would be responsible for someone else in the cockpit as clueless as I was. Previously, of course, I had only ever flown with instructor pilots, solo, or with the grand total of one instructor nav.

I don't think I have ever spent so long doing my checks on that first trip with Les. I was petrified of screwing up and killing him, which was probably a good attitude to have all told. I know he would have appreciated it. The trip was basically a repeat of the previous trip with Uncle Tony, including a bit of medium level navigation culminating in a practice diversion to Lossiemouth and a couple of instrument approaches and circuits back at Leuchars. I remember very little of that sortie, other than it seemed very pleasant with both Les and I falling over ourselves to provide the best professional service that we could. All in all, we didn't enter any restricted airspace, didn't crash, and didn't make fools of ourselves, so all good there. I was also able to take Les supersonic for his first time—me being a veteran of supersonic flight by this stage of course! As far as flying as a single aircraft went, that about covered it on the course apart from night flying which would come a little later on. Now it was time to fly in formation.

Wow—That Is Close!

I had done plenty of close formation flying on previous types and tactical formation flying on the TWU on the Hawk. Should be just the same then right? Apparently not! The brief was massively complicated and my head was spinning at the end of it. We were going to do a pairs take-off, followed by some close formation manoeuvring. Pairs take off meant we would line up together on the runway and roll together so that I was in close formation all the way through the take-off. It is a hyperventilating nightmare, but a huge, huge thrill.

Once the close formation part of the sortie was done, I would be waved out by the leader into a fighting wing position for some more aggressive manoeuvring. Fighting wing allowed me to move in a cone around the leader but trying to anchor in a position about 300 yards swept on either wing by about 30 degrees. This allowed the leader to move around the sky more aggressively but still know where I was throughout. It was also close enough for me to quickly close to a tight formation position should we be about to enter cloud. I used to love fighting wing—close enough to the leader to be amazed at seeing another aircraft that close, but not too close that it took all my capacity and sweat to stay there.

Finally, on the trip, I would move out to battle formation 2–3 miles line abreast and up to 10,000 feet split in height. This was a standard formation for a pair of fighters going into an intercept. The height split made it harder for an enemy aircraft to see both of us at the same time, and the azimuth split allowed us to check each other's 6 o'clock position—the vulnerable space behind the formation. Manoeuvring this formation while maintaining formation integrity and therefore mutual support was both difficult and essential to master. If you can't do it, you will be chopped as it is a life-saver in tactical situations.

Turns included 90s, turnabouts, and rotates, which are relatively easy to master followed by more difficult 30s, 45s, and 60s. All of these were flown with a 4-G pull and were a physical and mental nightmare. I'll spare you the maths of how these turns are done, but take it from me when I tell you this trip is a complete mind explosion. All of it helped by the fact that I am flying with Coops again and his laid-back encouraging manner. Halfway through, Coops took control to 'give me a rest', which I definitely needed as my brain was like spaghetti by this time and I was sweating buckets. All too soon my rest was over, and it was back into close for a formation approach and then a circuit and landing all in echelon formation.

It is an amazing sight and feeling being on the wing of another aircraft. The F4 is a huge piece of metal to be that close to in the air, and we were only a few feet away from it. I formated into the correct position by lining up the leading and trailing edge of the wing with the anti-collision light on the spine of the aircraft. That triangle gave the correct forward and back position, which I adjusted by 'walking the throttles' back and forth as previously taught by Coops on the first trip in the circuit. The correct up/down position was achieved by 'splitting the wing' so I could see both the upper and lower surfaces of it. In and out was mostly a feeling in the water, but involved squaring off the view of the tailplane. Put all three of those together and you have a solid close formation echelon position, or in my case, you flash through it from time to time constantly trying to correct the many errors Coops was pointing out.

We practised this on both sides of the leader. The main reason for this is that when we did formation take-offs and approaches, we had to be on the upwind side of the leader as any crosswind flowing through them to us was even more turbulent and could lead to handling problems for the wingman. In one known case in the F4, a full-blown accident occurred because the leader had his wingman on the wrong side during an approach in a strong crosswind and the wingman and his navigator had to eject close to the ground. If you don't mind, I have to tell you a story of a close formation trip I flew way back in flying training on the Jet Provost.

SPLEET THE WEENG WEELSOHN!

I was flying with a French Instructor who was over on a three-year exchange posting with the RAF. He had flown Mirage F1s with the French Air Force and was the epitome of a cool fighter pilot. Unfortunately, his English was somewhat limited and he had a peculiar turn of phrase and an outrageous French accent, which was hilarious on the ground but a nightmare in the cockpit.

The sortie was a three-ship with us as Number 3 and had included the usual close formation manoeuvring in Vic formation (like geese—one either side of the leader), line astern (like ducks in a row), and tail-chasing (sorry, no more bird analogies left), which was us pretending to be fighters chasing a target to shoot it down. All the time in close formation, Frenchy would be shouting 'Weelsohn! Relax!' which had the opposite effect of course and I gripped the stick even harder as I tensed up and sawed the throttle like mad. It didn't help that he kept gripping my thigh to feel how tense my legs were.

The final act of the sortie was a run in and break for individual circuits. The leader called us into echelon formation which put the Number 2 on his wing and me on the Number 2's wing. Everyone on the ground will watch formations running in to the break and will offer instant criticism if you are not in position properly, so there is some pressure on you to be in the right place. You really stick out like a sore thumb if you aren't. Frenchy is going apeshit at me as I try to get into position and we get closer to the airfield. 'GET IN ZERR WEELSOHN. GET IN ZERR. SPLEET THE WEENG!' In the middle of all this shouting, he also called, 'RELAX WEELSOHN,' which didn't help at all. 'SPLEET THE WEENG WEELSOHN! YOU EMBARRASS ME WEELSOHN! GET IN ZERR OR I WEEL BITE YOU LIKE A DOG!! LIKE A DOG I SAY!' The last comment destroyed any concentration I had and I bucked my way up and down on the wing. I knew it looked like shit to everyone watching on the ground.

I tell you what though—I would pay good money to replace Coops with Frenchy in the cockpit right now. Coops got more direct as we got closer to the ground and went through the approach. The leader used hand signals to indicate when to put the gear down. I have always loved watching bits move on other aircraft while formating on them. When you see the landing gear drop out of the bottom of the aircraft, it is a wondrous thing. Then the flaps moved on his signal and the attitude and trim of the aircraft changed as we get ready for landing. Coops took these simple pleasures away from me with his helpful comments on my ability. To be fair to him, I was not hugely smooth at this point, but he could do with looking up positive reinforcement in the dictionary.

As I have already said, when the gear comes down, the hydraulics dissipated so much that we would often get a 'UTILS' caption come up with the flashing attention-getter. I would have to change hands on the stick to cancel the flashing lights and then quickly change hands back again. When the flaps came down, we would get a 'BLC' (boundary layer control) caption. The F4 had air blown over the wing to help with lift at low speeds. This would also bring on the flashers, which needed cancelling. Hopefully, you get the impression that it is a bit of a faff in the cockpit, changing hands while trying to not crash into the leader. During the formation circuit, I was so maxed out just trying to fly, that I couldn't cancel the flashers as well, so to alleviate Coops' worries I said, 'Don't worry about the attention getters, it's just the bleed air'.

'It's not that I am worried about,' said Coops, 'it's you hitting the bloody leader I am worried about!' There we are then. Despite Coops' lack of belief in my ability (or lack of), I managed a pairs landing and survived the debrief. I did one more of these trips, then a further one with Andy in the back, and I was cleared to start intercept training—proper fighter pilot stuff at last!

Downtown

The weekends at Leuchars usually began with getting shitfaced in the bar at happy hour on Friday night, possibly followed by a drunken taxi ride into St Andrews if we could be bothered. If we didn't want to meet real people, then happy hour would become happy hours involving an athlete's tea of beer and mess chips and then more beer until bed called. Alternatively, St Andrews offered up the only two things a fighter pilot needs in a local town—a decent bar and a curry house. MaBelle's was the bar of choice and was usually populated by Phantom aircrew and the local girls, and the curry house was the Bulaka. When I joined the RAF, I didn't particularly like the taste of beer and had never eaten Indian food. Now, four years later, they were like the staff of life to me. The Bulaka was like any other curry house in the 1980s, and most Leuchars aircrew had been thrown out of it and banned for life, only to pitch up the next weekend and be welcomed in to eat. Business is business, I guess?

MaBelle's was a cool bar and usually very welcoming of RAF folk. There were four local girls always in there. These girls were known as the 'crash divs' and befriended most courses that went through Leuchars. In aviation, a crash diversion (crash div) is another airfield close by to your own where you can divert if you cannot land at home due to a crash on the runway. The runway is said to be 'black' and is unusable. Therefore, you can always go to the crash div. The girls were supposedly of easy virtue, hence their title. To be completely honest with you, it didn't matter how easy their virtue was, I was so hopeless with chatting up girls that it didn't really make any difference to me. However, the girls were at every party in the mess and seemed to know their way around better than our course.

Dundee was the town of choice for half a day out shopping with a hangover and was a short train ride or drive away. It also had a public swimming pool with some wicked water slides. I always found it funny to see a load of drunk twenty-year-olds queuing up with the young kids to get on the slides. The novelty of the slides wore off a bit after some local hooligan had wedged a razor blade in one as a joke, and following news of some horrific injuries, our forays to the pool dried up. There was of course the lure of golf. Leuchars is on the doorstep of the most famous golf course in the world at St Andrews, and most aircrew took up golf of varying levels during a tour there. I bought some cheap clubs off a mate and set out to conquer the game. You can insert any of the usual golfing jokes here regarding handicaps, etc., and will get a picture of how good I was. Still, a round of golf was a welcome diversion from the stresses of the OCU, or should have been. Being as crap at golf as I was, it just added to the drama.

In Trouble

It was almost to be expected on every course in flying training that *ab initio* students would get into some sort of trouble with the staff, and the OCU was no different. Usually, it would be not cleaning up the coffee bar or not locking up the squadron properly at the end of the day when duty student. This time, it was my fault we ended up in the shit. Every morning began with met brief, where all the aircrew on the squadron would gather together to be given a comprehensive brief from one of the met men on the day's forecast weather. Being a Met Man seemed a thankless task. Met is not an exact science (according to met men), and forecasting the UK's unique island weather patterns is fraught with potential disaster.

As pilots, we all studied meteorology through training and basically found that most of it was on the toss of a coin, depending on which way the wind decided to blow. To be fair, the Met Office was correct 80 per cent of the time in those days, but most pilots only ever called the Met Man to bollock him when he got it wrong. Anyway, the rest of met brief included an ATC brief, parish notices about the airfield, and a bit of squadron admin. There was always a quiz for the students on the 'Emergency of the Day'. The staff pilot or nav running the met brief would pull an emergency from the FRCs and then ask one of the *ab initios* for the drill. This particular day was my turn.

Each course was allocated a course commander—one of the staff detailed to look after us from an admin and welfare point of view. Gouldy, one of the navs, was ours and was running met brief. Gouldy asked me what the drill was if we were to hear a whining noise and vibration coming from the right footwell in the rear cockpit. I knew this was the equipment cooling fan, and the drill was for the nav to pull the circuit breaker for the fan on one of the panels down by his right foot. I think I even said what number circuit breaker it was and that it had yellow paint on its end to easily identify it. Pleased that I had passed this very public test in front of all of the staff and students, I was then side-swiped by Gouldy, who asked what I would do if that didn't work.

This was not something that was taught in ground school or the sims so required a bit of lateral thought. With only about fifteen hours on the jet, I was lost. Will Phillips, one of the old sim instructors, was trying to mime the actions to me, but either his acting or more likely my limited knowledge left me short. Gouldy then asked me as I foundered, 'Is there anything else that can be done?' I didn't mean to be flippant, but that's exactly as it sounded when I replied, 'I guess there must be.' Gouldy's head went purple and he spat the drill at me.

'RAT out, Gennies off!' he yelled before shaking his head and sitting down. I'm not sure I would have worked that out for myself even with 100 hours on the jet, but I felt hot, bothered, and thoroughly chastised nonetheless. I saw the Boss talking to Gouldy before he stood up and bollocked all of our course for not knowing our stuff and stormed out. Gouldy told us to wait behind as everyone filed out of met brief to go flying.

'Right, you lot! I am furious with you! You've embarrassed me and yourselves in front of the Boss,' though I'm not sure why Gouldy was embarrassed, 'so on Friday afternoon, you are all going to have some extra exams and emergency quizzes. Now fuck off out of here!' As students in the flying training system, we expected to be in trouble and to get bollockings, but this was going to be an issue for me this time. I had already been cleared for a day off on Friday to go home and take my father to hospital following one of his many heart scares. With that in mind, I went to see Gouldy. My *mea culpa* speech and subsequent apology including a plea for me alone to be punished fell on deaf ears. I also asked if I could take the punishment early so that I could make my father's appointment.

Now, as students, we expect our course commander to stick up for us when he can and also to shield us from some of the shit that comes down from above. Gouldy proved his worth by denying my requests and telling me I shouldn't have screwed up in the first place. The next time I saw him was Friday afternoon as he supervised our whole course taking test after test after everyone else on the squadron had stacked for the weekend. You could cut the atmosphere with a knife, and I know that all of us were looking for a chance to get even with Gouldy. Brave is the man who pisses off a whole course of flying training students. When our moment of revenge came, it could not have been sweeter.

Gouldy's Coffee

Starting the intercept phase of the course meant that we were due a few more lectures—radar theory and intercept theory as well as practical employment of the radar, and weapons lectures on the Skyflash missile, the Sidewinder missile, and the gun. When I say gun, I mean of course the 6-barrel Gatling-style cannon that we carried in a pod under the aircraft.

The biggest, longest, and most tedious of these lectures was the technical lecture on the Phantom radar—four hours of bewildering tech language and abbreviations, all delivered by Gouldy. To say we were a hostile crowd would be wholly accurate, and Gouldy's briefing style left a lot to be desired. He was one of those classic people who are not at all funny but persevere with humour despite this crippling disability. He was also labouring under the impression that we liked him and had forgotten about throwing us under the bus and the extra exams a few days earlier—alas not, Gouldy my friend! If there is one thing I have found out about fighter crews (including students), it is that we know how to hold a grudge.

Gouldy slogged his way through the first two hours of OHP slides and then mercifully gave us a tea break. As we stood up to go to the crew room, he held his mug out and said, 'Coffee for me. White with 2 sugars.' To a man, we walked past him and ignored his mug until Joel picked it up and said, 'I'll make your coffee Gouldy.' We were incandescent with rage that Joel had split ranks during our silent protest, accusing him of brown-nosing and all sorts of other things until we got to the tea bar in the crew room. Joel then proceeded to make Gouldy a 'special coffee' including anything he could find in the cupboards—brown sauce, mustard powder, salt and pepper, five teaspoons of coffee, a bit of washing-up liquid, and a wring out of the dishcloth all went in there.

Joel went straight to legendary status and we couldn't wait for the second half of the brief where Gouldy would drink his 'special coffee'. As we left the tea bar, we were vaguely aware of Joel zipping up his flying suit, having held the coffee mug below the counter for a little while. 'Did he just piss in Gouldy's coffee?' whispered Ivan.

'Don't ask,' I replied. 'Nothing we can do about it now.'

The second half of that lecture was a blur. We couldn't do anything except stare at Gouldy's mug. I have no idea what Gouldy was saying, which is probably why I know bugger all about how the radar worked.

Gouldy kept picking up his mug and then putting it back down without drinking from it, while he lectured and we held our breath. We were mesmerised, and I am sure Gouldy was convinced it was his brilliant lecture that kept us rapt. Then it happened—he took a huge gulp and his face contorted into a look of agony. 'Shit! That's a strong coffee,' he said.

'Sorry, Gouldy, is it too strong for you?' asked Joel.

'No, no,' replied Gouldy, who probably saw it as a bit of a challenge and downed the rest of it all in one go. So, there we had it—a small victory for us, albeit a silent one. Revenge was a dish best served lukewarm, with a bit of mustard powder, washing-up liquid, and possibly some of Joel's bodily fluids.

Intercepts

Starting this phase was pretty daunting in that if we didn't get it, we were screwed. The rest of my life as a Phantom pilot would be based around what I would learn in this phase. There was even more pressure on the navs. Actually, just getting a radar contact was a skill in itself and a very intense procedure. The navs would hunch over the radar screen in the back with their right hand on the hand controller and their left on the radar control panel. Then they would move the scanner up and down as they scanned thousands of feet of airspace, out to 60 miles or more, hoping a big fat blob would appear on the scope. Once they had the blob, it was a case of trying to work out its height, speed, and heading all the while trying to keep it on the scope while the pilot flung the aircraft around the sky trying to make the intercept work for either a head sector Skyflash shot, a rear sector approach to visual identification (VISIDENT), or Sidewinder shot.

I am getting way ahead of myself here though. First off, we need to learn a bit of radar theory and then intercept theory. Now I am not (nor ever was) a technically minded kind of guy, so radar theory was not the easiest thing for me to grasp. Basically, it is just a load of hard physics involving the electromagnetic spectrum. The radar scanner at the front of the jet fires out pulses of energy that travel at the speed of light. These pulses hit a target and get reflected back into the receiver bit of the scanner and you should get a big fat blob on the scope. The range of the target from you is worked out by using a time distance speed calculation divided by two for the out and back journey of the pulse.

It sounds kind of simple until you realise that the scanner has to switch between transmit and receive many times a second, and the transmitter switches the frequency of the pulses per second to aid with detection at various ranges, and all this has an effect on how good the radar is at finding and tracking targets. As the scanner moves left and right constantly and up and down when commanded by the nav, it generates its own internal noise that the radar has to mask otherwise it would paint a load of targets on the scope. Therefore, it has to set a threshold of noise below which it ignores. If you get energy returned from a target, it will always be higher than the internal noise, hence the target appears on the scope. Confused yet? Maybe not, but I haven't mentioned what pulse repetition frequency actually does, what PRI and CHIRP are, electronic scanned arrays, or jamming, etc.

However, it is incredibly important to realise that if the target is below you, and you motor the scanner down, you are going to get a big fat return from the ground. This is called clutter and it will mask any target you are looking for. To get around this, the Phantom had another radar mode called pulse doppler (or PD as it was known). This gave us a 'Look down, shoot down' capability that a fair few other aircraft did not have and gave us a bit of an advantage in some arenas. I did doppler theory at school in physics, so thought I understood the concept. The pulse of energy hits the target and comes back as normal. However, if the target is travelling towards us, the pulse is flattened a bit by the forward speed of the target hitting it. This flattening shows us an apparent change in the pulse's frequency. That change is measured by the radar as a speed.

So, now, rather than getting a blob on the scope at a certain range, we get a blob at a certain speed. The higher up the scale, the faster the target. If we wanted to know the range of the target, the nav would need to lock the radar onto it and the scope would turn into a range scope again. As the radar was reading a relative speed in PD, it could differentiate between a target and the ground. The only issue now is that the ground itself has a closing velocity that matches our own speed, so we would see a thin arch on the PD scope called main beam clutter, or MBC, or 'The notch'. If a target was coming towards us, it would appear above MBC. If it was going away, it would appear below MBC on the scope. If the target then turned sideways onto the beam, we would lose the contact into MBC as it would now have the same closing velocity as the ground. I am sick of explaining this now. There is a lot more to it as you can imagine, but that is more than enough for this book.

Much more interesting, and important, is how we conduct an intercept. We first did simple intercepts at the TWU, and I was pleasantly surprised to find they were all to do with maths, specifically geometry. I was a young man of limited abilities, but one thing I did excel at was mental arithmetic. All those early years at school doing times tables paid dividends, and a natural ability for simple maths gave me a slight advantage as a fast jet pilot. For example, we simplify time, distance, speed calculations by turning our speed from knots (nautical miles per hour) into miles per minute. Therefore, if I am flying low level at 420 knots, which was the standard cruising speed, I know I am covering 7 miles a minute. So, if my turning point is 21 miles away, I know it will take three minutes to get there and I can work out how much fuel I will use and what time I will get there. I still do time, distance, speed calculations when I see road signs on the motorway—60 mph is 1 mile a minute so I can make an accurate prediction of how long it will take me to get home. Sat Nav? Pah! As you can imagine, it is a lot of fun in my car. Back to flying though—intercepts are all conducted using simple maths as a foundation.

The 1 in 60 Rule

Skip this bit if you don't like maths! I find maths and numbers fascinating. They dictate the order of the world and, in particular, aviation, such as time, distance, speed, altitude, and geography—especially latitude and longitude. The 1 in 60 rule states that if you turn through 1 degree of heading and travel for 60 miles on that new heading, you will end up 1 mile laterally away from where you would have ended up had you not changed heading in the first place (think of a long, thin, right-angled triangle). Therefore, if we get a contact on a target 20 degrees left of the nose at 60 miles, we have 20 miles of lateral separation, also known as displacement. If that target is only 30 miles away, we have half of that (30 is half of 60) so only 10 miles of displacement. We can use this formula all the way down using fractions of 60 on the range.

This works in the vertical also, which gives us a method of working out target height. If the nav is looking 3 degrees nose up on the radar and sees a target at 60 miles, he knows the target is 3 miles above us. A radar mile is 6,000 feet; therefore, the target is 18,000 feet above us and we can quite accurately state what its altitude is. We use the old adage of 'why measure with a micrometer, when you are cutting with an axe?' In intercepts, this 1 in 60 calculation is more than accurate enough. So, once we have these basics down, we introduce geometry into the act.

When the nav detects a target, we will watch it for a little while. This is called blip track analysis and will involve watching it over a few miles to see how many degrees it drifts left or right on the scope. Using the 1 in 60 rule again, we can make a rough guess at its heading. We get its speed from the PD, and adding it to our speed will give us a closing velocity.

My job as the pilot is to hit the stopwatch and count down my best guess at ranges based on our closing velocity. If the nav locks to the target, we will lose any chance of detecting other targets out there, and we may also alert the target that we have seen them. At a certain range, based on my calculations, the nav will then lock the target, hopefully just in time for an optimum range Skyflash shot in the face. If we do not have clearance to kill, we will probably turn the intercept into a 'stern attack' to close on it for a VISIDENT (VID). This involves us setting up on the reciprocal heading of the target (180 degrees out) with 5 miles of displacement. This is known as a 180 by 5. We hold that heading and will see the target drift outwards on the scope, and when it gets to 8 miles from us, which should coincide with 40 degrees off the nose (1 in 60 again), we turn towards it at 45 degrees angle of bank. This gives us a controlled 'final turn' to roll us out about 2 miles astern. This is the heart of the envelope for a Sidewinder shot or a starting point for the VID procedure (more of which later). We try to be 0.1 Mach faster than the target to make the geometry work and can either ease or tighten the final turn to make the picture work and get that rollout correct.

That is about as simple as I can tell it. If we are looking to shoot the target at range in the face, we manoeuvre to put the target on a 160-degree track crossing angle (TCA). This is the angle between his tail and our nose. That seems a bit complicated, I grant you, and modern-day intercepts are done looking at reference from both aircraft noses, which is a lot easier to fathom. Anyway, we work out the TCA with reference to the compass in the aircraft, our own heading, and maths again.

Getting the impression there is a lot of maths flying around here? Modern fighter radars do all of this maths for you and all you have to do is fly a picture on the scope rather than crunching the numbers yourself. A 160 TCA gives a radar tracked missile like a Skyflash or Sparrow a lot of closing velocity (good for tracking), yet still retained some separation to convert to the stern for a Sidewinder shot. This is very basic intercept theory, but to us, at that stage, it was a gobsmacking mix of hard sums, complicated geometry, and tactics, as well as a sheer orgasmic thrill of practicing shooting somebody down for real.

The Harsh Reality

Of course, the OCU had to find a way of sucking this fighter pilot enthusiasm out of us, and they did this with a device called the air intercept trainer. In a cold and noisy room somewhere in the hangar was a training rig that had a desktop style set of displays—one for the nav and one for the pilot. My station had a stick and throttles, a set of flight instruments, and a radar repeater scope as well as a missile management panel (MMP). The nav station had a radar scope, radar control panel, hand controller, and a rear seat set of flight instruments.

In between us sat one of the staff navs, and he would set up targets for the nav to search for, and then we would conduct an intercept to either shoot or VID. The aim was to put all the radar, intercept, and maths theory we had just learnt into practice using the kit. It rapidly became apparent that this was going to be a lot harder than we thought. Just communicating between us was a nightmare as we tried to speak the new standard language of the intercept. There were various checklists to complete before every intercept, including radar set up for the navs, such as range scale and radar mode, and missile and fuel checks for me.

I had to make the standard calls as if we were talking to our ground controller. I would declare that we were, 'Charlie 44+8 Tiger Fast 40,' or some such. Charlie was a C-fit Phantom (i.e. two external fuel tanks under the wings, known as 'Sargent Fletchers'). A-fit was no tanks; B-fit was a centreline tank; and D-fit was all of the tanks fitted. '44+8' meant that we had four Skyflash, four Sidewinders, a gun with over half of the rounds remaining (this could be minus or zero if the gun was not fitted at all), and the '8' meant that all of our missiles had a head sector capability. Tiger Fast told the controller we had enough gas for a supersonic intercept (Tiger Slow meaning subsonic only), and the '40' was the minutes of duration we had after that. It was all very punchy and cool, apart from when you are just learning the language and are so maxed out you can't remember how to calculate the endurance time.

The instructor would then generate a target, and it would take the student nav ages to find it. When he did, he would lock it up (in the early exercises) and make the appropriate call to me and our simulated controller. 'Contact nose, 260, 40 miles (on a good day!)' He would then tell me to come hard right or left to start the geometry of the intercept. I would watch it all unfold on my repeater scope, silently matching the maths of the intercept to the way the blip moved on the screen as we got closer to the target.

The first AI trainers were designed to teach us the mechanics of the stern intercept, and as we started the final turn in behind the target from 40 degrees off the nose and 8 miles (we hoped), the nav had to convert his PD lock into a pulse lock, otherwise the radar would lose the lock as the target went into MBC. This switching of modes was complicated for the navs, hence it was important for pilots to be able to work out how the intercept was going in the final turn and fly accurately.

We would roll out astern with some overtake, and the nav would select VID mode. I would see a small steering dot on my scope and I would fly to put it on the centreline and on the range marker second from the top. This would then lead me to a position 300 yards from the target either left/right by about 45 degrees, and up/down by about 10 degrees, depending on what I had requested from the nav. He set all these parameters on the radar control panel. All the way in, the nav would call speeds, headings, and overtake, and we would gracefully end up in the position mentioned above—yeah right! Again, this was just instrument flying for me with an extra instrument to monitor and scan along with some inputs from the nav to process. For real, I would have made the decision on where to approach from based on ambient conditions such as star or moonlight and how high the target was. Obviously, I would not want to approach from below if the target were at low level.

Having scraped through a couple of AI trainers, we were destined to take it all airborne and use the radars for real. Most of my trips were now going to be with the staff navigators rather than instructor pilots, so there was always the added pressure of having someone else's life in my hands, who had no way of flying the aircraft. My first such trip was with Punchy.

Punchy's Pet Project

Punchy had only just qualified as an instructor and still had a lot of front-line adrenaline flowing through him. He was exceptionally professional and sharp, and I took an instant liking to him. He actually pre-briefed me, helping me to put together the sortie briefing I would give. I would be leading another aircraft that would pretend to be my target and *vice versa*. Therefore, I would be assessed on how well I could lead a pair of aircraft as well as how well I did on the intercepts.

I would brief up the domestic part of the sortie including take-off, transit, and recovery, and Punchy would then step up to brief the tactical part of the trip. In the other aircraft was a newly qualified instructor pilot, Robin, and in his boot was Andy from our course. We would take turns pretending to be the fighter and try to do enough intercepts between us both to pass the trip. These trips were so much harder for the student navs to pass. As student pilots, we could get away with two decent intercepts as we weren't doing the hard bit of handling the radar. Okay, so just not crashing was still a challenge for us, but the student navs needed three good intercepts to get a pass and that was much tougher.

The brief seemed to go well, as did start-up, taxi, and take-off, and before I knew it, we were up and ready to do the first intercept. Of course, Punchy was awesome; got contact straight away; and rolled me out 1.5 miles astern ready for my first ever VID. Once we got to 300 yards, he called, 'Target, 45 left, 10 down, my instruments.' I froze my inputs on the controls and looked out to where Punchy had called. 'It's a Phantom,' I said and we knocked it off and separated from our number two by 50 miles to start the next one. We bat and balled the role of fighter until both of us were good, then joined up and headed home—job done, though not quite (more on that later).

This trip was a bit of a life-changer for me. Punchy showed me how a fighter crew worked—mutual respect and reliance, good communication, and when we were separating out to our start points or being the target, he would lighten the mood by chatting.

It was during one of these periods that he asked me which front-line squadron I wanted to join. At the time there were two squadrons at Leuchars (43—the Fighting Cocks, and Treble One—The Tremblers); two at Wattisham (56—The Firebirds, and 74—The Tiger Squadron); and two in Germany at RAF Wildenrath (19 Squadron—The Fighting

Dolphins, and 92 Sqn—The Cobras). I told Punchy I didn't care as long as I got to Germany. He asked me why, and I told him that I thought being on a fighter squadron in Germany was the proper front-line of the Cold War.

Punchy was over the moon. He had been on 19 Sqn and regaled me with tales of eight-ship formations of Phantoms attacking twenty-four Tornados, Jaguars, and Harriers at low level, and how much sharper I would be than the dullards of UK Air Defence squadrons. He was raving about the life out there and did a great sales job on me. By the end of the trip, there was only one destination for me and that was the land of beer and sausages. I'm sure there was more to Germany than that, but racial stereotypes were *de rigeur* in the 1980s. More importantly, I think I became Punchy's pet project, as no one else on my course, from the *ab initios*, wanted to go to Germany.

So, I brought my formation back to Leuchars and we set up for a visual run-in and break. A VRIAB is the most expeditious way of getting your aircraft on the ground after a trip. I called Robin into echelon starboard and descended to 500 feet for the run-in and accelerated to 350 knots. As we passed through the initial point (which is about 1–2 miles on the extended centreline of the runway), I called 'Initials' to Air Traffic Control and they cleared us to join the circuit, while warning me there was one aircraft just turned downwind. I saw the other Phantom, and about halfway down the runway, I breaked hard left at 4-G and climbed to 1,000 feet, which is circuit height to roll out downwind.

I knew that Robin would break three seconds after me to ensure he had clearance on the runway to land behind me. Punchy called out the pre-landers, and I responded by putting the wheels down and the flaps to half, turned finals with full flap, and hauled it to the doughnut. I actually carried out a half-decent landing, popped the chute, and came to a graceful taxi speed to clear the runway. Robin cleared a few seconds later and I switched us to ground frequency to taxi back to the squadron line.

On the taxi back, Punchy switched to the squadron ops frequency and called in our aircraft and radar serviceability. He did this so that a technician could be waiting for us to get a debrief and also to give the duty authoriser (the instructor running the flying programme) a heads-up if our aircraft should not be used on the next wave of flying until it is fixed. A jet with a broken radar can't fulfil a mission as a fighter, but it could be a pure target for another aircraft. Once Punchy finished his call, the auth then said, 'Tell Tug the Boss wants to see him in his office soonest.' This was a highly unusual call and meant one of two things—either there had been a death in my family or I was cosmically in the shit.

Thank God—I Am in the Shit!

Having shut the aircraft down, I left Punchy in the backseat, wrestling with our errant INAS. I walked into the line hut to sign the aircraft back in, and with some trepidation, I walked into the squadron. As I signed the authorisation sheets with our take-off and landing times, no one seemed to be giving me any sympathetic glances, so I wandered up to the Boss's office to find it empty. Hot-footing it down to the ops desk again, I asked the duty authoriser where the Boss was. 'Oh, he's airborne.'

'But I thought he wanted to see me soonest?'

'Yeah well, he'll see you when he lands.' Given that would be about two hours away, I asked if he knew what it was about. 'Beats me, but he sounded pretty pissed. He was just starting up and called over the radio that he wanted to see the leader of your formation.' I now figured all my family were still alive, but somehow, I was in the shit. I couldn't for the life of me think why, though. The debrief went well for me, but not so good for Andy. His radar work had been a bit patchy, and once Punchy had checked his film, it ended with Andy failing the trip. This was the first failure on our course so far, and it was thoroughly unpleasant.

There is a well-known phenomenon on flying training courses where everything is great while we are all passing our trips. As soon as one of us fails a trip though, it flows through the course like a disease, and we all feel vulnerable from then on. It is then a measure of how good a course we are as to how well we recover and support each other. Andy was a good guy and we all felt his pain. Following the debrief, I had an anxious wait until the Boss could see me. Neither Punchy or Robin had any idea what I had done wrong in the circuit, so it was just a case of seeing what happened.

I knocked on the Boss's door and his 'Come in,' was laced with disdain. It probably wasn't, but you know how your brain works when you are waiting for a bollocking. With no offer of a seat, I stood to attention in front of him and took it straight between the eyes. 'What the hell was that on finals?!' he shouted. I was a bit perplexed and asked what he meant. 'You flew right through the centreline yet still continued with the approach!'

'Sorry, Sir, but I didn't. We rolled out right on the centreline.'

'Are you calling me a liar, young man?!'

'No, Sir, but I think you must have seen the Tremblers jet in front of us. We didn't fly through.'

'Bullshit! I saw it myself from the pan.'

Ah, so he had made his mind up it was me, having seen the event from about 2 miles away. I was convinced it was the Treble One jet he had seen, but it was pointless trying to argue, and I adopted the survival attitude of the flying training student throughout history—'Yes Sir, no Sir, sorry Sir.' He then bollocked me for being too close to the man behind me in the circuit. By his logic, that was my own wingman, Robin, who had broken into the circuit three seconds after me. How the hell I was responsible for that, I have no idea. I zoned out a bit while staring at a point 2 feet above his head and was then summarily dismissed with a flea in each ear and a warning that he was watching me.

I had had bollockings before many times (part of military life then), but whenever it was one I did not deserve, it just hardened me up. If I had any doubts about the Boss before, I certainly didn't now. As I exited his office, Punchy and Robin took me aside. They had heard the shouting and wanted to know the story. Punchy was incensed, and then something happened that taught me more about flying as a crew and fighter squadron spirit than any other event: Punchy stormed into the Boss's office and fought my corner—a staff nav standing up for a student whom he saw as a crewmate wronged.

Punchy achieved legendary status with our course that day, I can tell you. The knock-on effect was that in the future, I fought like an animal to stick up for my navs, even when they had messed up. Believe me, in my time on the Phantom, my navs had to stick up for me a lot more often. That support was one of the most beautiful things about flying a twin-seat aeroplane. There has always been a saying that whenever you arrive on your first squadron, you should take a look around the crew room, and if you can't spot the wanker, then it is you (because every squadron has one). However, if you are flying with him, then he is your wanker and he is worth more than any of the wankers on the other squadrons. You don't have to like anybody in this game, but you have to be able to fly with everybody.

Chopped

There were two courses on the OCU at any one time. We were the junior course at this point, and our senior course were about two months ahead of us and close to graduating. Like us, they had a couple of re-treads on their course, one of which was a wing commander who was refreshing after a ground tour and was going on to become the Boss of 74 Squadron at RAF Wattisham. We didn't really know him, but he seemed a nice chap (that will never catch on in a Boss). What we definitely didn't know was that he was struggling to get to grips with the jet again after his break from it. The upshot was that out of nowhere, we heard he had been chopped! If they could chop a wing commander with previous experience on the jet then surely, we had no chance. It really shook the senior course and, to a certain extent, us as well. They were so close to finishing their course and the most experienced guy got chopped. Immediately, our pet wing commander was bumped up to their course and ended up as OC 74.

At about this time, 56 Squadron at Wattisham were in a bit of bother with the RAF. They had recently lost two jets in separate incidents, where the pilots had mishandled the aircraft and the crews had to eject. I think the accident investigations showed that the pilots had used aileron inputs at a high angle of attack, which had led to departure from controlled flight. Fast jet aircraft don't spin. They are inherently unstable, which means they can manoeuvre quickly, but also means that if you mishandle them, they will depart from controlled flight and tumble around the sky pretty violently.

In the Phantom, if you were manoeuvring hard and the angle of attack was building, there was a rule that you could not use the aileron to turn the aircraft if you were above about 15 AOA. What kind of design is that? So above 15 AOA, we turned the aircraft using bootfulls of rudder. That is why Phantom pilots are so good on the rudder, as in most fast jet aircraft, it is just a footrest in the air. Anyway, these guys had ejected, and the RAF had a paddy that they didn't know how to fly the aircraft properly so came down hard on the whole squadron. Their solution was that all of the pilots on 56 had to go back to the OCU and fly a dual check with an instructor pilot majoring on high AOA manoeuvring. This included their QFIs and QWIs, which must have been embarrassing for them.

Of course, they all passed their check rides and in true fighter pilot style, they had a patch made up with 'Cleared to 19.2 Units' on it, or some such. I am sure this was a way of sticking two fingers up to the RAF and good for them. It was good for us to see some current front-line pilots in our crew room, mainly because we were only about two months away from possibly flying with these guys.

The intercept sorties moved on apace, with the radar work getting more complicated for the navs, and the film debriefs even more so. The navs were using search modes only, to do intercepts, so had to use a bit of blip track analysis on the scope and the 1 in 60 rule to determine height and heading of the target rather than locking it up to get the information. All the time, they were heads down in the back, getting extremely hot and bothered.

We were doing a mix of stern intercepts to VID and also attack reattacks (ARAs). These involved manoeuvring for a head sector Skyflash shot and calling 'Fox 1!' as we pulled the trigger, then breaking hard after that trigger press to put the target on the edge of the scope (any further and the radar would break lock and the Skyflash would lose tracking and fail, as it needed supporting by the radar all the way to impact with the target). Then we would reverse the turn and convert to the stern and select Sidewinder to get the growl from the seeker head; check we are in range; hit the SEAM button on the stick top (Sidewinder expanded acquisition mode) to lock the seeker head onto the target to give us a steady tone; pull the trigger and call 'Fox 2!' and a kill; knock it off; and separate 50 miles from each other and start again.

One of these trips I am flying with Put Put, a staff nav who absolutely adored the Boss. He was so far up his arse you could barely make out the soles of his flying boots. The Boss was leading the sortie and briefed it up to comprise a thirty-second stream take-off into some radar shadowing, and then Put Put briefed the intercepts and what he expected of me. The Boss had Stain in his boot, and after the intercepts were complete, they were going to clear us off to return the Leuchars, while they went and practiced a flypast route they were going to fly over St Andrews at the weekend, supporting some sort of parade. The sortie went well and Put Put called that we were complete on the intercepts. The Boss cleared us to split from him and I headed away back to Leuchars. I guess Put Put was heads down making notes at this point, but as he looked up and saw the umbilical from him to his beloved Boss stretch out beyond his comfortable limit, the following conversation took place:

'Where are you going, Tug?'

'Back to Leuchars.'

'Why? Join up with the Boss now!'

'He's cleared us back to Leuchars, Put Put.'

'No? Why would he do that? Join up now!'

'They are off to practice the flypast. He's told us to go home.'

'Come left now! You never leave your leader! Don't leave the Boss!'

At this point, he tried to call the Boss on the radio, but they had already changed frequencies and he couldn't raise them. That was not enough evidence for him, and he went into a tailspin, shouting at me in the cockpit. I had already had this kind of experience at the Tactical Weapons School at RAF Chivenor, and amazed myself with how calm I was.

'Turn your microphone off, Put Put,' I said, then muted my own mic. He continued to rage at me so I put him on cold mic (meaning I couldn't hear what he was saying) and headed back to Leuchars as if I was single-seat, speaking only to Air Traffic Control. I finally pulled him off cold mic after breaking into the circuit, and asked him to check his straps. He quietly said 'tight and locked,' and I landed on and taxied back to dispersal in silence. Put Put blanked me until we got into the debrief with the Boss and Stain, which suited me. We acted like nothing untoward had happened in the debrief and the Boss asked if there were any other points. I pointedly stared at Put Put, but he refused to speak up. So, I did it for him. Having asked the Boss to confirm that he had cleared us to split back to Leuchars as a singleton, his reply was something like, 'Of course I did. Weren't you paying attention?' or words to that effect, and he and Stain swept out.

Put Put stood and tried to follow, but I pulled him back. 'Anything to add Put Put?' I asked. He looked suitably embarrassed, and then launched into how my crew co-operation had been really poor, before I asked if we should discuss his mistake with the Boss and the way he had reacted in the air. He compromised by giving me his word that he wouldn't mark me down for crew co-op, and this would not be mentioned again—lesson learned and all that. He kept his word for all of one hour I think. He wrote a supervisory note in my file criticising my crew co-op and it was brought up as a point in my mid-course interview with Nails, my flight commander—what a bastard!

It's Dark Out There

It got to the part of the course where we had to go night flying. The night phase had four flights which obviously started with a dual check. I did mine with Stroker, who was well-named. No one—students or staff—liked this guy, and I drew him in the programming lottery. Actually, he was okay in the end. He gave me the usual flying instructor spiel about flying at night being exactly the same as flying during the day (which is bullshit by the way), and we roared off into the Scottish night with our afterburner chucking two bright blue, red, and yellow flamed spears into the sky, not that I could see them of course—I only had twenty hours on the jet at this point and was still just about hanging on during take-off.

We floated around for a bit looking at the lights on the coast and generally having a much better time than I was expecting with Stroker in the boot. As I have already said, I had a bit of a knack for instrument flying, and night flying involves a lot of reference to instruments. We did four instrument approaches and a few night circuits back at Leuchars and Stroker got the impression they were safe enough for me to night fly with a student nav.

My crew solo was a bit false in that I was crewed with Odo for the next trip. What a hoot—flying with someone who had way more experience, but who wasn't assessing me was the easiest trip I did on the OCU. I still had some pressure on me not to kill him with my incompetence, but he was immensely professional, yet still managed to keep me relaxed enough to thoroughly enjoy myself. We did plenty of instrument approaches and Odo conducted an internal aids approach using the INAS and onboard radar to navigate us around the radar pattern and to bring me nicely onto finals. Two more trips would see the night phase done, but I couldn't have envisaged two more different trips.

The next night, I was flying with Spencer. He was the staff nav that we all dreamed about flying with. Cool, relaxed, and very funny, he had a way of relaxing us and convincing us we actually enjoyed flying the Phantom, even though we were being assessed. Of course, we loved flying it, but in the melee and stress of a training course, it was nice to be reminded of it once in a while. Officially, it was a night navigation exercise, but all told it was nothing short of a gag fest with Spencer joking his way around Scotland and bantering with me about whatever came to mind. We carried out a practice diversion to Lossie with a simulated birdstrike, which would have ended in me doing a circuit or two there had there not been a proper emergency aircraft on recovery.

A Buccaneer had gone single-engine and we held in the overhead in the twilight as it took the approach end cable. There was a huge explosion of sparks as the hook hit the ground and the Bucc went into the cable. I called Lossie to depart, and straight away, Spencer said he felt ill with some fumes in the cockpit. It was a bit odd to get another simulated emergency so soon after the last one, but I guess his test was to see where I would go with Lossie's runway out of action. I dialled up Kinloss, but before I could call them, Spencer groaned and said, 'No Tug. Take me home. I want to see my family.' Playing up to him dying in the cockpit, I started back to Leuchars and got ready to call an in-flight emergency. Spencer said he was feeling worse and we should get a move on. I continued roleplaying the emergency when Spencer obviously lost his patience with the subtlety. 'Tug. If we don't get a shift on, the bar will be closed by the time we get back!' I almost died laughing as I put the burners in and raged back to Leuchars at about 0.95 M and plonked it on the deck. Spencer debriefed me walking back to the mess, and we got there just in time for last orders—what a legend!

My final night trip was close formation. None of us believed this was a real trip as surely no one would be daft enough to fly close at night. This was going to be the first training sortie to prepare us for air-to-air refuelling and VID at night. I was up with Freddie, who was a nice relaxed QFI (the opposite of Stroker), so things were looking good. He took me out to the aircraft during the day to show me the night time references he wanted me to fly, basically making a triangle with the leading- and trailing-edge lights on the outboard of the wing and something called a grimes light on top of the spine of the aircraft. I wasn't convinced and still thought this was madness, but it looked like we were going to do it anyway.

We lined up on the runway next to the leader and then he rocked them outboard and the roar took the enamel off my teeth as I watched his burners scorch the night in front of us. Thirty seconds later, I went brakes off and followed him into the sky to carry out some shadowing on the radar before being called to join in close. Basically, it was like doing a VID and then completing the last 300 yards into echelon. I have hyperventilated a lot before in the cockpit, but nothing compared to this. My oxygen indicator was clicking so fast I almost blew the doll's eye indicator out of the glass.

Freddie was calm throughout, although I am pretty sure he was bricking it looking at the way I was sawing the throttles and breathing like I was pushing a baby out. There I was—in close formation, at night, in charge of 25 tons of screaming death, just a few feet away from 25 tons of screaming death! They say that when you die, your whole life flashes before your eyes. Well, when that happens, I will be looking to see what the hell we did on that trip because I have no recollection of it once I got into close. I am guessing we survived, and I ticked off another life experience, having lost a fair few heartbeats along the way.

From the Ridiculous to the Sublime

Back on the day waves of flying, my next intercept trip was with Spencer—lucky me, especially after Put Put and the madness of night close formation. As we separated out for another intercept, Spencer asked if he could take control of the aircraft. We were flying a twin-sticker, so he had a set of throttles, but the rear seat stick had been removed for better access to the radar. Therefore, he had no way of flying it, or so I thought.

Spencer had a trick of jamming his chinagraph pencil into the rear stick housing on the floor of the cockpit and using it as a makeshift control column. He happily flew it around, upside down at times, and seemed very grateful for the opportunity. It turns out he harboured a desire to train as an airline pilot after leaving the RAF, having already paid for a private pilot's licence at a local flying club. Years later, he achieved his aim and flew professionally for an airline. At that time, though, I was just gobsmacked that he was flying a fighter with a pencil; it was trips like this that cemented my love of flying the Phantom, especially with guys like Spencer.

Don't get me wrong—it was still a huge ball-ache doing the course, but this was a moment of pure gold. Rather than feeling like he was assessing me, it felt like I was flying with a good mate. I even tried a bit of banter and told him how shit his handling was. He paid it back by laughing his head off at my somewhat firm landing, telling me it was a good job he had his gumshield in.

However, while I seemed to be having the time of my life, Andy was still struggling and had only just scraped through to the crew solo intercept sortie. We flew together on it, and once again, I was worried about either killing him or screwing up his radar work with my incompetence. There was no cockpit voice recording then, so whenever I got tally on the target, I would try and help with the final turn to the stern so that we achieved a decent rollout. The staff navs knew their stuff though, and gave Andy a hard time in the film debrief again, and it looked like he was in the gunsight. When the end came for him, it seemed swift and brutal. One more trip and he was gone. We were gutted. He was such a nice guy and part of our course, and then we saw him in his blues, having his suspension interviews. Before we knew it, he had left Leuchars altogether.

Back to the Ridiculous Again

As we adjusted to one of our number being chopped, the intercept sorties and AI trainers came on strong. It was at one of these AI trainers that I made my first acquaintance with QWI navs. Tac Weapons had soured my attitude towards QWIs, and Fat Billy perpetuated this by the way he treated myself and Les on this particular exercise. He gave Les a really hard time about his radar work, but I seemed to be doing okay—that was until he told us to change seats and try each other's jobs for once.

This was my first time handling the radar, and it would have been a bit of a hoot had it not been for Fat Billy. He railed on Les for poor and inaccurate flying (not surprising given that Les was not a pilot) and leathered me for poor radar work. I eventually found the target after a couple of resets, locked it up, and talked Les around the sky to make the stern intercept work. Of course, I completely forgot to re-lock from PD to pulse and as we got onto the beam in the final turn, the radar broke lock as the target entered MBC. I stared blankly at the screen, then at Fat Billy before Les shouted to me to change to pulse, but by then, it was too late. Fat Billy delivered the standard constructive QWI debrief, which consisted of telling us both we were shit, and sent us off with a scraped pass on the exercise.

I think instructors forget sometimes the collective support and power that a course of students can generate following incidents like this. We always talked things like this out with each other in the crew room. This 'band of brothers' mentality sustained us through some tough times and marked some of the instructors for life (such as with Gouldy's coffee). As Les and I were recounting our experience, I spoke of the unfairness of

Fat Billy expecting us to do each other's jobs with such little experience, when we barely knew our own.

At this point, our re-tread pilot squadron leader piped up. 'If you come to my squadron as a pilot and can't do an intercept, I'll rip your fucking lips off!' he helpfully intoned. As he was heading to 56 Squadron as a flight commander, we all mentally ticked off the Firebirds from our list of squadrons to volunteer for. By the way, Fat Billy went straight to the top of our shit list. It would be a couple of years before I was able to nail him though.

Postings—Or Not!

Our senior course was almost finished—just a couple of trips to do and they would be off to the front-line. Our junior course had just started ground school, so we were about to become the senior students on the OCU, which was amazing given that we still felt we knew bugger all about the aeroplane or the job we were supposed to be doing.

It was a tradition that course postings were handed out through the medium of alcohol. No. 228 OCU would set out the squadron drink of each front-line Phantom squadron, then blindfold the student, and whatever number he called out, he then drank it down in one. He kept going until he got the drink that matched his posting. Then it was cheers and back-slapping all round, and lots of beer to see the evening off. The drinks involved using coloured spirits to replicate the colours of the squadron. For example, 92 Squadron was a shot of red bols with a shot of advocaat poured on top (red and yellow, known as the Snakebite), while 74 Squadron replaced the red bols with Kahlua to make it black and yellow. This all fell down of course when 56 Squadron (red and white) had the dreaded green lemonade, which seemed to be all the white spirits in a glass with crème de menthe. Of course, the staff always fixed the selections so that no student managed to pick the correct drink first or second choice.

It is difficult to explain just how important an event like this is. This is the moment that will dictate the next three years of your life—where you will live, who your friends will be, and how hard your life will be, etc. With that in mind, we all piled into the bar to watch the senior course get posted. All was going well, with quite a few slots going in Germany to 19 and 92 Sqns, and then the final student stepped up to drink. He had specifically asked for a posting to stay at Leuchars and was adamant that was all he would accept. His girlfriend was based at Leuchars, and he also had elderly parents in the UK. The RAF seldom took any of this personal stuff into consideration, and as he downed the 92 Squadron Snakebite, his blindfold was whipped off amid much cheering and back-slapping. As the reality of a new future in Germany dawned on him, he went absolutely batshit crazy. I had never seen anyone lose it as badly as that before, and the evening took on a much less celebratory feel as we shuffled about embarrassingly, staring into our beers.

Luckily, the Boss gave Ivan and I a wide berth (suede brogues are pretty expensive, I guess), and we sloped off to the Bulaka in St Andrews, leaving the carnage in the bar still raging. We all agreed in the curry house that we would accept any posting at all, just so long as we passed the course. This is just survival instinct thinking on flying training courses. We just wanted to pass to the next stage, as each one is closer to being a proper front-line pilot. That very incident in the bar impacted on me the following week.

Posting? Now?

The following Monday, I was up to fly the hi-flier intercept sortie—airborne as a pair and tactical manoeuvring to the play area. Every minute of every sortie had some form of training attached to it—formation flying; formation leading; instrument approaches; visual circuits, all bookending the actual job of the intercepts. Just when I thought I was getting to grips with handling the jet, we took it into the higher reaches of the part of the atmosphere we punted around in. The air is much thinner the higher you go, which means we generate less lift. Therefore, we need lots more speed and as such, our turns will be much wider. This time, we were looking for 8 miles of displacement to make the stern intercept work, so slightly different maths for me to contend with.

The intercept started with a 70-mile split from the target with both of us having to conduct a supersonic acceleration and climb profile. This Rutkowski climb profile (apologies if I remember it slightly wrong) started with us bunting over in full afterburner and diving until we hit 1.2 Mach, then gently bringing the nose up to accelerate to about 1.3 until we made the rough height of the target. The acceleration would continue to about 1.4, and we would do the intercept from there somewhere in the mid-40,000-foot mark. This was by far and away the fastest I had ever gone, and I had to be relatively gentle with my handing as my usual chimp-fingered baboon approach would wash off all the speed.

It was gently round the final turn and keeping the overtake to carry out the VID. The speed and the height made the whole thing completely awesome. It took a bit more anticipation on the throttle to stabilise the position for the VID. Just a slight over-cooking of it would see us shoot past ahead of the target. I did think, 'if they chop me now, at least I have been 1.4.' With debrief done on that one, it was another trip ticked off, leaving me one more sortie closer to the front-line.

After the debrief, my flight commander, Nails, came into the crew room and asked to see all of the *ab initio* pilots in his office. The four of us filed in, thinking we were probably in the shit, but he asked which one of us wanted a posting to Germany. I immediately raised my hand to find I was in a majority of one. 'Right Tug. You will be taking the slot on 92 Squadron that has just unexpectedly become available from last Friday. We'll try and rush you through if we can, once the Air Combat phase is done.' In short, the OCU had argued with RAF Personnel Command and secured the guy from our senior course who didn't want to go to Germany, a posting to 56 Squadron at Wattisham leaving a gap on 92. So that was a done deal. I was going to be a Cobra, so long as I passed the air combat phase and the advanced intercept/operational phase. Piece of cake? Ha!

The Boss's Revenge

I spent three glorious days in early June just sitting on my arse while the senior course took all the jets for their operational phase, revelling in the fact that I was going to be a Cobra. Punchy was chuffed for me, but bantered that I was going to the inferior squadron at Wildenrath. That Friday morning saw me flying again, on my twenty-fourth birthday, with the Boss on my mid-course general handling ride. This is a trip common to all tactical flying courses such as OCUs and Tac Weapons. As all we had been doing in the air for a while was tactical flying, the MCGH sortie was a check that we could still do the basics of flying the aircraft accurately and smoothly. Therefore, it would have some low-level nav, aerobatics, instrument flying, and circuits with maybe some stalling and practice emergencies in it.

I briefed up with the Boss and walked to the aircraft, showing him my knowledge of the external checks and the readings for hydraulic fluid and oil levels, before crewing in. At the start of all flying training courses, we are taught to call out the checks we are doing over the intercom so that the instructor can check we are doing them correctly. There are tons of checks to call out, but a few trips into the course, the instructors trust that we are doing the right thing and we go to silent checks. I carried out my checks meticulously and silently, only speaking to the Boss to check the intercom. He sat there, knowing I was doing this, but saying nothing until I signalled that I was ready to start the APU. 'Stop!' he shouted. 'You haven't done any checks!'

'I have, Boss—I just did them silently as we have for the past two months.'

'How do I know you have done them correctly?' I was stumped by that one.

'Do you want me to call them out?'

'Yes! I want to you call them out!' So, I began them again from scratch, calling out every single check, feeling small and totally patronised, particularly as my checks were interrupted by 'Stop!' whenever I got a check slightly out of order or did not use the exact words he wanted. For example, the normal way to check the oxygen was to read out the contents (marked on a dial in eighths), then check the flow—so something like 'oxygen, eight eighths, winking and blinking.' The latter part referring to the doll's eye flow indicator, which would go from black to white and back again as you breathed in and out.

'Stop! The way you check the oxygen is as follows. Oxygen system. Connections all secure. Contents. Eight Eighths. Flow normal indicator winking and blinking.' I repeated what he said word for word and continued on. I reached breaking point when it came to starting the engines. The engines were labelled 1 and 2 for the left and right (no idea why, but there it is). We started 2 first, so I held up two fingers to the ground crew, rotated them, and said to the Boss, 'starting number 2.'

'Stop! The correct terminology is "starting the right-hand engine."' I quickly turned off my microphone and shouted 'Arsehole!' into my mask, then calmly switched it back on and called, 'Starting the right-hand engine,' and getting it going. By the time I eventually reached the runway, I was a cross between a Tasmanian Devil and a condemned man.

I could blame the Boss for all of my subsequent woes on the sortie, but I should have been able to put all of that drama behind me and still perform despite the pressure. However, my ineptitude came to the fore in front of the most important man on the squadron. The sortie began with a short low-level nav route starting near Perth and taking us up through Loch Ness and beyond. I had not done any low-level navigation for five months or so, and it is a perishable skill. I made a mistake in not formally planning a heading and time to the start point from take-off. The start point was on the extended centreline of the runway so I figured I would find it easily as we blasted out as it was only about 30 seconds away. Anyway, I missed it and floated off beyond Perth, working myself up into a fizz.

'So, we are less than two minutes into the flight and you are already lost! Not very impressive is it?' said the Boss helpfully. As I froze a bit, he snatched control of the aircraft and hauled it round to point me in the right direction. All the way round the route, he criticised my flying, and in particular for flying at 300 feet rather than 250 feet. Anyone who has tried to fly at 7 miles a minute while trying to judge your height on visual clues alone will understand how nit-picking this was. The end of the route culminated in the Boss giving me a simulated engine failure, leading to me diverting to Lossiemouth for an approach. That seemed to go okay, and we climbed out of Lossie for some upper air work.

My aerobatics have always been described as 'spirited,' which is a nice way of saying 'lots of G, but still a bit shit,' so the Boss remained unimpressed. This continued through a badly executed stalling package. Not soon enough, the fuel ran out and I recovered to Leuchars for a circuit to land. Thank God, we didn't have enough fuel to bash the circuit. I taxied us in, pretty sure that I had failed the trip. My dreams of becoming a Cobra were about to take a huge knock. I don't remember much about the debrief other than the Boss telling me how poor my handling of the aircraft was and how I would really need to be better going forwards. I have always loved the 'Be better' comment whenever I have heard it from instructors, but with no practical advice on how to do it. Anyway, the shock news was that I had passed the trip after all.

This definitely called for a few birthday beers in the bar, and as it was a Friday, we could make it a big night. Ivan was doing his MCGH with the Boss in the afternoon, so I hung out in the crew room for him. He came out of his debrief looking like he had been stabbed in the chest. The Boss, despite passing the trip, told Ivan he was so shit he should be flying something slow like a Hercules. I am guessing the MCGH was supposed to rein us back in from our fighter pilot mindset and get us back to being professional academic style pilots—either that or the Boss was getting his revenge for his ruined shoes.

Virgin

That night was epic in the bar. I suppose I should take this opportunity to apologise to everyone who lived in St Andrews in those days, especially the staff at the Bulaka, for the behaviour of all of the fighter crews at Leuchars. Our pressure relief valve was operated by drinking heavily, singing bar songs, vicious banter, and generally acting like animals and idiots from time to time. The evening started at 5 p.m. with happy hour, where Ivan and I began drowning our sorrows. We had never felt so depressed after passing a trip, so we ignored the Boss in the bar and got some speed on with our junior course mates who had just started flying.

After many beers, flying songs, and pyrotechnic activity involving the mess cannon, we started to banter each other. Just to point out here what the mess cannon was—it consisted of five or six catering-sized baked bean cans, with their tops and half of their bottoms removed. These were then stacked on top of each other and taped together into a long tube using lots and lots of speed tape to give it some strength. The half-removed bottoms provided baffles inside the structure that helped to accelerate the air through them. The bottom bean can had a full bottom with a small hole in it, into which was poured a good portion of lighter fluid. In the top of the tube, we would place a speed-tape ball that just fit inside the can. The lighter fluid was then lit and the resulting whoomph would fire the ball across the bar, accompanied by much cheering, spilling of beer, and 'holy shit!' if you happened to be at the wrong end of the room when it went off. After a few shots of the cannon, there is usually a duty adult on hand to confiscate it before it hurt someone or, in some cases, splits open altogether causing a whole lot more damage. Therefore, as I said, our entertainment moved on to personal banter.

It started with Ivan and I coming in for some heat about how shit we were on our MCGH trips, but somehow it came out that Les was probably a virgin. He probably wasn't, but beer-fuelled banter is rarely bothered with accuracy. In fighter squadrons, you are known for how good you are in the aircraft, but also how good your banter is in the bar and the crew room. Being a pilot of limited ability and a bit of a lightweight in the drinking stakes, I needed to make sure I used whatever wits I had on being a banter superstar to make up for it. Squadron banter usually starts when a pilot or nav has made a mistake, had an odd haircut, said something stupid, or had a car accident—you name it, it is fair game.

I had been on the receiving end numerous times, so I enjoyed Les taking a hit or two, and his indignant reaction to being called a virgin only fanned the flames. It just so happened that Les had a female friend staying the weekend so obviously, this was going to be his big moment. The rules on having guests of the opposite sex in the mess were still pretty draconian in the 1980s, so Les had booked a separate room for his guest. As drunk as we were, we decided that one of us should witness Les's coming of age, and we hatched a plan to secret one of us under his bed. As Les went off to the guardroom to collect his friend, we broke into his room, and Joel tried to get under his bed. Joel was a bit more portly than the average man, so we had to jack up Les's bed using a couple of his books and Joel squeezed under. We left him there with a beer and some snacks and went back to the bar. Les joined us with his friend, and while chatting to her, it became apparent that she was merely a family friend visiting the area and not his paramour at all. I can't remember if we gave Joel another thought, but we continued drinking until the bar closed and then retired to bed.

Breakfast was interesting. Joel was pretty pissed with us. Apparently, he had fallen asleep as it took so long for Les to go to bed. Les was very OCD and noticed straight away that his room looked different, with the bed being higher than usual. He rumbled Joel straight away—Joel's snoring didn't help.

'Joel. What are you doing under my bed?'

'It was the others, Les. They forced me under here!' Joel pleaded.

'But you have a pint of beer and some pork scratchings under there.' Joel had no answer for that and sloped off to bed suitably embarrassed and chastised.

The Sport of Kings

Next up was the air combat phase. Whereas the student navs had had a hard time on the basic intercept sorties, it was time for a load of trips that would see me, Ivan, Joel, and Willy put through the wringer. The first trip of the phase was an odd one—a singleton aircraft with a QFI, to just explore handling the jet in full burner at high angles of attack. The pre-phase briefing laboured the use of rudder rather than aileron over fifteen units, and some performance figures regarding how much height above the simulated base was required to roll over and pull through. This stuff would be re-briefed in the sortie brief itself.

I looked at the programme for the next day and saw that I had drawn the Boss again. Right, well at least I knew what the old bastard wanted this time. After crewing in, I started singing out my checks, only to be stopped by him telling me he didn't want to 'Hear all that shit.' Following another shout into my muted oxygen mask, I continued on and out to the runway. This was the first time I had flown alpha fit—a clean aeroplane with no external fuel tanks. There were only a couple of pylons under the wings to hold the dummy Sidewinder acquisition rounds. I pushed the throttles to 80 per cent, holding it on the brakes, then let my toes off, and we leapt forwards up to mil power, rocking the throttles outboard and pushing to full burner and shitty death. This was an absolute rocket ship. The jet was airborne in seemingly half the time and distance, and we were barrelling out over the glinted sea of the Moray Firth. I was almost whooping with delight; this was like the first trip all over again.

'See how slick she is, Tug?' the Boss asked. He should have flown a clean jet everyday if this was the effect it had on him. With the Boss in such a good mood, I relaxed and really got into hauling the jet around at high AOA and the highest G I had pulled in absolutely ages. My God, the fuel went in an instant though, and I had made a point of doing lots of fuel checks (as warned in the phase brief). The rear cockpit had no fuel gauge in it, and obviously the navs were somewhat touchy about it and would pimp their pilot if they weren't given enough fuel checks. However, they did have the same 'low fuel' warning caption in the back as we had in the front. If that was the first thing they knew about the fuel situation, then woe betide that pilot when they got on the ground afterwards—and rightly so. I landed off that trip absolutely buzzing, but better was to come that day.

Going Abroad

Our German Air Force exchange officer, Odo, needed to head back to his old airfield at Wittmundhafen in northern Germany to sort out some admin regarding his three years in the UK. The squadron was very accommodating and gave him an aircraft for the trip, flying out of Leuchars Friday afternoon and back first thing Monday morning. Our flight commander, Nails, thought that seeing as I was posted to Germany, it would be a good experience for me to fly Odo there and back. I was over the moon (and bricking it). This would be my first time as the captain of an aircraft flying outside of UK airspace.

Odo planned the route and gave me the map a few days before, so I could study it and the approach to Wittmund. We had packed a bag each for the weekend, and I was very carefully briefed by Nails before he authorised the sortie for us. A lot of the brief centred around warning me not to screw up, and off we went. The bags were stored in a baggage pod hanging off one of the pylons, along with a spare pre-packed drag chute. Reloading an unpacked drag chute was a nightmare so I was glad of this. The baggage pods were old napalm cannisters that had been modified with doors on the side that could be opened up for storage. These doors were held closed with quick release fasteners, although most of these were so old and bent that a wise pilot usually speed taped around the whole cannister just to be safe.

Odo and I blasted airborne and headed towards a navigation point on the border of UK and German airspace called Mike Charlie Six. This was a really important trip for me in some respects. First, I had been trusted by the grown-ups to do it and come back on the Monday after a weekend away. Secondly, Odo had become a really good friend to everyone on the course, but also remembering that he was a very experienced Phantom nav, having 1,000 hours on the German F4F, I did not want to let him down or look like an idiot at his home base.

The weather was typical June in Northern Germany—hot, but with poor visibility due to the industrial haze in the air. We got lined up about 10 miles out, and I got sight of the airfield at about 5 miles. This was made all the more difficult by the fact that all NATO bases in Central Europe were deliberately toned down in colour to drab greys and greens so that they were difficult to spot by Soviet bombers. There were no flight lines like at Leuchars as all of the aircraft were dispersed into HASs and revetments around the airfield. We landed safely and were instructed to taxi to one of the HAS sites by the tower controller. We were marshalled into an enclosed apron and parked up next to a Dutch F16. This was the first time I had seen one up close and it looked a bit small compared to our lumbering beast. Lots of Odo's old squadron mates were at the jet to meet him, and I was introduced to everyone. For the first time, I was being treated like an equal by proper front-line Phantom crews, and it felt great.

The weekend was one long round of beer and barbeques, and Odo had something close to celebrity status as all his old friends wanted to see him and probably check that the RAF was treating him properly. The overriding memory of that weekend though was that almost everyone I met asked if I had seen *Dinner for One*. I had never heard of it (which they found unbelievable) but apparently it is shown every year on German TV around Christmas or New Year and is a cult tradition in most households. It is a thirty-minute sketch of an old aristocratic English lady who holds a dinner party. She has no real guests, so the butler pretends to be all of them and gets drunker and drunker as the sketch goes on, as he has to drink for each of them during the many and varied toasts. Anyway, one of the guys found a copy on video at a barbeque and we all sat down to watch it, I think mainly so they could see my reaction. It is a funny sketch, but a bit more of an old-fashioned style than I was used to; I was really into Rik Mayall and Ade Edmondson at this stage. However, I think I laughed in all the right places, and this gave Odo a good feeling that he had enriched my life with *Dinner for One*.

When we got back to Wittmund, first thing Monday, we had breakfast at Odo's old squadron, filed a flight plan, and went out to the jet to find it was gone. The ground crew had towed it away on the Friday after we had left and parked it snugly in a HAS. I had never operated from inside a HAS before, but Odo assured me it would be okay. As I did the walk round, I was acutely aware of how tight it was and how close to the walls of the HAS the wingtips were. At the back of the HAS, there were two huge gaps with an angled concrete splitter in between, to syphon the exhaust from the jet pipes outwards and upwards once we had started up. The splitter was jet black caked with soot.

As we were crewing in, the ground crew fired up the big generator and the noise in the HAS was horrific. This only got worse when I started the APU and the engines. I have lost a fair bit of my hearing over the years, and some of it must be down to operating in HASs. The noise of jet engines in confined spaces is almost otherworldly; it is so shocking. Anyway, once started, I inched my way out of the HAS. The ground crew looked a little non-plussed with how slowly I was moving, but there was no way I was going to have a wingtip strike, especially after Nails's 'don't screw up' brief the previous Friday. That was the most difficult part of the trip in the end. The transit back to Leuchars was uneventful, and after landing, I couldn't thank Odo enough for such a great weekend. It seemed that Germany consisted of beer, barbeque sausages, and quirky old comedy sketches—should be a good first tour then, as long as I could get through the last couple of phases of the course.

Failure

Having had a go at fighting ourselves as a singleton on ACT 1, it was time to fight someone else. Basic air combat training begins with set-piece exercises so that the instructor in the back can demonstrate the manoeuvres, then hand control to us so we can try and replicate what we just saw. I couldn't have wished for a better instructor. I was programmed to fly with the head of the QWIs. As I have already said, I usually had very little respect for QWIs, but this guy was different. As head of the QWIs, he should be one of the best at air combat (and he was). His nickname was 'Guns'. He was approachable, enthusiastic, and cool as hell. How the hell he passed the QWI course with that kind of reputation I will never know. This is a guy I really want to impress. True to form though, I make a dick of myself almost straight away.

The trip called for a pairs take-off with us on the wing. I lined up next to the leader on the runway, slightly swept back in the close formation position, and gave him a thumbs-up. I watched him give the wind-up signal and pushed the throttles to 80 per cent while holding on the brakes. After another thumbs-up from me, the leader nodded his head as he let the brakes off and smoothly went up to mil power. I worked hard on the throttles to maintain my position and then rocked the throttles outboard into burner on another head nod. I could see the burner flames coming from his jet pipes and as we approached take-off—all kinds of shit happens.

My aeroplane decided to get airborne before his and I struggled to keep in position by pushing on the stick, then pulling to match his jet taking to the air. I was now up and down on the correct formation position, trying to get the undercarriage up and not crash into the leader. This up/down motion is what we call a PIO (pilot-induced oscillation) and must look like a sack of shit to Guns—not a good start. I got the flaps up and tried to catch a breath. Guns was cool about it all and we flew out to the play area and set up for the exercises. Initially, we would do some 'perch' work. The leader would set a pre-briefed speed around 400 knots and we would sit on a perch about 1,000 feet higher and swept back about 1.5 miles.

At the radio call of 'commence', Guns selected burner and got a Sidewinder lock and pulled the trigger, calling 'FOX 2!' The bandit broke into us and set up a 4-G turn. As we closed, we selected the gun, and Guns put the sight on the pilot's cockpit. If we just continued like this, we would probably fly through to the outside of the bandit's turn, giving him the chance to reverse his turn and threaten us. To prevent this, we first had to recognise the high closure rate and the high angle off the bandit's tail. Then we rolled off the bank to wing level and aggressively pitched up to stop the fly through. The bandit would now extend away from us as soon as we had stopped the fly through, so we then overbank back towards him.

We were aiming to get into a guns position about 300 yards behind and within about 30 degrees of his tail. This manoeuvre is called a 'high-speed yo-yo' and is a classic basic fighter manoeuvre. A hi yo-yo will quite often leave us out of range for the gun (we call this 'stretched'), but if the bandit is still turning and has some height below him, we can use this to cut across his turning circle to get closer. So, as soon as the hi yo-yo is done, we point across the circle in front of the bandit and push forwards going below him to gather speed. This is called a 'low-speed yo-yo'. Now we may end up approaching the bandit with lots of overtake but with a lower angle off his tail. To kill the speed, we can now use a 'lag pursuit roll'. This means flying a tight barrel roll behind the bandit, using lots of G and a bit of three-dimensional geometry to roll out gracefully in guns range. There are a few other aspects to air combat, such as flat and rolling scissors, but we all have to start somewhere. Guns executed the whole set piece perfectly then handed me control for a go.

I did okay on the weaponeering and had done plenty of hi and lo yo-yos in the past, so I made a decent stab at those. I had never done a lag pursuit roll before, and I guffed my way horribly through that one, rolling out about half a mile behind, so I had to lo yo-yo across all over again before finally gunning the bandit. I had another go at the full procedure and it hit me just how difficult this phase of the course was going to be. There was so little fuel that I didn't get the chance to hone my skills. I passed the trip, but I knew I hadn't covered myself in glory. However, a pass is a pass, and sometimes that is all that counts.

All too soon though, I ran out of talent—on the very next trip as a matter of fact. I was up with Nails on ACT 3, and once again, I rode the bucking bronco on the pairs take-off. In flying training, any 'trend' seen with student performance becomes an 'issue', and I had just given them something to concentrate on and target me with. The take-off was not the only thing I managed to screw up, and after about twenty minutes of some of the worst flying I had ever done, I knew the game was up and this would go down in the auth sheets as a DNCO (duty not carried out—namely, a failed sortie).

The auth sheets had lots of columns for things like the people flying, the type of exercise to be carried out, take-off times, and length of sortie, etc., then each aircraft's captain would sign their initials followed by the authoriser's initials (this could be someone who was part of your sortie or may be the duty authoriser on the ops desk). We were then legal to fly the sortie. After landing and signing the aircraft back in with the engineers, we would sign back in the auth sheets with our actual take off time, landing time, duration of flight, time spent in cloud, type of approaches, time spent on instruments, number of landings, and then sign in again with your initials. The column before the initials was the one that really told the story in flying training. If the instructor wrote DCO then the duty was carried out and we had passed the trip. We could DNCO due to weather (DNCO WX), serviceability of aircraft (DNCO AC) or radar (DNCO RDR), but DNCO on its own meant a failed sortie.

I was absolutely gutted when I saw it in the sheets after this trip but not wholly surprised. I had failed a few trips in the previous three years of flying training, and every time it was like a hammer blow. The axe was getting nearer and the chop was more real. The key after a failed trip was how you bounced back. Well in this case, I had the re-fly of the trip to bounce back as a subsequent fail could well have seen me chopped.

Obviously, the formation take-off took a fair chunk of the debrief, but to his credit, Nails tried to get to the bottom of why I had started to struggle with it, having not had a problem before. Basically, as I fell behind on the runway, I was accelerating to catch up and reaching take-off speed before the leader's jet was ready to commit to aviation.

Nails told me to hold my stick just off the backstop to stop my jet from leaping skywards and pull it the last bit as I saw the leader leave the ground. He also suggested I sit a bit further forwards on the runway so I didn't get left so far behind on the release of the brakes. He put a lot of the rest of my poor performance down to being rattled by the take-off. I wasn't convinced at that point but appreciated him trying to help. None of the other guys had failed an ACT trip at that point, so I felt even more isolated. It is a desperate time when you fail a trip. Flying is a great leveller, and waiting for the re-fly has always been a horrible experience. However, I did what I always did and prepared as much as I could for the next day, prayed to the gods of military aviation for some help, then tried to apply all the advice I had been given from the debrief.

Success and Failure

Nails flew with me on the re-fly and his take-off technique worked a treat. You can't buy the confidence I gained from that or from the praise that Nails gave me at the time. The rest of the trip was good enough to pass and let me loose doing air combat with a staff nav in the back. My sense of relief was huge, and my reward for passing the trip was that I flew with Spencer on the first of those trips. Once again, he was a joy, and it was amazing to see him as a nav get his teeth into the fight as much as me. It has always been a surprise to me how much navs loved flying and fighting in the Phantom, and their enthusiasm was infectious. Coming through the failed trip had given me a big dose of confidence. I really got into the ACT phase and was able to show off a bit of aggression.

However, as I was growing into the phase, Willy began to struggle. Despite my valiant attempt on ACT 3, it is rare that a student on a flying training course will get chopped towards the end of a course due to a pure aircraft handling problem. More often than not, it will happen because of a mental processing issue. This ability to think outside of the cockpit and/or think ahead of the aircraft is a key element for an aviator to excel and to remain safe. Willy walked into the crew room having failed an ACT trip by almost running out of fuel. As I have already said, there is no fuel gauge in the rear cockpit, and his staff nav was obviously very upset when his 'low fuel' caption came on, but Willy continued to press the fight in full afterburner.

A shout from the back seat to cut the burner got Willy's attention, and they flew an uncomfortably quiet transit back to Leuchars on fuel minimums. Willy had compounded the situation by not calling that he was 'fuel priority' with ATC, which could have got them sequenced ahead of other aeroplanes recovering at the same time. Willy seemed somewhat unconcerned even though the trip was a fail. His handling during the trip had been fine, so I guess he just saw this as a minor issue that was easy to sort out. His staff nav did not share his view, I think. Funny thing, but the navs' union were pretty sensitive about young pilots running them out of fuel.

That weekend was the summer ball in the officers' mess. The summer ball was the social event of the year and was a twelve-hour blowout of food, drink, live music, and a horrific hangover that destroyed the whole weekend. We had the following Monday off, so it was a good chance to let our hair down. The mess was decorated like a cruise ship, complete with lots of entertainment and food options, including a brilliant seafood bar, main buffet, and a Mongolian BBQ, a casino, a disco, and a couple of live bands.

The mess was chock-full of Phantom aviators from Treble One and 43 with their wives and girlfriends—guys that I was about a month away from serving with. The big news from the ball for our course though was that Les had brought a girl along, and she was one of the crash divs. So, this was it; Les was finally going to break his duck and his virginity was going to be consigned to history.

The ball was awesome, and breakfast came around for the survivors at about 5 a.m. Drunk food inside me, I retired at about 7.30 a.m. and spent the rest of the day sleeping it off. I was about to enter the final phase of the course—about a dozen more trips to get through and I was done. By the way, Les's date did not stay the night, so his virginity remained intact. My hangover was so bad I couldn't even muster the enthusiasm to banter him about it.

The ACT sorties became a lot more aggressive with the staff pilots, who were our opponents, turning up the pressure on us. It is relatively easy for a staff pilot to beat up on a student pilot in ACT, but the key was to up their game to such an extent that whatever shot opportunity we got against them, we had earned. They were no longer making deliberate mistakes for us to capitalise on, and they would severely punish any errors that we made. I was absolutely loving it though. I can't say I was any good, but I had plenty of aggression, worked well with the nav in that dynamic environment, and was buzzing with enthusiasm. The RAF loves a tryer, and that effort and joy can cover a multitude of sins if an instructor sees that you really want it. I also had a pathological hatred of being shot down, which was probably a good attitude to have looking at what my future job was going to be. Instructors hated students who just gave up when it looked like they would be shot down. I kept fighting even after the simulated missiles and bullets had ripped me to shreds, and I was more than happy to cheat given the chance.

Willy had failed his re-fly. Once again, he had almost run out of fuel, this time with Uncle Tony. When the caption had come on, Uncle Tony, who was always very mellow, had shouted for the burner cut. When he asked Willy how much gas they had, Willy had replied, 'Not a lot,' which went down like a shit sandwich. This made for an even more uncomfortable recovery than the last time as Uncle Tony could not get a straight answer out of Willy regarding their fuel situation. Willy looked a bit more worried in the crew room this time as he had been bollocked really badly in the debrief. He knew that the next trip was definitely a chop ride so things were serious now. It has always been shocking to see how quickly a guy can go from doing okay on a course and feeling confident to having him prepare for a chop ride. It was made all the worse for him, being so close to the end of the course and tantalisingly near to the front-line.

I had never really been close to Willy through our previous training courses together, but course student spirit kicks in and we usually band together against the common enemy—in this case, the staff who want to chop us (none of the staff really want to see anyone chopped, unless they are a complete arsehole, but that is a survival mentality for flying training that comes through). None of us were acing the course, but nonetheless, we tried to combine our thoughts and help Willy plan for his chop ride. The general consensus from us was to forget about the fighting of the aircraft and just concentrate on the fuel and give the staff nav more fuel calls than he has ever had in his life—not rocket science I know, but difficult to do for real when you are maxed out trying to fight someone in air combat.

Willy was flying with Dennis Outlaw, who was a QWI nav and a right hard bastard. The result was inevitable, as Willy once again ran out of fuel, but this time in a spectacular fashion. Obviously, Dennis was going to concentrate the whole sortie on Willy's fuel management and loaded him up with pressure until the 'low fuel' caption came on. Willy didn't notice it again and just kept on fighting. Dennis let him go until his ass started puckering and then knocked it off. Apparently, they were so low on gas that they recovered on vapour. That was that. Willy was chopped and his time on the Phantom came to an end.

As usual, this meant a big night in the bar, almost like a wake. Some of the instructors joined us for a beer or two to commiserate with Willy, but made themselves scarce in the usual manner shortly after. When a student is chopped from a course, we go through a self-healing process where the instructors are not welcome. Actually, that is a little harsh as the instructors understand that this is not their time. The students had to 'grieve' and then move on, becoming more resilient in the process. Willy was distraught, but he held it together until the instructors left the bar. He then burst into tears and got steaming drunk.

One of our coping mechanisms through flying training is to banter our way through our troubles. In typical gallows humour style, we renamed the 'low fuel' caption the 'take me home Willy light', and that has stuck for us to this day. At the end of the night, Willy was in no fit state, so we put him to bed. Our band of brothers ethos kicked in and we sat up drinking in his room all night making sure he didn't choke on his own vomit or some such. That ethos then duly upped and buggered off as we got drunker and more bored, and we systematically moved all of his furniture and belongings —and him—outside onto the mess lawn. Of course, we had to move it all back in the next morning, but we hadn't thought of that at the time.

Bollocks

We were now onto 2 *v*. 1 combat where we had to work as a coordinated pair against a single bandit. This involved lots of tactical formation flying with big height splits, to intercept the target and shoot them down using 'free and engaged' tactics. The idea was to get one of the fighters into the fight, unseen by the bandit, and then have that fighter tie him up while the other one disengaged, and then re-engaged unseen with massive advantage to shoot the bandit down. As the engaged fighter, it was my job to fight as hard as I could to pressurise the bandit, all the time calling to my wingman over the radio about where the fight was and if I was winning or losing. The idea was to get the wingman's eyes onto us so that he could re-enter with me making the bandit predictable.

As the free fighter, I would take a huge height split while trying to keep my eyes on the fight, and then reposition to enter from an unseen area and kill the bandit.

It all sounds pretty straight forward, but all of this took disciplined standard communication over the radio to coordinate—all while aggressively flying the aircraft, trying not to get shot down, and conducting lots of effective weaponeering to take shots as they presented themselves. Add to this the comm in cockpit between myself and my nav to keep sight of the target and get it on radar and you can see how complicated and dynamic these trips were.

Our knowledge of the radar and weapons had to grow to match this complexity and this was tested daily as the sortie briefs became in-depth quizzes to check we knew our stuff prior to flying. We all got a shock when Joel failed a brief and didn't go flying. Dennis was in a bad mood—or a standard QWI mood—and didn't like Joel's laid back attitude so quizzed him to within an inch of his life, expecting QWI levels of knowledge. When Joel came up short, he was given a massive bollocking and the flight was cancelled.

Speaking of bollocks, that evening, I was soaking in the shower, absolutely exhausted from the sortie I had flown earlier, when I felt a dull ache in one of my balls. As I investigated, the ache got more pronounced and I grew more concerned. Then I felt a small hard lump and instantly thought I was going to die from bollock cancer. With no internet in those days to put my mind at rest (or put me closer to the grave), my imagination worked overtime and came up with the worst outcome.

As luck would have it, I had my annual aircrew medical the next morning. Annual medicals always went the same way. You would arrive early to memorise the bottom line of letters on the sight chart when no one was looking, then impress the nurse by reading it backwards to her. This was followed by a hearing test where you could score highly by just guessing the rhythm as the beeps got quieter. You then did a urine test and went in to see the medical officer, who would ask how you had been over the past year, check your reflexes, and listen to your chest before declaring whether you were good for another year.

I figured when the doctor asked how I had been, I would say something like, 'Ok, oh apart from one of my bollocks,' and that would break the ice and I could get it sorted with little embarrassment. All proceeded as expected until I walked in to find that Leuchars had a female MO. I completely lost my ability to speak properly, and when she asked how

I had been, my eloquent reply was, 'Er... okay Doc. Well, I say okay. Apart from ... you see, I have a ... well it's a bit embarrassing really.' She let me squirm a bit, and I took a deep breath and pressed on. 'You see I have a problem with one of my erm...' I just couldn't bring myself to say bollocks in front of her.

'Testicles?' she asked.

'Yes! That's the word I was trying to think of!' The ice broken, I then told her the problem and the next thing I knew, I was on the bed and trying to think of anything other than what was happening down below. After what seemed like days, she finished her examination and gave me the good news that I didn't have cancer, but some sort of calcified deposit in my tubes—thank God! I was prescribed some pills, and then she gave me the awkward news that I was grounded for the rest of the week while I took them. This meant I would have to fess up to the squadron. With any luck, I could keep it between myself and Nails.

Thirty minutes later, I was sitting in his office, telling him I was grounded. He immediately called the MO to see if I could fly with a pilot instructor in the back seat so I could continue with the course on schedule. This is the one side of the phone conversation I heard while Nails spoke to the MO: 'Hi Marie. Yes, it's Nails here from the OCU. I'm great thanks. I've got young Wilson here in front of me and wanted to talk about his [long pause] condition. So, he has a lump in one of his erm... Yes! That's the word I was looking for!'

He continued to discuss me in this way, but the end result was the same—grounded for three days. To tell you the truth, three days away from the stress of flying did me good, but waiting to go flying is almost as stressful, especially when the rest of the course is progressing without you. My errant testicle became the latest object of ridicule, and even some of the staff bantered me about it. Three months I had been on the course, and my bollock was more popular than I was. Dinner in the mess that night was interesting, especially when the MO sat down next to me and asked how I was feeling. As my coursemates cracked up laughing, all I could think about was whether she had washed her hands before dinner.

Final Push and Postings

The last phase of the course was advanced radar and was going to be difficult for both the pilots and the navs. We were now looking to take all of the skills we had learned in the basic radar phase and use them down at low level. This would be an eye-opener for me for me as the job in Germany was mostly conducted at low level. I still had a couple of 2 *v*. 1 combat trips to complete as well, so the next couple of weeks were going to be pretty intense.

Within all of that, our postings night was arranged and we donned the blindfold and drank the drinks to find out our futures. It was a bit anticlimactic for me and Odo in that I knew I was going to 92 Squadron and the German exchange posting was always on 56 at Wattisham. However, it was nice to have it confirmed, and as I yammed my Snakebite down, there was much cheering and pats on the back. Our senior officers on the course had already left for their postings, so it was left to Ivan, Joel, and Les to get theirs. All three of them were picked out for 74 Squadron at Wattisham and would be flying the Phantom F4F rather than the FG1 or FGR2 every other Phantom squadron had. The RAF had bought a whole squadron of F4Fs some years earlier, and the guys on it had the thrill of wearing cool American flying kit. They were also the Tiger squadron so had cool badges too. However, they were UK-based and so obviously dull and shit; I was already talking the hard man, front-line Germany talk.

I did the next 2 *v*. 1 trip with Uncle Tony, and it was the closest I had been to flying like a normal crew. The experience of us working together to coordinate with our wingman and shoot the bandit repeatedly was a beautiful thing. Recovering as a three-ship and breaking into the circuit with me in the lead almost seemed routine, yet only three months ago, I was still thinking the aircraft was trying to kill me. I had always loved how the Phantom looked, but now, I was getting on top of handling it; I was really smitten and couldn't imagine having to fly anything else. I took pride in how ugly it looked and revelled in the fact that it was a proper proven war machine, having thrown its weight around in Vietnam. My mates from flying training were flying Tornado GR1s and Jaguars, and one was even on the new fighter version of the Tornado (poor bastard as it really was a bit shit in those days). The two aircraft that had the kudos in those days were the Buccaneer and the Phantom, and I was so lucky to be flying the Phantom.

Bow Your Head in Shame

There was no time to pat myself on the back though as the sorties came thick and fast. AD14 was the first low-level intercept sortie and I was programmed to fly it with Dennis. The advanced phase came with lots more rules and weapons knowledge attached, and it was a serious workload to get up to speed with it all. We needed to learn the standard UK rules of engagement, which were complicated at best, dimensions of friendly and threat surface-to-air missile engagement zones (SAM MEZ), recce features of Soviet aircraft, low-level ranges, and limits of the radar and weapons—the list seemed endless. All this stuff was written down in 'secret' documents kept in the secure cabinets in the squadron registry. These were all subjects that the instructors would test us on in sortie briefs.

Cognisant of the fact that Dennis had failed Joel in a brief for not knowing his stuff, I swotted all night before my trip with him. He fired weapons questions at me, and I answered every one confidently. After a few, he switched tack and when I gave my answer, he would ask, 'Are you sure?' This started to freak me out a bit, and my confidence evaporated. To this day, I know I got them all right, but I could see the blood rising in Dennis as I ummed and erred my way through his latter questions.

At the end of the brief, he seemed to be fuming and I knew I was headed for failure, but couldn't understand how I had ended up in that position. It was at this point that the natural survival instinct that all student pilots have kicked in. Mine was honed in the shit pit of Tac Weapons and told me I had to find some way of avoiding this flight. Unfortunately, there were tons of jets available and I couldn't fake illness (sticky ears was always a good one) at this late stage. This would take some thought. Dennis had gone full bastard mode by the time I checked comm with him in the cockpit. Then, the inspiration came to me. On the right-hand console, was the CADC switch (combined air data computer). The CADC fed all sorts of clever data to the radar and INAS and was essential for flight. If I switched it off a few times, we would have to abort the flight. However, if I did it on the chocks, they would send us to a spare aircraft and I would still have to fly. Therefore, I went through a full start up and check in with the leader, keeping my powder dry. As we taxied out of dispersal, I flicked the CADC off. We both got the CDC caption and the attention-getters. I called it out and reset the switch and the captions went away. On we continued with the pre-take off checks and I casually flicked it off again. Dennis wasn't happy, but I reset it again.

'If it goes again Tug, we will have to abort.' Bingo! Just as we switched frequency to tower for take-off, I took the switch off again and we had to call it a day. I am not proud of the fact that I had allowed two very expensive jets to taxi all the way out and then all the way back for nothing, but this was about survival. In retrospect, I should also apologise to the ground crew for snagging a perfectly serviceable aeroplane and causing them a whole heap of investigative maintenance. The irony is that as we walked back in from the jet, Dennis said, 'I'm sorry about that, Tug. I was really looking forward to flying with you— you sounded like you knew your stuff'—shame he hadn't told his face that in the brief. That whole episode is not the most shameful thing I have done in an aeroplane, but it comes close.

Anyway, all's well that ends well as I got to do the re-fly with Bungle, and he was brilliant. Bungle was badly named. He was a tall, wiry guy who had thinning hair, wrinkles, and a Gaucho-style moustache that made him look older than he was. He was incredibly fit, having played basketball for the RAF (and excelled in a wide range of other sports too) and was extremely capable in the air. He was the course commander for our junior course and they loved him. They almost killed him I think, as they were a hard-drinking, hard-partying course.

There was a tradition in flying training that students would TACEVAL their course commanders from time to time, usually after happy hour on a Friday. TACEVAL was the name for the no-notice exercises on the front-line where stations 'went to war' for a few days and were evaluated on their drills and procedures by teams of NATO auditing staff. TACEVAL in flying training meant a group of students banging on the course commander's door late at night, demanding beer and food. Woe betide a course commander who could not or did not provide copious amounts of booze and egg and bacon sandwiches. Bungle and his wife were the perfect hosts and were almost constantly bombarded by their course. They never once failed to provide. In the big scheme of things, it was a huge compliment to be TACEVAL'd by your students. Bungle was a legend with his course, and no matter what trouble they found themselves in, he waded in and protected them as much as he could.

Suffice it to say that our course didn't TACEVAL Gouldy once during the course. On numerous occasions, he hinted to us that he was up for it, but we always gave him the big ignore, preferring to stay in the bar until we were broken and went to bed. Hopefully, Gouldy got the message. Students have long memories, and the fact that he had thrown us all under the bus at the first opportunity was not lost on us. The trip with Bungle was great, just like flying in a proper crew again. Bungle was a brilliant instructor, but he was also smart enough to realise that at some point, he would be posted back to the front-line and may well be crewed with one of his students in the future, hence he acted like a decent human being. A couple of the other staff navs weren't that smart or didn't care, and that caught them out later on when they returned to the front-line.

I really got to grips with handling the Phantom at low level, and even with the G restrictions (especially with full tanks), I loved raging around at 250 feet, hauling it behind the target and taking kills, or closing in to VID—all with the ground rushing past at 400 knots or more. What a buzz! This was going to be my life in Germany? Bring it on. As we mixed these low-level trips with the last couple of 2 *v.* 1 ACT missions, I thought I had died and gone to heaven. The front-line was just a sniff away and for the first time, I thought I was going to make it. I was flying with good navs—even another trip with Put Put went well—and seemed to have cracked the handling of the jet. Okay, I was still a bit agricultural on the controls, but I think that suited the Beast that lurked in the aeroplane's guts. The pair of us now had an understanding. It had stopped trying to kill me, and I was being much more sympathetic in my handling. This could be the start of something special.

Another One Bites the Dust (In More Ways Than One!)

However, just as my life and love affair with the Phantom was coming together, Les's was starting to come apart, and he was having trouble handling the radar at low level. He had failed a trip or two and was in the spotlight. On the flipside, as we went into the weekend, it looked like his virginity was in even more trouble. Odo had invited both courses to his house for a Saturday BBQ, and Les was bringing along the girl he had invited to the summer ball. We promised Les we wouldn't camp out under his bed again and left the path clear for him to finally pass the ultimate trip.

Odo's wife, Sabine, was an amazing cook, and the BBQ was absolutely rocking with us being up to our eyes in German sausages and Bitburger beer. Les and his girl were becoming somewhat amorous, and this attracted the attention of our junior course mates who took it upon themselves to sabotage his special moment. Les had already drunk a fair amount to settle his nerves, but the added spiked drinks he was given sealed the deal. The next thing we knew, he was on the roof of the shed with his trousers round his ankles, declaring his love and describing what he was going to do once he got his girlfriend back to his room. Fortunately, we managed to talk him down off the roof, and he instantly fell asleep in a corner of the garden.

Les was still unconscious when it came time to call it a night, so the two biggest guys off the junior course (Lurch and Bros) got him upright between them and started to drag him back to the mess from Odo's married quarter. On the way back, a RAF police car drove past and stopped about 100 yards past them before turning around to investigate. Quick as a flash, Lurch and Bros threw Les into the nearest front garden and tried to look innocent as the police car pulled up.

'Can we offer you a lift, Sir?'

'No thanks, Corporal, we are just walking back to the mess.'

'What about your colleague, Sir?'

'Who?'

'The body in the garden, Sir?'

'Oh, er no—we can manage him thanks.'

'Very well, Sir,' and off they drove. The guys deposited Les on his bed, and both of our courses sat round him on vomit-watch while drinking and joking about the state of him. His girlfriend, who was a nurse, seemed unconcerned, having seen it all before in A&E on a Friday night. However, as we got drunker and drunker in Les's room, the evening took a turn for the downright bizarre.

Les was an incredibly clean and smart guy and was always ironing his flying suits and polishing his boots. My boots had been Phantomised in that they looked a bit scruffy and had the odd oil stain on them, and Ivan's were just plain evil, smelling like something or someone had died in them. They were so foul he had to leave them outside on his window ledge at night. Les's were immaculate, and he had a full and neat care kit for them. Bros, who was well and truly bored at this point, found a plastic bottle full of boot polish that had a small sponge on the end. Taking the top off, he squeezed out some polish on the sponge and started painting Les's face, muttering something about dragging Les's lazy arse all the way back from Odo's house and how he 'deserved it'.

Not content with painting his face, he lifted Les's shirt and painted a big cock on his stomach in black boot polish. This brought a huge round of laughter that turned to horror in an instant. Ivan had picked up Les's razor and shouted, 'Let's shave off one of his eyebrows,' before jabbing it down and cutting a gouge out of Les's left eyebrow. I have never sobered up more quickly in my life. I jumped on Ivan and wrestled the razor out of his hands before he killed Les. After much arguing, Les's girlfriend agreed to shave one of his legs to appease the drunken crowd. To be honest, I think she was pissed with Les as their special night together had turned out to be not so special, and she just wanted rid of us. She had not expected to be nursing him through the night, so the leg was a bit of punishment for him.

In the time-honoured tradition of drunk people everywhere, we all lost interest and decided to call it a night. Just as we were filing out, Ivan got a touch of conscience or something and worried that Les would exact revenge on us all, he decided to cover our tracks. He put the razor in Les's right hand and the boot polish in the left, and then sellotaped them together. It was at this point I had my one moment of clarity. 'Ivan. There is no way in the morning Les is going to wake up and think he has shaved his own leg, blacked his own face, drawn a cock on his stomach, and then sellotaped his own hands together. Leave it mate.'

I was right. My room was next door to Les's, and at about 10 a.m., I was woken by him banging on my wall and shouting. 'You bastards! You bastards! I am going to... Jesus! Look at my fucking leg!'

Sunday was a bad day all round. We had a students *v.* staff cricket event in the afternoon, but to be honest, our hearts weren't in it and Bungle slaughtered us with his cricketing prowess. The biggest loss was later that night though, as Les's virginity finally succumbed to the inevitable.

Les faced the inevitable in the cockpit also that week. He never quite got to grips with the low-level trips and got chopped in short order, a mere handful of trips from the end. It was a great shame as Les was a good guy. It was obvious at the end that he was struggling to enjoy the flying though. This happens a lot when students struggle and start failing trips (I know that from my own experience), but underneath that, a student must have the motivation and drive to pull them through that bad time. Without it, they are destined to fail and be chopped. The rest of the course can help up to a point, and the best courses were those that banded together really well. This is hard to do at an OCU as most of your best mates from flying training had probably been posted to different jets and your OCU course took their place as surrogate mates, banded together by necessity depending on how grim the OCU was. We were a good course in that respect I think, but nowhere near as tight as our junior course. They did seem to rely a lot on the bar and Bungle's beer fridge to gel themselves together, but so what? It worked for them.

Fill Her Up!

We had lost both *ab initio* navs and one pilot off our course, so 50 per cent of the *ab initios*. This is a really poor average at this late stage of the flying training programme. Joel, Ivan, and I entered the final mini-phase of the course called CAPEX. This consisted of us 'going to war' for the last three trips. We would launch out to a medium-level combat air patrol (CAP) and set up a two-minute racetrack pointing down threat. Every fast jet squadron in the UK had been invited to fly towards us, and we would be vectored towards them and instructed to either engage or identify them by our GCI (ground control intercept) controller. The targets could be at low level or all the way up to high fast fliers, and we had to deal with whatever was thrown at us. It also involved departing and recovering to the airfield with the Rapier SAM system 'live', meaning we had special navigation procedures to ensure we weren't looking hostile to our own defences.

I flew the first CAPEX sortie with Bungle, and he was brilliant. We were all over the sky, and I was disappointed when it was all over and we had to come home. Afterwards, I looked at the programme and saw that the next day was a day off flying for me, then two trips the following day to finish the course. However, my day of mellowing out took an odd turn when I pitched up for met brief and glanced at the programme board to see my name on it.

I was on the programme with Nails as a singleton, and the sortie profile was AAR—I had never heard of it (I had, but had consigned it to the very deepest pit of my memory, thinking it was definitely 'Future Tug's' problem). AAR stood for air-to-air refuelling, commonly known as 'tanking', and was something that was taught at the front-line and definitely not on the OCU. Part of our ground school had been that almost criminally boring lecture on AAR given by the pensioner from Brize. Ignoring that brief was about to catch up with me.

I asked the duty auth what AAR meant while pointing to my name on the board. He gave me a withering look and told me I was doing a dual check on tanking. I laughed and said something along the lines of not fooling me, etc., but he remained deadly serious. 'We've got use of a tanker and are trialling student refuelling. It's you from your course and Animal from the junior course.' Sure enough, Animal was programmed to fly about thirty minutes after we took off with Stroker. As I have already said, Stroker was the biggest cock of the pilot instructors, and ordinarily, I would have had a bit of sympathy for Animal, but I was convinced this was just a spoof. I still thought it was a spoof as I taxied out with Nails—an elaborate spoof, I'll give you that, but a spoof nonetheless. I think it was only as we intercepted the tanker that I fully accepted this wasn't a spoof after all and I was actually going to refuel for the first time.

The tanker was a Victor and it was absolutely huge. I had done plenty of close formation in the past, and even in the Phantom, but this was like formating on a small town. There were some standard operating procedures (SOPs) to join the tanker, which involved them clearing us to an echelon position on the starboard wing (we still called it port and starboard in those days) and then going through the pre-tanking checks. Nails called out the checks and I moved all sorts of refuelling switches that I had never touched before. Nails then called, 'probe out,' and I repeated it back to him and hit the switch.

This huge cock-like appendage emerged from just under the canopy on the right-hand side and extended forwards, up, and right. I had to retrim the aircraft to adjust for the drag and must have stared at the probe for ages. Then we were cleared in behind the Victor to prepare for contact. It was a Victor wing-hose, which Nails pointed out was the worst one for turbulence (great) and the fact that the wings had an anhedral droop made it a bit tricky to formate on.

I was tense on the rudder pedals and squeezing the stick so hard I must have almost popped all the buttons out of it. Nails got me to take a few breaths and just hang out a while behind the basket before encouraging me to move forwards into the 'waiting position'. The idea was to move into a position a few feet back from the basket and wait for it to settle down in the airflow. Nails gave me 'up a foot' and 'left two feet' type instructions as I picked a reference point on the Victor's wing to fly on. I did this by putting the pipper of the gunsight on the bottom left of the hydraulic drum unit (HDU, where the hose came out of).

Nails then told me to push and I walked the throttles forward a smidge to get a little overtake going. He had told me not to look at the basket so I didn't. The next thing I knew, I heard and felt a clunk and we were in. 'Push! Push!' said Nails, and we moved further forwards until one of the coloured bands on the hose disappeared into the HDU, and the small lights either side turned to green to tell me we were taking on fuel. I don't think I had ever been as excited in an aeroplane. The first time I tank and there I am—in straight away and taking gas. I think I even stopped hyperventilating for a while and took in the scene—a big aeroplane trailing a hose and me attached to it. Then the Victor started a turn to the left and I followed in formation as smooth as you like. Nails was almost as happy as me, I think.

'Rim, No... Oh Dear'

I was aware of a bit of chat on the radio, and shortly afterwards, two Tornado F2s joined on the right wing. We were asked to unplug and hold on the port wing while they tanked, so I slowly pulled back to unplug. This had to be done relatively slowly, otherwise it had been known for baskets to rip off a probe (or *vice versa*) if the manoeuvre was too fast or violent. So, I wasn't a tanking virgin anymore, and I relaxed in a loose formation on the left to watch the front-line guys have a go.

The Tornado F2/3 was the fighter version of the Tornado GR1 bomber. The GR1 was a well-regarded aircraft, perfectly suited to its role as a low-level bomber. The F2 (subsequently the F3) was shit as a fighter, being optimised for low level and therefore underpowered at medium to high levels. Despite it being manned by lots of former Phantom crews, there was already an intense rivalry between the fleets. In essence, the Tornado was destined to replace the Phantom, and Phantom crews were not best pleased about it, so any chance to beat up the new kid on the block was eagerly welcomed. We were cruising at about 25,000 feet, and the Tornados were struggling for power. They were having to light one of the afterburners just to keep the height, which made tanking difficult.

Next thing, we hear the F2s asking for toboggan. This was a request for the Victor to descend while tanking to get to a lower level where the F2s would have more power. Nails was laughing in the back-seat and offered up some choice insults to me about the Tornado, pointing out how lucky I was not to be flying 'that heap of shit. No power and a concrete radar!' Some of their jets had concrete ballast in the nose as their radar was not fully up and running at the time. I lapped up everything that he said. Eventually, they were full of gas and ready to depart. We asked for permission to refuel again, and the Victor asked us to hold while they climbed back to 25,000 feet.

'We can tank in the climb if you like?' said Nails, specifically to piss off the Tornado mates. They quickly called that they were leaving and went off frequency and I dropped in behind the port wing for some more prods. Buoyed by my previous success, I was convinced I would just pop back into the basket and that would be that. However, I then proceeded to joust with the basket for a few minutes with no success. A couple of times, I hit the outer rim of the basket with the probe and just withdrew and called 'Rim, no damage,' to let the tanker crew know the basket was still intact.

In my defence, it was a very bumpy day with a lot of turbulence, but I made things much worse by having a sneaky look at the basket rather than just flying my references and listening to Nails's commentary. What turned out to be my last prod was somewhat hairy. As I withdrew from missing the basket again, it disappeared under the radome of the aeroplane. I was about to call 'Rim, no damage' again when I saw this mangled gob of metal spokes and white material at the end of the hose.

'Ah,' we both said in the cockpit and reported the serious damage to the Victor boys. The basket had gone under the radome and caught on the lower UHF aerial. The bored and disappointed voice of the tanker captain came over the radio telling us the standard patter that we may have ingested some foreign object damage (FOD) down our intakes, and their recommendation was that we return to base carefully. Animal just arrived on the wing as we were getting our admonishment, and I pulled the probe in and sheepishly slunk away from the tanker back to Leuchars. To be fair, Nails wasn't bothered and had a bit of a chuckle when we were taxiing back in and ATC informed us that we had 'something dangling' from the nosewheel area. I had managed to bring a fair bit of the parachute-style material from the end of the basket back with me, which obviously made me the target of some major banter for the next few days.

This Means War

The final two days of the course, we went to war—sort of. We had a full day's worth of briefings on rules of engagement, recce, weapons, etc., and the staff ramped up the readiness state. It was all very exciting and we were itching to go flying the next day. The idea was that we would be brought up to cockpit readiness and then launched to a CAP to face God knows what. I checked the programming board the night before, and to my horror, I saw that I was flying with Dennis. This trip was going to be my end-of-course check ride and they had put me up with a complete bastard. I had pulled the CADC trick with Dennis earlier on in the course, so had no option this time but to tough it out.

I did so much prep the night before that if I did fail the trip, I knew it wouldn't be down to lack of effort on my part. Dennis asked me a couple of tactical questions to kick off our crew brief (we had a big squadron-wide war-type brief in the morning) and when I got them right, he nodded his head and said, 'Right Tug. As far as this trip goes, we are a crew, so let's act like one. You know your stuff so we will just try and have as much fun as we can.' The first thing I did was check that the sky was not falling down and then followed Dennis in a bit of a haze to get kitted up. I signed out the aircraft and then we sat in the crew room waiting to be called 'to cockpit'. One by one, the crews were brought to cockpit readiness and then 'scrambled' in slow time, so we didn't screw anything up by rushing.

I remember very little of the trip, as no sooner did we make it to CAP, we were vectored off to intercept a pair of Buccaneers that were so low over the sea, they might as well have been underwater. Once we had shot the shit out of them, we reset back to CAP and were straight into the next engagement. Dennis was awesome. He really got into the aggression of it and patted me on the back whenever I did something well. I wanted to say, 'Who the hell are you, and what have you done with Dennis?' but we were way too busy. He was heads-in the radar for the whole trip so I could have got away with most things, I guess. All too soon, the fun juice ran out and we had to head home. I think there had been talk about setting up a tanker for us, but my recent adventure probably put paid to that idea.

As I climbed out of the cockpit, Dennis shook my hand and said I had passed the course. 'Maybe see you on the front-line sometime, Tug,' he said, and that sealed the deal. This was not my last trip on the OCU though. The final trip was supposed to be a crew solo in the afternoon as a sort of freebie. However, they had chopped both *ab initio* navs, so Ivan and Joel did their last trip with other staff navs and I lucked in to fly with Odo. As usual, he was great to fly with, and we had the added bonus that the radar was knacked, so we just took vectors from GCI and took lots of Sidewinder and guns shots—what a hoot!

That night was a big one in the bar for the three remaining pilots and Odo. All of our retreads had been accelerated through the course and were already on the front-line. We had a week or so of admin ahead of us before we were due on our first squadron. That admin period at the end of a course is a golden time. You can swan around patting yourself on the back having passed the course, watch the junior courses still struggling and studying, get shitfaced every night, and know that you have no pressure on you until you start the next course (or in this case, squadron work-up).

Ivan and Joel had it easy in that they could just load up their cars with kit and make their way to 74 Squadron at Wattisham in Suffolk. I had to get to Wildenrath in West Germany. This consisted of putting all my worldly goods into three big boxes and taping them up so R&D section on station could pick them up. I had written 'FG OFF R A WILSON, OFFICERS' MESS, RAF WILDENRATH, RAFG' on them. RAFG stood for RAF Germany, which was pretty much a separate air force in those days. I saw them load onto the back of a panel truck and had no idea if or when I would see them again. All I now had in my possession was my car (which I sold just before leaving for Germany); a kit bag with all my flying kit in it; another kit bag with my uniforms in; a third kit bag full of civilian clothes; and my wits (on this one, I was poorly placed I think). I also had a flight ticket for the military trooper aircraft that flew out of Luton to Düsseldorf and a train ticket to get to Luton.

3

92 East India Squadron, RAF Wildenrath

What Are You Doing Here?

I don't mind admitting I felt thoroughly alone boarding that aircraft at Luton and was apprehensive about what I would find at the other end. RAFG was a notoriously hard school, and not for the first time, I questioned why I hadn't pushed for an easier option of one of the Leuchars or Wattisham squadrons. There were no easy options, of course, but your mind plays tricks on you in these situations. Anyway, Punchy had sold Germany to me so well, and now it was up to me to make the best of it. More pressing was that I had scant detail of what to do on arrival. I had called 92 Squadron beforehand to tell them of my arrival and had been assured that there would be a car and driver waiting for me at the airport.

Except there wasn't. Having collected my luggage, I searched for the driver and he was nowhere to be seen. They had announced on the flight after landing that there were coaches ready to take people to Rheindahlen, and I managed to jump on one at the last second before it left. I guessed the squadron were testing my resilience and resourcefulness by seeing what I would do, so I figured I would get to Rheindahlen (HQ RAFG) not really knowing where it was, but figuring it was better to be on a RAF base rather than stuck at Düsseldorf airport. I hoped I could commandeer some sort of vehicle and driver to take me to Wildenrath.

I looked a bit of a sorry site dragging my kit bags to MT Flight at Rheindahlen and asking if I could get a lift to Wildenrath. I think the desk sergeant took pity on me and said he would sort something out. The next thing I knew, I was perched in the back of a Land Rover driven by a couple of army corporals from some regiment or other, driving through the German countryside, until arriving at the main gate at Wildenrath. Security was tight as a couple of British soldiers had recently been murdered by the IRA in Roermond, which made the whole thing a lot more real for those serving in Germany. The two guys giving me the lift had spent most of the journey complaining about officers in general, so when they asked me where I wanted dropping off, it went a bit quiet when I said, 'officers' mess please'.

The silence allowed me plenty of time to take in my surroundings. Wildenrath was a drab green, grey, and brown camp that looked a bit like a quiet town with lots of trees and not much evidence of buildings, or indeed, life in general. Of course, this was the idea. The base was deliberately low-key and difficult to see from the air, as I would later find out when flying.

I warned in at the mess reception, and the receptionist showed me to my room. Gisela was a lovely middle-aged German woman who mothered all of the young aircrew in the mess and was a wonderful, welcoming face in the middle of the distinctly unwelcoming 'who the hell are you?' environment I seemed to have entered. My room was in a drab, single-storey block just across the mess car park and was a standard single officer's room—functional and not at all homely, with a single bed with sheets and blankets; wooden wardrobe; desk and chair; chest of drawers; and a sink. That was it. Given that my flying kit would be housed on the squadron, my two bags of kit looked a bit pathetic. I unpacked, which took all of five minutes, changed into a flying suit, and wandered back to the mess to ring the squadron and let them know I had passed their arrival test.

The most bizarre thing happened to me as I got into the mess. I bumped into a young woman who said, 'I know you!' It turns out, we had been in sixth form together six years previously, and she was now married to a pilot on 92 Squadron. Small world, and it gave me a modicum of comfort that there was someone I knew here in Germany. After chatting for a few minutes, I heard my name called out and turned to see Harry and Von, who had been on my senior course at Leuchars and posted out to 92 about a month before me. They were all badged up in 92's red and yellow colours, and my generic F4 badge and RAF wings looked a bit ordinary in comparison. There was much shaking of hands and smiles, and they gave me a lift to the squadron which was on the south side of the airfield.

We waited at the traffic lights at the end of the runway as two Phantoms came into land. This was my first sight of the F4 in Germany, and it looked awesome. They crunched into the runway, and I saw the drag chutes stream behind, slowing them down. The jets were from 19 Squadron as most of 92 were away on detachment in Cyprus and not due back until the following day. A few guys were back already, including the Boss, so there were plenty of folks to meet. We drove through the trees for a couple of minutes and arrived at Delta Dispersal—the home of 92 Squadron.

The first thing I noticed was a concrete guard box with a yellow cobra and red maple leaves painted on it. This was the squadron badge—a cobra because of the East India Company buying our Spitfires during the Battle of Britain, and maple leaves commemorating the Canadian pilots on the squadron when it formed in 1917. The guard box was only for use during war or exercise, but it was a reminder of the world I had entered. The squadron buildings were low-slung, single-storey, and green, surrounded by hardened aircraft shelters (HAS) and high-walled revetments. Harry and Von led me into the squadron, and the first person I saw was OC B Flight, who had been on my OCU course. 'Tug! What are you doing here?'

'I'm posted here, Sir.'

'I know that you idiot. I thought you were due next week.' That explained why there was no lift from the airport then. I don't know if I was more relieved that there hadn't been a test to see how I would get to Wildenrath or pissed off that they had forgotten about me. Anyway, next up was a cup of tea in the crew room. No. 92 Squadron had a typical fighter crew room—lots of pictures from the squadron's history on the walls and tons of memorabilia on every shelf and table top. Most shockingly, there were a couple of stuffed cobras in glass cases ready to strike and a huge 92 Squadron nameplate from a steam engine dominating one wall. Around the outside edges, there was a roomful of red leather armchairs.

Harry made me a cuppa, taking a mug down from the squadron board behind the coffee bar. Every pilot and nav had their own mug with the squadron crest on it and their name or nickname. As I sipped my tea, the

Boss walked in. I introduced myself (feeling a bit insignificant as I looked at his 3,000-hour Phantom badge) and got a less than warm welcome. 'Are you the one that didn't want to come here?' he barked.

'No, Sir,' I blubbered, 'that was a guy on my senior course. I am his replacement. I was the only one on my course who wanted to come to Germany.'

'Right [long pause] well, welcome to 92 Squadron then.' That was some welcome.

After hanging around for a bit, Harry gave me a guided tour of the squadron. There were a few offices for the Boss, flight commanders, admin, and QWIs, and these along with the crew room were known as the 'soft'. Then you went through an airlock into the 'hard'. The hard was everything I had expected from a front-line squadron in Germany. It looked punchy, and it was ready for war.

Everyone's flying kit (helmets and life jackets, g-pants and immersion suits) were up on a set of pegs in a liquid hazard area (or would have been if the squadron hadn't been mostly away), then there was a vapour hazard area before entering the planning room. The hazard areas were set up for life operating in a nuclear biological and chemical (NBC) environment.

Walking past the standard big map-planning tables, I could see lots of info on the walls that was definitely restricted or classified information—lots of threat aircraft pictures and diagrams and surface-to-air missile (SAM) stuff. There were a couple of briefing rooms, toilets, and showers, and 'The Submarine', which I would come to know and hate later on.

The heart of the squadron was the ops room—a large raised platform that the duty auth and the ops clerk would sit on in front of the huge programming board that filled one wall. Separating the auth from the general public was an equally large ops desk that ran almost the length of the room with auth sheets and documents on it. This would be where I would out-brief before going flying. Everything was just like the outside—green, brown, and grey, apart from a cheap plastic yellow wall clock that looked completely out of place with its mad splash of colour. The whole building was eerily quiet, but this wouldn't last for long once the squadron got back in tomorrow. In the meantime, OC B tasked Harry and Von to oversee my first official duty.

The Dort Convex

Every new joiner went to the mess bar on their first night to undertake the Dort convex. This was the conversion to Dortmunder beer and was a military way of stating that I was going to get shitfaced—and shitfaced is what I got. No. 19 Squadron were in the bar in force, and they had another couple of guys that I knew, so there were plenty of folks to drink with. After a few Dorts, I was vaguely aware of some cheering behind me, and I turned around to see a short, oldish guy in a flying suit, jumping off the top of the fruit machine into the arms of a few 19 Squadron boys. 'Who's that?' I asked.

'That's the station commander!' shouted Harry over the din.

'You are shitting me!' The next thing I knew, I was shaking hands with him, having been introduced as the new pilot, and he took over control of the latter stages of my Dort convex.

So, that resulted in me lying on my bed, still in my flying suit and boots with the room spinning around my head. I have a gift when I am drunk in that I always recognise the clues that I am about to throw up and can always make it to the bathroom. I crawled from my room to the toilets in the block and gave up most of the Dort I had drunk earlier. The drunk mind works in strange ways, and tonight was no different. This was the first time I had had a close up look at a German toilet and the fabled 'continental shelf'. For some unknown reason, European toilets didn't just fall away gracefully from the seat to the water but had an interim stage where whatever was deposited was put on show for you to examine if you wanted—the contents of my stomach being the latest thing.

Before too long, it was time for the southern end of my alimentary system to be heard, and I settled onto the loo and promptly fell asleep. I was woken by the urge to throw up again (I always vomit twice when drunk), and it was at this point that my drunk brain came up with a plan. I looked down to see a triangular gap made by my thighs and the front of the toilet, and it definitely looked big enough for me to just hurl through without having to get off the seat. Alas not, and my first night on my first front-line squadron ended with me consigning my boxer shorts to the dustbins outside.

I cadged a lift back to the squadron late the next day to find the jets returning from Cyprus. Everyone looked a bit weary after two weeks away and 'welcomes to the squadron' were a bit muted. My flight commander, Welshy, took me into his office for a half-arsed arrival brief, but I could tell his heart wasn't in it. He just wanted to get home to his family for the weekend. He asked a few cursory questions, then asked pointedly if I liked a drink. 'Love it, Sir,' I replied, eager to show I was ready for the 'work hard play hard' partying lifestyle that Germany was famous for.

'Well, we don't go in for that sort of thing on 92,' he said, bursting my bubble a little. It turns out that the squadron was returning from Cyprus in disgrace, having made drunken fools of themselves during an all-day drinkex a couple of days before—lots of very drunken antics including boats, the sea, and upsetting the general public, culminating in a hospital visit and stomach pump for at least one of the navs. Therefore, happy hour in the bar that night was going to be a quiet affair—thank God, because I was still struggling after my Dort convex the night before.

A Red and Yellow Badge

The next day, I was helped by Von to do some personal admin around the station, starting with opening a bank account at the Sparkasse and depositing the cash I got from selling my car. The upcoming weekend would see me getting right into the German lifestyle before starting my simulator and flying work-up. First up at the weekend was a trip to RAF Rheindahlen, the home of RAFG. It had a huge NAAFI shop that was a Mecca for all service personnel in the area. I walked in and almost immediately walked out again with a huge stacking hi-fi system (this was almost a rite of passage for a young officer in Germany). I then had to go back in and buy my first-ever CDs to play on it as all my tapes were still in transit. Therefore, for the next few weeks, all I heard was Michael Jackson's *Bad* and Madonna's *Like a Prayer*. I know every stinking word to every song on those two albums, having played them for three solid weeks.

Sunday saw my first outing to the Fuchsbrau—a traditional German country restaurant (I remember lots of wood panels and beer steins)—for the best crispy chicken and chips in history. What the hell was it with mayonnaise on the chips though? I was being ferried around by the guys I already knew on both 19 and 92, but I would need to get myself a car soon.

On the Monday, I was back on the squadron, and although the guys were a little chastened following their bollocking for the Cyprus booze-up, the welcomes were extremely warm. A lot of the guys were young and only a couple of years ahead of me—a mix of married guys who lived out in quarters and a few singlies who lived in the mess. All of them had a look about them though—like they knew what they were doing and how good they were. I was desperate to be a part of this.

Nearly all of them asked if I had met the Beast yet. He was a retired officer who ran the F4 sim, which oddly enough, was based up the road at RAF Bruggen. He had been a very capable and experienced Phantom QWI in the old days of the really hard school, and he often put young aircrew through the wringer during the monthly emergency drill check in the sim. I was the next man up, of course, and everyone seemed to be offering me advice and sympathy. Anyway, a great thing happened to me on that first day in that I was given a name badge.

Normally, name badges took a few weeks to order and make, so you look like an outsider for a while before getting your squadron colours on your chest. However, just a few weeks previously, one of the pilots called Scooby had inadvertently pulled the manual separation handle on his ejection seat rather than the drag chute handle on landing. The man sep handle releases the pilot from his seat after ejection by firing off lots of small explosives in various places around the seat, to sever the restraints and help deploy the parachute. It all happens automatically anyway, but this is a back-up should the seat not work correctly. Anyway, Scooby had pulled it by accident, and the story is that his nav had transmitted something like, 'Help! My pilot is trying to eject!' as the cockpit filled with smoke from the assorted pyros. As expected, Scooby attracted a lot of banter, and part of that was a name badge with 'Tuggy' on it rather than Scooby. On meeting me, Scooby and Jimbo (one of the young navs) took the badge and tried to block out the 'gy' at the end with a red felt tip pen. Our name badges on 92 were red background with yellow border and wings and the name below the wings embroidered in yellow also. To be honest, it looked a bit shit, but I was absolutely beside myself with joy. I was wearing the squadron colours—awesome!

Books and the Beast

While the squadron got down to its normal daily routine, I met the QWIs and got briefed on how my convex was going to go. The first week would be lots of reading and a couple of sims, then day and night dual checks with the squadron QFI the following week. After that, it would be intercepts, low-level, and air combat—the usual stuff. The QWIs on 92 seemed like decent guys, but I held my judgement, having been burned badly before. The QWI leader was a nav who turned out to be one of the sharpest people I have ever flown with. He was achingly cool also. The QWI nav was just as sharp and seemed like a great guy too. At the time, 92 did not have a QWI pilot. The QWIL took me to the 'secret' cabinet in the registry and got me to sign out two massive documents— SUPPLAN DELTA and SUPPLAN MIKE. 'Right, Tug. Read and learn these two this week.'

'What? All of them?'

'Yep. This is our bread and butter.'

I carried the two huge tomes through to the crew room and started reading. As far as I remember, Delta was full of SAM belt info that detailed how high and wide the friendly SAM zones were and the rules of engagement at various levels of readiness. Our job in war was to plug the gaps between these SAM zones in FAORs (fighter areas of responsibility). Looking back, I might be wrong about all of that as I pretty much fell asleep reading it. Military documents are a bit dry at the best of times, but even with all the 'do it right or you will die' warnings, it just didn't grab me. It didn't help seeing big badass Phantoms taxi past the window almost close enough to touch from the crew room. I was really missing flying my big, fat, ugly bird and moped around the squadron like a lovesick teenager.

SUPPLAN MIKE was something else though. This detailed all the safe routing that would be in force during the next war when the Russian hordes came streaming over the border and our own bombers were trying to return from their missions—low-level transit routes, transit corridors, minimum risk levels, etc., all wove together and changed shape and dimension at the forward line of own troops (FLOT), forward edge of the battle area (FEBA), and included IFF off and on lines etc. It was mind-boggling, and I struggled to comprehend it all. However, I really needed to tuck this away as sooner or later, I would be expected to fly within this framework.

It was while I was sat in the crew room cuddling SUPPLAN MIKE that I met Massey for the first time. He was a really quiet, nice, unassuming guy who was towards the end of his first tour. He was about as far removed from the stereotypical F4 fighter pilot as you could get, and this made him all the more likeable. 'Struggling with SUPPLAN MIKE?' he asked.

'Yeah, pretty much.' He then told me he had put together a briefing on it and would happily take me through it if it would help. At this stage, I would have tried anything, so off we went to the briefing room and Massey brought out a set of about fifty OHP slides. I inwardly groaned, but as soon as he put the first one up, I was mesmerised. In his previous life, Massey had been a car designer for Jaguar and was a brilliant artist. He had hand drawn these OHPs that depicted MIKE as a three-dimensional model, showing height and width of all of the corridors in glorious technicolour, and it was a thing of beauty. More to the point, after a couple of viewings, it cemented SUPPLAN MIKE in my head. I couldn't thank him enough. 'No problem,' he said. 'Have you met the Beast yet?'

I met the Beast the next day. One of the younger navs, Bouncer, drove me over to Bruggen, and we were crewed together for my first sim. As far as I recall, there were two pilots and two navs teaching at the sim. All of them were older guys, either semi-retired or going that way. One of the navs was the guy who had been involved in shooting down a Jaguar for real by accident, years before, so was quite famous. He and the other two instructors were quiet gentle souls. Then I met the Beast.

He was tall, well-built, and imposing with grey hair and a huge smile—a bit like just before a shark bites your arm off. I introduced myself, and he immediately called me 'young man,' which came across as patronising and a bit demeaning. I later found out this was a bit of a test, but at the time, it went over my head. Anyway, off we went to the sim itself. The cockpit was up about twenty metal steps, and after we had strapped in, the Beast handed us our headphones, took the canopy safety strut out, and went down to his control console.

Bouncer and I went through our start-up procedures, and I think I was a bit ropey having not flown for two weeks, but good enough. We had an engine fire on start, which I handled okay, and then got on the runway for take-off—no visuals again, so all instrument flying. With the stick hard back and the power up, off we popped. We handled the engine fire on the roll okay, and the Beast sent us back to the end of the runway.

This time I crashed on take-off, and again, and again. The Beast was unsympathetic when I told him the sim felt nothing like the aircraft or even the sim at Leuchars, and after a short set-to, he put us airborne so we could crack on with some upper air work and emergencies. The rest of the session was a blur of emergencies, crashes, swearing (on my part), bollockings, and fury until, sweating like a pig, I was finally released from the torture.

The debrief was brutal, and despite trying to argue my case about how unrealistic the sim handled, the Beast was unmoved. We drove back to Wildenrath with me in a depressed state and Bouncer trying to tell me the Beast was like that with all young pilots. As soon as we got back to 92, Welshy asked to see me in his office. 'I've just had the Beast on the phone and he says you weren't very good in your sim.' The rotten old bastard had grassed me up almost as soon as I had left the building. I told Welshy how bad I thought the sim was, and he listened quietly, obviously smelling bullshit in his view. 'Well that's as maybe. So, you can go back tomorrow and do that one again. The Beast has suggested that as you don't seem to be able to get the jet off the ground, he will just start you airborne and then freeze the sim when you get an emergency so you can do the drills without having to fly at the same time.' Welshy was telling me I had failed the first sim. This was bad enough, but the Beast was saying I couldn't fly at all. I was fuming with that patronising old bastard.

I hadn't calmed down a bit the next day either and had worked myself up into a frenzy by the time I got to the sim with Jimbo. I could almost see the look of glee in the Beast's eyes as I walked in, pretty sure he could smell blood in the water. 'Okay, Young Man. Do you think you might be able to take-off without crashing today?'

'Dunno, Beast. Is your piece of shit sim anywhere near replicating the aeroplane today?' I found myself saying. I think I heard Jimbo gasp.

The Beast went into full-on patronising mode and in almost a sing-song voice said, 'It's a computer. Fly it like a computer.' It was at this point I made my name with him.

'I didn't join up to fly computers, Beast. I joined up to fly fighters!' There it was—my balls right there on a plate for him. I guess it was only a couple of seconds of silence, but it felt like an age.

The Beast's face broke into a grin, and he said, 'Right then young man. Let's turn you into a fighter pilot then.' From that moment on, I was okay with the Beast. Rather than torturing me, he taught me. I would love to say that the sim went well, but it probably didn't. However, it was better than last time, and I felt as though I had leapt over a huge hurdle. I also enjoyed a short period of legendary status, having gobbed off to the Beast, but my thoughts now turned firmly towards flying.

Back in the Saddle (At Last!)

Standard procedure on joining a squadron is a dual check with the QFI. Jimmy was a thoroughly nice chap and was extremely relaxed all through the brief and walking out to the HAS. The jet fit snugly in the low-slung concrete cave and looked as hard as shit. Jimmy took me round the HAS, pointing out various hazards and told me to take particular care at the end of the trip when being pulled back into the HAS by the winch or pushed back by the tractor. A few weeks previously, he had been pushed back and had banged the stabilator at the back of the HAS. The ground crew would attach a steering arm to the nosewheel and use it to manoeuvre the jet back into the HAS. They had screwed up a bit, but it was down to Jimmy to make sure the aircraft was pushed back safely.

I climbed in the front and had a bit of banal chat with the Liney, but my mind was completely on the impending flight. It all got a bit noisy as I fired up the APU, and then it was time for the main event. I cannot explain how shockingly loud it was when the engines sparked up—every rock concert you have ever been to times ten and I was in control of it (barely). Jimmy was cool and talked me through all of the procedures for unplugging the external power and then taxiing out and around the HAS site. ATC gave us our clearance into the upper airspace, and we pulled onto the operational readiness platform (ORP—a large rectangle of concrete just off to the side of the threshold of the runway) and prepared for take-off.

As I said, it had been a couple of weeks since I had flown, and the airspace round Leuchars was pretty open and easy to operate in. I was now about to launch into some of the most congested airspace in the world. There was no time to fret though. As we took the runway, I went through my last chance checks of pins and flaps, the jettison safety switch was live, brakes were on, and power was up to 80 per cent. The engines looked good, so the brakes came off and went up to mil power. Rocked outboard and kicked in the arse, we powered down the runway. I bloody loved this jet. We leapt airborne, knowing that folks on the ground could see and hear us, then gear up, flaps up, and pushed the op erase button (see how much I have learnt?). I was now a RAFG pilot. I still didn't see myself as a fighter pilot yet; that would come later.

Tower handed us off to departure, but we were moving so fast that we were given to clutch radar almost immediately for our climb into our designated training area. I had the feeling that the aircraft hadn't missed me as much as I had missed it, but it was early days again in our relationship, and I was more than happy with unrequited love. Jimmy put me through my paces with all sorts of general handling and instrument flying, but he did it in such a pleasant way that I barely felt as though this was a check ride. This was a world away from the OCU, and I instinctively knew that 92 was the perfect fit for me.

Jimmy pointed out various landmarks and we recovered to Wildenrath for a PAR. This gave me a chance to look out of the window and see the airfield for the first time from the air. I could barely see it with all the camo and low visibility design and colouring. Jimmy pointed to Bruggen just to the north and showed me a couple of navigation features that helped to prevent misidentification between the two airfields (probably stuff I should have listened to, but more of that later). I could see the HAS sites break out at each end of the airfield as I settled down on finals. It was not a bad landing, and we rolled into the air again and joined the visual circuit. I did two half-decent circuits and we landed off the second one.

I was actually really pleased with myself and my performance, and I thought it just showed how well I could fly when the QFI was not a complete bastard. The trip wasn't over yet. I shut down one engine and we popped the canopies. Jimmy coached me through the re-entry to the dispersal and how to get back into the HAS. We were given a HAS number by the duty auth and taxied slowly round to it. Each HAS had a large circular revetment in front of it where I was supposed to taxi around to point my tail towards the shelter. I say a large revetment—it was only large when you weren't trying to turn a Phantom around in it. Once we stopped, the ground crew attached the winch to the main landing gear legs and a steering arm to the nosewheel and started winching us back into the cave. I looked out the back to the left, and Jimmy was watching the rear right. I held the stick hard back in my guts, so we could both see the stabilator and that it was not going to hit anything (Jimmy was understandably nervous about this). There was also one of the ground crew watching each wingtip doing the same. Once we stopped, it was chocks in, external power connected, and engine off. My first trip was done. I was signed up as being unlikely to kill my navigator through incompetence, and a couple of days later, Bouncer and I launched into my low-level system familiarisation trip.

'Don't Even Think About It!'

The low-flying system had a series of set routing leading to and from the low-level training areas that almost simulated what it would be like if SUPPLAN MIKE were implemented during wartime. Collectively, the routing was known as CODEC, and there were two versions that alternated every six months. That day, we were in CODEC A, and Bouncer showed me all the navigation features that acted as turning points for the routing. It was a beautiful gin-clear day, and we saw tons of other military aircraft, such as Tornados, Jaguars, Harriers, F16s, and even a F104 Starfighter.

Bouncer was locking some of them up, and I was pulling the trigger, taking Skyflash and Sidewinder shots as we floated around the North German plains. We went a long way east towards the Inner German Border and the buffer zone between East and West, then turned back for Wildenrath. On the way, we happened upon two huge road bridges spanning a gorge. 'Don't even think about it!' laughed Bouncer, and it was pleasing to know that even though I was a brand-new pilot, Bouncer still couldn't be sure I wouldn't try and fly under the bridge. Perhaps there was a bit of fighter pilot in me that he could see? Either that or he thought I was just a knob and stupid enough to give it a go. I got to see the low-level recovery to Wildenrath this time and broke into the circuit to plop it down roughly near the numbers. That would do me for the week apart from another sim the following day before Friday's happy hour.

Happy hour at Wildenrath was something else. The bars in RAFG were heavily subsidised, and beer was little more than a number of pence per pint and gin something ridiculous like tuppence a tot. We all arrived *en masse* to find 19 Squadron out in force, and it just exploded from there—lots of shouting and boozing interspersed with random rounds of squadron drinks. Somebody from 92 would order a massive round of snakebites and antidotes (Red Bols with Advocaat and a separate shot glass with Schnapps in it) and take them round the bar on a tray. Once we all had one, the buyer would shout, 'Is there a Cobra in the house?!' We would then reply, 'You bet your sweet ass there is! *Yam sing*!' *Yam sing* means 'Drink all,' and you would drink the snakebite down in one. Then, the buyer shouts, 'Who owns this bar?!' to which we would shout, '92 Squadron!' and yam the antidote. There were huge cheers from us afterwards and lots of braying from 19 Sqn.

A few minutes later, the roles are reversed and 19 are passing around their Blue Bols yammers, having a shout and taking abuse from us. Then out of nowhere, the whole bar comes together to sing 'The Flag', an old Nazi song that was banned in the German Air Force, but was the signature tune for RAF fighter squadrons (maybe for bomber squadrons too, but who gave a shit about them?). It is basically a love song from a German soldier to his sweetheart, just before he 'marches against England'. Of course, the regular shouts of '*Sieg Heil*!' spoil it somewhat, but I was mesmerised as everyone sang at full volume. This was a defining moment for me as 'The Flag' then led into a whole range of bar songs singing the praises of the Phantom and deriding other aircraft such as the Jag, Harrier, and Tornado—all of them incredibly clever and funny and the vast majority, absolutely filthy and disgusting. I made a pledge to myself there and then that I would learn every single word of these songs and become a big member of the unofficial bar choir. I could hold a tune and thought that this would be a good way to make a name for myself.

Out of nowhere, a load of pizzas and garlic bread arrived from the local pizzeria. I handed over 5 Deutschmarks to somebody or other and ended up with a handful of pizza and Dort—a real athlete's dinner. I had no idea what time it was, but all of the squadron wives arrived in the bar to inspect the damage to their husbands. As the new boy on the squadron, I had a bit of celebrity status and was introduced to everyone's other halves. No doubt I wasn't looking or smelling my best, but everyone was very nice and I felt like the latest addition to the family. One by one, the married guys were removed from the field of play, and the singlies like me were left to tough it out until last orders. Another weekend was consigned to the hangover, and I found myself itching for Monday to come around so that I could fly again.

Cream and Shit

It was my night dual check with the QFI. This was a double-edged sword of course. I wanted to pass it and get it out of the way, but it would qualify me to fly on the night waves. I have always had a love-hate relationship with night flying. It is brilliant when the weather is clear, but thoroughly miserable when it is cloudy and raining. However, we actually launched in daylight and logged just twenty minutes of night at the end of the trip to get me current. I was liking this squadron even more—talk about a painless way to get the job done. The following day's trip with the QFI was going to make me cream my pants and shit myself all in one go.

I had to do a high AOA manoeuvring sortie to prove I didn't use aileron at high AOA and crash (thank you 56 Squadron), but at the start of the flight, we were going to do a MOS take-off (minimum operating strip). This meant taking off from the taxiway. In wartime, if the Russians bombed the runway, we could still get airborne and land from the taxiway that ran parallel to the runway. As we lined up on the very end of the taxiway and called for take-off, three things struck me:

First, the taxiway was barely half the width of the runway, so looked horrifically narrow. Keeping straight would be critical, and I shuddered to think what we would have done if the nosewheel steering failed.

Secondly, the trees surrounding the HAS sites were very, very close, so there was no margin for error.

Thirdly, read points one and two again, and remember it was me (barely) in control of the jet.

The Phantom didn't care, of course. Concrete is concrete, and it gave me an even bigger thrill on take-off than normal as I saw the trees rush past and we leapt airborne, cheating death once more. My aircraft and I cavorted around together in full burner, without a care in the world. This was no longer the first throes of passion—I truly loved the fat, ugly, loud, and dirty cow. The fuel didn't last long, and due to a couple of guys needing the jets to complete their operational work-ups and four-ship lead checks, I was done flying for the week. The next week would see me back flying with navs as I really got my teeth into my own work-up.

The rest of the week gave me chance to catch up on some personal admin, but I have to say, I mostly hung out in the crew room, chatting to my squadron mates. My boxes arrived from the UK, and my initial euphoria at being reunited with my kit was cut short as I realised how little I had to show for my twenty-four years, four of which I had spent in the RAF. I did manage to buy a car though. Massey was a huge car freak and had a classic Datsun 260Z in black. I absolutely loved it, and we found a sleek black 280z in a local garage so I went and bought it. This was a proper fighter pilot's car—powerful, mean-looking with a bonnet that went on for miles, and totally unreliable. I have had some shit cars in my past, and this one just joined on to the end of the list.

God, I had some dramas with it, but nonetheless, I loved it and it looked very cool indeed.

The trips came thick and fast through the rest of August, and I flew with a variety of navs. I loved flying with every one of them, but especially Jimbo, who did a lot of my work-up, and Bobby. Jimbo was only a couple of years older than me, but he was extremely proficient and sharp—so much so that he later went on to command a fighter squadron on the Tornado F3. Bobby was a fair bit older, having originally been a nav on the venerable old Shackleton before re-rolling to the Phantom. A fair few Phantom navs had trodden this path, and it was actually the sharp ones who had been on the Shack (Bungle from the OCU for one).

Bobby had a bit of a rep for not being the sharpest on the radar, but I loved flying with him. His pure enthusiasm and his sheer doggedness in the face of the criticism and banter he attracted was absolutely amazing. He didn't help himself with some of the bullshit he used to come out with, but if I could describe him in one word, it would be 'legend', though legendary for possibly the wrong reasons sometimes.

My sorties were filled with pairs take-offs, close formation, intercepts, VIDs, and visual and instrument recoveries by day and night. Initially, I was the wingman, but I quickly started leading the pair myself. My op check in a few months would see me leading at least four Phantoms, possibly more, and some F16s on a low-level CAP against who knew what was going to try to get past us. Therefore, I needed to be a leader early doors. My first lead seemed to go well until I turned early for the runway in the murky weather and started heading for Bruggen. 'It's Bruggen!' shouted my wingman over the radio, and a 4-G break later, we were setting up to join at Wildenrath—if only I had paid attention on my dual check with Jimmy. That brought me a fair bit of banter, but it was small beer compared to my next adventure.

Crash!

I had about ninety hours total Phantom time, with about ten at night by this stage, and was up with Jimbo doing intercepts to VID. I completed my VID phase one check during the daylight part of the sortie, then my phase two check as it turned dark. Phase two was night time with the target's lights on. Our leader had landed ahead of us, and everything looked nice and controlled around finals to me. The main wheels touched the deck, and I reached for the drag chute handle. A split second after, the nosewheel touched down and immediately snapped forwards with a huge bang. We were now cutting a groove in the runway with the nose of the aircraft doing about 160 knots, with the warning panel lit up like a Christmas tree.

I was vaguely aware of Jimbo transmitting a mayday call, saying we had crashed on the runway. In the cold light of day, I can reflect on how I coped with it all, but at the time it was a thing of fury—sparks, graunching noises, and flashing lights. My hands were a blur as I stop-cocked the engines and turned the fuel cocks off. We had no brakes as the hydraulic fluid was pissing out behind us, but I still needed to stop the aircraft before the overrun cable otherwise the high tensile cable cord would go over the nose and possibly shatter the canopy and me with it. There was a mechanical back-up mode to the brakes called 'elephant foot braking', (yes, really), which stated that if you put 1 million pounds of pressure through the toe brake pedals, you can mechanically push the brakes on. Okay, it's not 1 million pounds, but I can't remember how much it was, having not paid attention in ground school. Whatever the figure is, guess how much pressure you can generate with your legs when you are covered in sparks and cutting a groove down the runway, illuminated by just about every caption on the panel? Correct—a shitload!

The aircraft came to a halt, and I put my seat pins in before raising my canopy. I could see the fire trucks on us already and slowly gathered my breath and started unstrapping. Out of the corner of my eye, I saw Jimbo jumping up and down on the runway, screaming at me to get out of the jet.

'Ok Jimbo!' I shouted. 'I'm just having a bit of a moment here!'

'It's on fire!' he shouted and I have never moved so fast in my life. As I joined him on the runway, I saw the firemen putting out a small fire at the back (some of the fluids apparently) and the jet was safe, as were we. Jimbo went a bit pale as the adrenaline wore off. By all accounts, I looked like a zombie. There was only one cure for the shock; we went to the bar with the other crew and got devastatingly shitfaced, having convinced ourselves we cheated death. We also convinced ourselves we saved the jet and are probably going to get the Air Force Cross as a reward.

Thing is, I went into work the next day to find out I had got the air force very cross instead—old joke I know, but I thought it was worth giving it another airing for old time's sake. There was no flying going on as the investigation into our crash was conducted. This started with a bit of engineering investigation, so the crew room was full. I told the story over and over and got questioned and patted on the back. As soon as Jimbo arrived, the Boss came out of his office and hauled Jimbo in. Fifteen minutes later, Jimbo came out and took me to one side. 'Has the Boss spoken with you yet, Tug?' he asked.

My reply was a no, and then Jimbo told me that the Boss had asked him, 'How hard was Tug's landing?' Jimbo had said it was normal, but the Boss had pressed him to state that I had screwed up the landing. To his credit, Jimbo had stuck to his guns, and it was obvious he was uncomfortable with the Boss's approach. So now it seemed my hero status was in doubt as the Boss was trying to blame me for what happened. This was made all the worse when he came out of his office for a cuppa and completely blanked me—something that did not go unnoticed by a number of the guys.

All of the old doubts from flying training resurfaced, and within the hour, I was convinced I was going to be chopped. Even at this late stage, they could chop someone from the squadron. In fact, 92 Squadron had just chopped a nav during my first month on the unit. The Boss continued to blank me, and I spent a miserable morning questioning my own actions and abilities. It didn't help that I had a hangover of epic proportions. Then came salvation.

We were all hauled into the briefing room and told by the SENGO (senior engineering officer) that the whole RAF Phantom fleet was temporarily grounded as they had found serious metal fatigue in my nosewheel strut and every aircraft had to be checked and possibly have the struts changed out. The Battle Flight jets here and the QRA jets in the UK had already been checked and now the engineers were systematically going through the fleet. Phew—I was in the clear. There was a bit more back-slapping for me, but nothing from the Boss, not even an acknowledgement. I tucked that one away. Survival instincts kicked in, and I decided to keep my distance from the Boss. He only had another six weeks before he was posted and we would then get a Boss who I would have followed into the gates of Hell—not sure I would follow this one now though, not even out of curiosity.

Anglo–French Relations—*Merde*!

The following week, 92 had been tasked to supply a static display aircraft at Limoges airport in France. During the Second World War, Leonard Cheshire had been part of a bombing raid that went a long way to liberating the area from the Nazis, and the locals had celebrated the anniversary ever since. Cheshire used to go each year and was treated like the hero he was. It had morphed into a small flying display, and for the last few years, the Tornado GR1 display aircraft had entertained the crowds. Jimmy had volunteered to go for the weekend but couldn't find a nav. He said it would be good training for me to fly in France, so I hopped in the boot and he flew us over.

This was my first time in the back seat, and it gave me even more respect for the navs. The rear cockpit was a black hole and a thoroughly unpleasant experience. Jimmy helped me to align the INAS and off we blasted. I tried the full nav experience of trying to fix the INAS at regular intervals to keep it accurate (failed) and spent a whole heap of time with my head in the radar scope trying to find targets and lock them up (also failed). All too soon, I felt a bit airsick so just looked out the window for the rest of the trip.

We arrived at Limoges to a medium-sized welcoming committee including the local mayor and dignitaries, and we were offered all manner of booze and nibbles. Our minor celebrity status was short-lived though as the Tornado display jet arrived and everyone flocked to see it. They had their own ground crew team who had driven there the previous night and were dressed in pristine co-ordinated overalls. I had not seen a GR1 up close before, and at first sight, it looked a bit stubby, but as it got closer to dispersal, the crew deployed the thrust reverse to slow down a bit. The thrust reverse 'buckets' (metal clamshell guards that closed over the rear of the jet pipes) were deployed with a high-pressure air system that made a high pitched and very loud scream as they moved. Well, the crowd went wild at this, and the few that were crawling over our jet and marvelling at how cool the Phantom was instantly ditched us to go and look at the new kid on the block.

The weekend's air show pretty much continued in this vein with everyone wanting to see and touch the Tornado (helped by the fact it was actually flying a display, which was awesome by the way) and looking at us with our dirty stained Phantom with expressions that bordered on sympathy and pity. Of course, our jet didn't really help itself by pissing fuel out of the dump pipes onto the lovely, smooth tarmac in the dispersal.

On the first night in the hotel, we received a small delegation pleading with us to come back to the airport with them. Jimmy and I both spoke a little pidgin French and ascertained that something was leaking out of our jet. When we got there, we saw the fuel dumping out at a slowish rate, but nonetheless, it needed sorting. Jimmy suggested starting up and throttling up a bit to pressurise the tanks to see if we could stop the leak. I jumped in the front, and with no helmet on or even flying gloves etc., I did an internal start on the battery and powered up. Hell's bells, the noise was brutal. I kept cycling the throttles until Jimmy was happy and then shut down. The leak had stopped and we patted ourselves on the back at a job well done. We had averted a diplomatic crisis with the French.

The next morning, we were back on duty in flying suits and surveyed the damage we had done in the night. The leak was back, and so our hosts had put two huge plastic drums under the dump pipes to catch the fuel. Worse than that, the fuel had started to destroy the tarmac on the pan, and my throttle exertions had blasted chunks of it all over the place, including the car park. We were now somewhat less popular than when we arrived and certainly a whole lot less than the golden boys on the GR1. However, the air show went well and we had lots of folks sitting in the cockpits having their pictures taken. Jimmy and I swapped seats on the Monday, and we blasted off into the glorious sunshine first thing. I don't know if the mayor had got our take-off time wrong, but neither he nor anyone else showed up to see us on our way. Turns out he was writing a snottogram to the RAF stating how we had damaged a load of cars with our antics the first night. Anyway, we didn't know any of this as Jimmy and I raged over France on our way back to Wildenrath. Jimmy conducted my instrument rating test on the way back, which I passed, and it was straight back into another week of flying on my long quest to get combat ready.

Making a Mark

The next couple of weeks turned out to be hugely important from a personal point of view as a couple of social events conspired to cement a bit of reputation and celebrity for me on both a squadron and a station level. First up was my inaugural dining-in night on 92. I have always loved the tradition and etiquette of dining-in nights. The squadron standard showing its battle honours is on display; the squadron silver (donated by, or in honour of, previous squadron members all the way back to its formation in 1917) comes out; and all of us don Number 5 mess dress with the wives in fancy cocktail dresses. Silver service comes from the mess staff and each member leaving the squadron gives a speech. This time, there were seven guys being dined out, including the Boss, the QWI nav, and Jimmy the QFI, so it was a big event.

There are a couple of traditions that I was caught up in, being the newest member of the squadron. This meant I was designated 'Mr Vice' and sat at the foot of one of the tables. The first duty of Mr Vice is to say grace before we all sit down to eat. The Boss called on me to speak, and I had prepared my own grace using a bit of Latin I had learned in school. Therefore, '*Gloria ad Deus. Cum grano salis, non-sequestra. Quantum ille canis est in fenestra*,' rang out and stunned the audience. As we sat down, everyone around me told me how cool it sounded and asked me what it meant. My Latin is sketchy at best, and I know the grammar was as bad as Monty Python in *Life of Brian* (People called Romanes, they go the house), but the thing about Latin is, hardly anyone knows any of it so you can bluff your way through it. I have used that grace all the way through my career, until I was finally bubbled years later at the XI Squadron reunion when a former Boss challenged me on it. He had studied ancient languages at university and saw through my thin façade. In short (with apologies to those of you who do speak Latin), it roughly translates as 'Glory to God. Take this next bit with a pinch of salt because it doesn't really follow. How much is that doggie in the window?'—complete nonsense, but it really does sound cool and it rhymes.

My second duty as Mr Vice was to toast the queen. Once the port and madeira had been passed around in their decanters, the Boss banged the table and said, 'Mr Vice! The Queen.'

I stood and announced, 'Ladies and Gentlemen! The Queen!' Everybody then stands and repeats, 'The Queen!' drinks and sits down.

My final duty as Mr Vice came straight afterwards as the Boss said, 'Mr Vice, tell us a joke.' This is a make-or-break moment for a junior officer on their first squadron. Usually, Mr Vice would get horribly shitfaced, mess up the loyal toast, and then tell a completely inappropriate joke (badly) and be instantly in the doghouse. I made sure I was prepared and had been careful with the drink so that when the Boss asked for a joke, I got a guitar out from behind the curtains and said I would sing a song instead. At Tac Weapons, I had bought a cheap guitar, and a navy student pilot had taught me how to strum a few chords. With a bit of practice and about ten chords, I was able to guff my way through just about every Bruce Springsteen song in the book. I thought that writing some words about 92 Squadron and each departing member would be a nice alternative to telling a joke and might put me on the map. It was all set to the tune of 'The River' by Bruce and had a chorus that I taught my drunken audience. It went down a storm, so that was me cemented onto 92 I think, and might even buy me some latitude were I to screw up or struggle in the air.

That episode also set me up for something similar, but station-wide. The officers' mess was putting on a revue night where each section was expected to write a skit and perform it in front of the mess members and their spouses. My dodgy guitar playing and catchy song catapulted me into the job of writing and performing 92 Squadron's offering. Word had spread quickly throughout the mess, and by Tuesday, I had been promoted to compère as well. That gave me just over a week to sort out something funny to deliver and to conjure up something to say about all the other acts.

In the meantime, flying continued apace and I was crewed with a variety of navs. After only two months on the squadron, I had flown with just about all of the operational ones. Things and people were changing rapidly around me, but this was the usual state of affairs on a front-line squadron. In the space of a couple of weeks, four or five aircrew left the squadron and were replaced by guys from other units. We also got a new Boss, who was brilliant, and a new station commander, who was just as cool as the last one.

My flying work-up continued and I seemed to be doing okay. It was still primarily upper air work, including all types of intercepts and VIDs, even in a jamming environment. We would regularly get a Canberra from 360 Squadron deploy for a couple of nights, so we could see the effects of jamming on the radar and hear comms-jamming techniques on the radio. I was flying days and nights, and it was interesting to see that night flying, which I had only been taught how to do in the Phantom a couple of months previously, was now a normal and regular part of my life and it was no big deal.

Northern/central Germany was generally raining with low cloud or steaming hot with poor visibility due to industrial haze, with very little variation in between. At night though, it was almost like the country wheezed away the dirty air of the day and all the lights of the towns and cities came out to party. As I said before, night flying was great on clear nights, but I hated the fact that the squadron seemed dead apart from the night flying shift. I could never get into the habit of sleeping late into the day either, so I always felt perpetually tired on nights. Squadrons didn't have enough people to run a proper day and night shift, so there was always overlap and you could find yourself flying two nights and then be back on the day shift the next day, so your body clock was all over the place. After debriefing, we would get back to the mess to find a beer waiting for us on the bar, ordered for us by some of the day shift (the bar would have closed long before we would get there). There was time for a quick beer and a shower, then we fell exhausted into bed.

The Clutch Beer Call

During that week, I was working on the skits for the cabaret night, and all too soon, Friday arrived with the show on Saturday. The only rehearsal was Saturday afternoon, so I would have a couple of hours to work out some compering words to introduce each act. Before that though, I had to survive Friday night. This particular Friday saw about fifteen–twenty aircrew from both squadrons clamber onto a service coach and head off to the clutch radar beer call. Clutch was the Air Traffic Control service that controlled the airspace in our region, and they held an annual get-together for all of the squadrons in that region. This included us, all of the RAFG Tornado squadrons, German Air Force F4Fs, and all manner of F16 units from Holland and Belgium. We all paid about DM30 and got a beer stein that was continually filled with free beer and soaked up with cheap German sausages and a pease pudding type of gunk.

Things started badly for us on the coach when 19 Squadron's NRL (Nav radar leader) opened up a copy of the *Daily Telegraph*. Every person on the coach, apart from him, thought this was outrageous. We were heading to a piss-up and already had some speed on, having loaded the coach with beer, and he was checking his stocks and shares? One of the 19 Squadron navs combat crawled on the floor of the coach and leant forwards to set fire to the bottom of the paper. The flames took a bit of time to lick up the broadsheet, and then the NRL eventually yelped as he ended up holding a small fireball. A quick dousing with a bottle of beer saw the incident finished and he grumbled the rest of the journey having hopefully learned a valuable lesson regarding young drunk aircrew.

The beer call was held in a vast, ornate, high-ceilinged hall and turned out to be a legendary frenzy of drinking and singing with the squadrons, fleets, and air forces singing disparaging songs about each other. Obviously, 'The Flag' was sung numerous times, and our hosts had laid on some competitions, such as wood-sawing, which is definitely not recommended with about 200 drunk men in the room. Various bits of wood lying around led to all sorts of other competitions, including a grand jousting event where two aircrew would ride bikes at high speed towards each other on a beer-swilled marble floor, while another guy stood on the back of the bike with a bit of wood to joust at the other crew. How the hell nobody got seriously hurt I will never know.

The pyromaniacs among us brought the evening to an early conclusion when they set fire to all of the wood a little too close to the floor-to-ceiling drapes. They burned pretty much as you would expect old heavy drapes to burn, and the vast hall filled with smoke. The fire engines arrived, and a halt was called to the proceedings. Every squadron crawled into their allotted bus for a raucous drive home. I don't mind saying that I was loving every minute of this fighter pilot life. I loved my squadron, my squadron mates, my shit car, and my two CDs, but most of all, I absolutely loved the Phantom. I was as proud as punch to be wearing my Phantom badges and my squadron colours in front of Europe's best, but admittedly drunkest, aircrew.

So, Saturday morning was a bit of a washout. I just managed to drag my sorry arse into breakfast at the last minute for some drunk food and had a quick practice of my main skit with my oppo before going to rehearsals to view the acts. As my style was heavy irony with deadpan delivery (think Jack Dee before Jack Dee), it was easy to come up with plenty of sarcastic comments to use for the evening's show. There were a couple of acts (me included) that didn't rehearse—saving it for the big night apparently—so I just figured I would make something up that was vaguely insulting about them and make do. I gathered my notes up and went for a couple of hours of shuteye before curtain up.

Juggling with the Station Commander

The ante room and dining room in the mess had been combined to make a pretty big auditorium, but as I walked out in front of the audience at the start of the show, it struck me how many people were there crammed into that space. With all the mess members and their spouses and older children, there must have been 250 people there at least. The problem with deadpan is you are never quite sure how it is going to go down until you get into it. Believe me, I have died badly using this approach in my time. There was no need to worry that night, though. The bar had been open for a couple of hours before we started, so everyone was well oiled, and my opening line of 'Good evening ladies and gentlemen' in a mildly pissed-off voice got a big laugh—no idea why, but I was happy to take it. The more pissed off I sounded, the better it went.

My premise was that we had booked loads of professional acts for the evening, but none of them had turned up, including the compère, so I was filling in, but only because I had been Joe'd by the station commander (who was sitting in the front row). I went on to introduce admin wing, who were doing a spoof *Blackadder* sketch, and was just about to pull the curtain back when we all heard someone say, 'Not yet!' So, the Adminers were on first, and had as much time to prepare as they wanted, yet still messed it up. Of course, the audience loved it as I was now on the spot.

Having done a few of these things in the past, I had a couple of things up my sleeve. I went on to say that the magician hadn't pitched up, but he had left me a couple of tricks. I pulled off the shittest magic trick in the book with a Tommy Cooper-style incompetence and I had it made. I pulled back the curtain and admin wing gave me twenty minutes to catch my breath as they flogged their way through their skit. OC admin (in the front row) came in for some tough banter but took it well, which meant he was ripe for more in my eyes. It was a good job he was because every sketch seemed to have a go at him, with the one from 19 Squadron being absolutely brutal. To his credit, he took it all on the chin with a huge smile on his face—good man.

Half time came and went, and it was coming up to our sketch. The previous group were making a hell of a racket clearing their kit off stage, and my act relied on the audience listening carefully to what was said. As a filler, I went into my rubbish juggling act that consisted of me demonstrating how to juggle from scratch. The key moment is when you choose someone from the audience to pick on. The place howled when I picked OC admin. Under the noise, I just managed to hear the station commander say 'cheap shot,' so in a moment of possible career-ending madness, I changed tack and got the station commander involved. The act revolves around juggling with one real ball and two imaginary balls and includes four separate gags that make the chosen person look a bit of a fool. The station commander was brilliant and really played up to it. He brought it to life for me really and the response was so good that I wanted to end the show there and then while I was ahead.

I gave the audience a minute or two to chat among themselves and calm down and then came back out in a trench coat and fedora to deliver my 'Private Investigations' sketch. I had a sort of joint New York/Chicago/North Yorkshire accent that probably wasn't so good, but I was delivering to very drunk people now so could have done it in any voice I wanted. As I went through my spiel, I had Basset behind the stage adding voiced sound effects using a microphone and the PA system. It all hinges on perfect timing and the guy out the front being able to react quickly if things go wrong. There are some set piece actions and reactions and the script is written so it looks like some things have gone awry. All of it is interspersed with old crappy jokes and banter about engineers, admirers, and suppliers. This was the defining moment of my first year at Wildenrath. I was amazed by the reaction, and now people around station were beginning to learn my name. Hopefully, this would help me stand out from the crowd; I certainly wasn't going to make my name being the best in the jet, but I hit the sack that night buzzing. That buzz stuck with me all the way into the cockpit on Monday.

Doggers and Bastards

My life in the cockpit could not have been more varied. In the space of a month, I flew a couple of high-flying supersonic sorties; a low-level nav exercise; delivered a jet to one of our sister squadrons in the UK on a Friday, and brought another back on the Monday after a weekend of partying; and then started my air combat work-up. Thank God, I loved doggers. The only snag was that every other pilot on the squadron was better than me at it, so I got used to flying while looking over my shoulder a lot. I really loved it, though.

The first trip of this work-up was a dual check with the new Boss to make sure I was safe enough to fight down to a simulated base height of 5,000 feet, which I was. Then it was back to fighting as a crew with the navs in the boot. Bouncer was first to fly 'Tug's vomit-inducing air combat extravaganza'. He was amazing—extremely aggressive and whooped when I managed to fluke a kill against the other jet. I had seen this before with some of the staff navs at the OCU, but Bouncer was roughly the same age as me and a proper squadron mate, so this was even more enjoyable.

In between the ACM trips, I found myself doing day tactics sorties. These were intercepts that ended up with aggressive manoeuvring at the merge (when the two aircraft pass each other visually). These could be 1 *v.* 1 or 2 *v.* 2 missions with the idea to practice the radar to visual skills of the navs talking the pilot's eyes onto the targets leading to air combat-style fights. Later on, I would be doing 4 *v.* 4s in this.

The designated target aircraft are only allowed a limited set of evasion tactics (turning, climbing, and speed change), but to be honest, that usually got blown off and it rapidly degenerated into full blown doggers. That is all well and good until you realise that the base height for day tactics was only 250 feet rather than the 5,000 feet for ACM. So, we could find ourselves doing almost air combat down at low level. My God, this stuff was crazy. Hauling my Phantom around the German plains at 4–5 G, taking shots, claiming kills, and they were paying me to do it.

I will remember the evening of 26 October 1989 forever. A few of us were having an after-flying beer in the bar when OC Ops came in and announced there had been a fatal shooting at the local Schnelli (fast-food place) just outside the main gate, and the station was on lockdown. These were the worst days of the IRA threat to military personnel, and it transpired they had murdered Corporal 'Mick' Islania and his six-month-old daughter. They were gunned down in cold blood with the IRA claiming they did not know there was a baby in the car and they regretted that she was killed—bastards. It put everyone on high alert, and the increased security measures seemed to last for the rest of my tour in Germany.

The very next day, our new Boss needed to get back to his house and family just outside London to help prepare for their move out to Wildenrath. He was short of a nav, so I jumped in the boot again as he flew us over to Brize Norton for the weekend. I have to say, it was like flying away from a blackness that hung over the base. I think my parents were glad to know I was away from it all, at least for a weekend if nothing else. The Boss's wife met us in their giant Volvo Estate, and the Boss sat in the back with his three children, the eldest of whom was about five or six and extremely precocious but in a very charming way. I heard some whispering from her and the Boss said, 'Why don't you ask Mr Wilson?'

I turned around and said, 'Just call me Tug.' As a family, they were very proper and the Boss told me they insisted on politeness from their children, to which she said, 'Can I call him Mister Tug, Daddy?' There it was. From that day forwards, I was known as Mr Tug. On the Monday, as the Boss prepped the jet, I headed over to station ops to file our flight plan back to Germany and was met with a somewhat frosty reception by the two ancient ops officers who worked in there.

Brize Norton was the RAF's main air transport base, housing the VC10 and the Tristar. In those days, a lot of truckie pilots and navs were guys who had been chopped at various points from the fast-jet stream. A few of them had chips on their shoulders because of this, and these two were obviously fully signed up members of the bitter brigade. They ignored me to start with, and when I asked for help, there were deep, patronising sighs as they shuffled off their commodes to accept my flight plan.

As the conversation progressed, I got more and more pissed off with their disdain for me and it all came to a head when they asked what type of departure we were going to do. There were all sorts of standard instrument departures (SIDs) from Brize. A SID was something we only did on bad weather days as it was an instrument procedure. The weather was gin-clear so I told them we would just do a visual departure. Well, I may as well have shat in the fingerbowl as the pensioners blustered and fizzed at me before declaring I had to do a SID. 'Nah!' I said. 'That's truckie shit.'

'Everyone is a truckie when they fly out of here!' shouted one of them, and I knew I had wound them up—it was a small victory. I do still wonder what they thought as they watched us get airborne and the Boss stuck it on its tail in full burner—they probably had a stroke.

Mr Tug It Is Then

Back at Wildenrath, the Boss started calling me Mr Tug and it stuck. The next name badge order saw me wearing 'Mr Tug' under my wings. No one knew where it had come from, but it seemed a cool nickname and I wasn't going to fess up to it being a five-year old's idea, certainly not when I heard people saying, 'That's <u>Mr</u> Tug to you!'

It wasn't long before the station held a memorial service for Corporal Islania and his daughter. It seemed that the whole of the station apart from those involved in supporting Battle Flight were stood down and crammed into the 60 Squadron hangar for the service. I have been to too many memorial services in my time and they have all been horrific. However, when they carried in the baby-sized coffin for his daughter, I don't mind admitting that it broke my heart. A quick look left and right told me that I was not alone as pilots, engineers, men, and women were unashamedly crying their eyes out.

At last, I was starting the low-level intercept phase. I would now be practicing my primary wartime role of low-level CAP, plugging the gaps between the Patriot SAM engagement zones in FAORs. My first go at it was with Lifford. He had been one of the navs dined out the month before, so only had a short time left before being posted to 56 Squadron at Wattisham in Suffolk. We blasted airborne as a pair and entered the low-level CODEC routing west of Wildenrath, heading south. We transited as a battle pair 2 miles line abreast down to Aachen and carried out a coordinated turn west towards the Ardennes low-level training area in Belgium. It was great to be back in the low-level arena, flying battle formation with my head on a swivel checking for enemy fighters dropping into our leader's 6 o'clock as well as looking out ahead while Lifford had his head in the radar.

We switched to the play area frequency and announced our arrival in case any other aircraft were in the vicinity. This was a standard call throughout 2 ATAF (the Second Allied Tactical Air Force) of which RAFG was a main part, and also set the hierarchy of the area. The idea in 2 ATAF was that we worked collaboratively with the German, Dutch, and Belgian Air Force fighters to man the low-level Caps. In extremis, this would include USAF F15s from way up north in Soesterberg and also the French Air Force Mirage F1s.

We rarely saw the USAF, so the pecking order had us at the top leading the Mixed Fighter Force (MFF) as we had the only capable look-down shoot-down forward sector shot with our Doppler radar and Skyflash or Sparrow missiles. Our callsigns all began with Mike-Lima, and that designated us as RAF Phantoms from Wildenrath. The numbers after that in our callsigns were unique to the airframe we were flying. Callsigns for other aircraft included Alpha-Lima, Alpha-Golf, and Alpha-Juliette to name but a few.

The area was clear of other jets so our leader split away from us by about 40 miles and we turned towards each other to start the intercept. Although it was a work-up trip for me, finding the target on the radar and keeping it painted to prosecute the correct intercept geometry over land was a tough ask, so Lifford was working harder than me. Bear in mind, he also needed to monitor my handling close to the ground and make sure I maintained safe procedures. He got contact and took a quick sample lock to get the range, before breaking lock and continuing in search mode. I hit the stopwatch as soon as he called the range and worked on a closure rate of 12 miles per minute to keep him updated on that range, hopefully giving him a decent clue as to when he should re-lock the target for our first Skyflash shot. These procedures were becoming second nature to me, having done them at medium and high level lots of times and were a big part of our standard crew-cooperation.

I gave Lifford a heads-up on the range and he went for the radar lock. The Skyflash steering circle, known as the ASE (allowable steering error), came up on my radar repeater scope along with a steering dot. I manoeuvred the aircraft to put the dot in the small circle, and as we got closer to the optimum range, the ASE expanded and Lifford called for the shot. I pulled the trigger and called 'FOX 1!' then paused for a second or two to simulate the missile coming off, then broke into the F-POLE manoeuvre. This meant turning hard left or right to put the target on the edge of the scope and then 'nibble' back towards it to keep it on the radar until the missile timed out (simulating hitting the target).

The idea behind this manoeuvre was to maximise the distance between you and the target at missile impact. It also gave us useful lateral separation to start the conversion to the rear hemisphere for the stern shot with the Sidewinder. We pulled hard in behind as I selected the heat-seeker and as soon as I heard the growl, I mashed the 'seam' button and took the shot at the tone. 'FOX 2!' followed by 'Knock it off. Knock it off' stopped the fight, and we separated out for the next engagement. This time, the target would be evading during the intercept and then turning to defend against us in the visual part of the fight. All in all, my performance during the intercepts was good, and my weaponeering and visual fighting were up to scratch.

The leader was obviously a bit bored of flying in roughly straight lines and wound up the last visual engagement such that we weren't far off doing a bit of doggers but down at low level. I have already said that day tactics was interpreted in a woolly fashion at best, and we ended up raging about the sky trying to shoot the living shit out of each other. You can imagine how much I was buzzing after that trip.

A Proper Bollocking

I think Lifford must have been happy with me as later that day, he asked me if I would fly him to RAF Valley on Anglesey for the weekend. He was going to a wedding in Chester and needed a pilot to take him to Valley, which was the nearest RAF airfield to the venue. No one else wanted to spend a weekend on Anglesey (and who could blame them?) so I was his last option—maybe I wasn't as popular as I thought?

As luck would have it, I had a set of pseudo-parents who lived in Llandudno, and a quick call confirmed that Ron could come and pick me up and I would spend the weekend with him and Meg before he dropped me off again on the Monday. Ron was ex-RAF National Service and had served in Suez during the crisis. He was RAF mad and I had spent almost every weekend with him while I was at Valley in their house in Penrhyn Bay. During training at Valley, everyone used to scatter to the four winds so the mess was dead at the weekends. Ron and Meg gave me much-needed respite from the stresses of flying training, and for that alone, I would be eternally grateful. I had booked Ron in with the RAF Valley guardroom, and as we taxied in to the visiting aircraft section line, he was standing there, his face absolutely beaming with pride as his 'son' brought this huge beast of an aeroplane to a halt on the chocks and went through the shutdown checks. I was actually quite choked as he greeted me, then stood like some cocky schoolkid as I showed him my jet. It was a golden moment for both of us and something I will remember for the rest of my life.

Lifford's ride had pitched up, and I told him that Ron and I would put the jet to bed so he could get on the road. We fixed a time for Monday and then I set to work putting all the undercarriage locks in; repacking the drag chute (nightmare); checking the fluids; and sending the liquid oxygen (LOX) pot off to the bay for refilling for Monday. Ron is a practical man, so I gave him an Allen key from the flyaway toolkit and asked him to drop a couple of panels on the underside of the fuselage while I fitted the intake, jet pipe, and canopy covers.

Once done, I went under the jet to read the fluids to find the underside looking like an advent calendar on Christmas Eve. Every panel it was possible to drop had been dropped. Ron was having such a good time that I didn't have the heart to tell him and just followed him around, doing them up again. He didn't stop talking about it all weekend and it was wonderful to see him getting so much pleasure from the fact that I had finally made it, sort of. There was still a lot of work-up to go before I got that operational patch on my arm. The op badge was the next big thing after getting your wings. Wings badges meant you were a pilot in the RAF. The op badge, though, meant you were a fighter pilot—come on!

That Monday was another step on my path to becoming a fighter pilot—my first proper bollocking to do with my flying. Ron dropped me off at the jet and watched as I prepped for flight. I got him to sit in the cockpit, and then Lifford arrived, having filed our flight plan for the return journey. As Ron and I shook hands, I told him to watch out for our departure as I was going to make some noise for him. He drove off to stand on 'Spotters' Hill' off the end of runway three-two and apparently told all the other spotters what I was going to do. They didn't believe him, especially when he told them I was a personal friend and had spent the weekend with him.

I called for 'take-off remaining for one and then depart,' meaning I would stay in the circuit for one go around and then climb out on departure. This is, of course, code for 'I am going to wazz through the airfield and do a burner climb,' or something like that, which is exactly what I did. Rocking the throttles into burner on take-off was extra special knowing Ron was looking on. I turned downwind once the aircraft was airborne and clean and cancelled the burner. 'Mike-Lima 69, downwind to low overshoot and depart.' ATC called me to continue and reminded me of the rules at Valley—'no afterburner until the airfield boundary'. I copied this as I turned finals, and when I thought I was inside the airfield boundary, I rocked them outboard again, and we roared over the runway at about 100 feet and then rotated to almost the vertical over Spotters' Hill, switching frequencies to departure. 'Valley Departures, ML69 with you in the climb to three zero zero.'

'ML69, this is Valley Departure, level at Flight Level 50.'

Oops—we were already passing flight level 150 so negotiated a bit higher before being handed off to London Mil. As we levelled off under radar control, Lifford said, 'Can I ask you a question, Tug? When they said no burner until the airfield boundary, which airfield boundary did you think they were talking about?'

'Well, the near one obviously so the noise stayed on the airfield.' There was a bit of silence, which was the clue that I was wrong, but I couldn't see that there would be any fallout from it. I mean, come on—I had used the burner on take-off anyway, so surely they couldn't complain? Also, let's not forget the morale boost I had just given all of the fast jet students going through Valley at the time. We used to love seeing and hearing front-line jets coming through the various schools during flying training. Yeah, I was definitely in the clear.

After landing, Lifford and I found ourselves standing to attention in front of the Boss's desk with our hats on getting a good tongue-lashing about my flypast. As we flew home, apparently, the phone lines to Wildenrath were glowing red, and the bollocking rippled down from the station commander to the Boss, ending up in my lap. I took full responsibility, but Lifford backed me to the hilt that Valley had been unclear with their instructions. The Boss had a bit of a grin on his face as he bollocked us (remember I had witnessed his departure from Brize Norton first hand) and the whole thing was remarkably pleasant. I walked out with my first bollocking and all was well with the world. Also, according to Ron, the spotters went mental.

New Faces

We continued our turnover of aircrew on 92 Squadron. The Phantom was flying a thin line, with the MoD looking for an excuse to bin it from service and save a few bob. Luckily for us, the Tornado F3 (our supposed replacement) was dogshit with lots of radar problems, meaning our old girl continued with various stays of execution. We, of course, revelled in this death row mentality as it just made us look harder. 'Come on, have a go at the F4 if you think you're hard enough!'

The fleet was in a slow wind down with the Leuchars squadrons being the first on the slope to be replaced by the F3. Accordingly, the F4 OCU was being pared back to little more than a training flight and lots of aircrew were looking at Wattisham and Wildenrath to try and eke out their Phantom careers. To that end, we ended up with Cliff Parsley and Bungle from the OCU (we landed on our feet there), an *ab initio* pilot and nav (Lurch and Poop) who were fresh off my junior course, Ginge and the Kid from Treble One, and a new QWI pilot called Lola. A couple of months after, we would get Fatty and Edge, and that would be it for the rest of my tour. Due to Lurch and Fatty, I was no longer the junior pilot on the squadron—I had become an old hand!

Harry and Von had just passed their operational check rides and that Friday, just before we decamped to happy hour, they had one more duty to perform and then their op badges would be fixed to their arms—the dreaded op pot. Op pots were rites of passage, and each squadron had their own traditional pot. It just so happened that 92's was a stein that held 4 pints of ice-cold Dort with a raw egg at the bottom. Von went first and stood by the open window in the crew room. He saw it off in just a few minutes (we had seen some guys take fifteen–twenty in the past), and he was presented with his op patch. There was then lots of oohing and aahing from the crowd as Von then stuck his head out of the window and barfed about 2 pints onto the lawn outside.

Cue much cheering and a look of absolute horror on Harry's face as he took hold of his pot. Harry was about half the size of Von, and watching him systematically drink and projectile chunder for about ten minutes was stomach-churning. However, he had a grin a mile wide as the Boss placed his op badge on the waiting Velcro patch on the arm of his flying suit. With any luck, it would be me next.

What Wall?

Happy hour that night was big—much as it always was after op pots. I barely remember hitting the sack, and Saturday turned into a bit of a hangover washout that seemed to run into Sunday. Coming out of dinner on Sunday night, I bumped into one of the young engineers in my mess block. When I asked him how his weekend had been, he gave me a bit of a blank stare and just said, 'Awesome. I was in Berlin.'

'Oh. Is it worth a visit then?' I asked.

'Holy shit, Tug! Haven't you seen? The Berlin Wall has come down!' I ran to the mess TV room to see people crowding round the set as news on BFBS (British Forces Broadcasting Service) continually covered the story from Berlin, showing scenes of people breaking down the wall. I didn't know it at the time, but this was the beginning of the end for my beautiful aeroplane, and it would change the world forever. Right then though, I had tons of prep to do for my upcoming trips and I got down to it straight away. Nowadays, young pilots call it armchair flying and it consists of thinking through the upcoming trip and visualising how it is going to go. It includes practicing the comm, learning intercept procedures, learning weapons limits and low-level route study, and all manner of other things related to the flight. I tended to over-prepare a little, but this was a hangover from my past struggles during flying training which drove me to work extra hard to make up for my lack of natural ability.

It was about this time that I got my first Ranger. Every year, each squadron would get twelve Rangers. These were landaway trips at the weekend (out Friday, back Monday), and we could pretty much choose any military airbase in Western Europe and spend the weekend there. The idea was that in wartime, we had to be able to land at any friendly and available airfield and so it was good to have experience of flying into different areas and speaking to foreign ATCs. I was going to lead two aircraft into Aalborg in Denmark, with OCB in my back seat. The other jet was our newly op crew, Harry and Von.

As an extra training task for the ground crew at Aalborg, 19 Squadron were sending three jets also, so there would be ten British aircrew raging around town for three nights. The prep for this trip brought it home to me how much I was maturing as an aviator. Both of our jets had baggage pods, but I insisted to our ground crew that they pack a full set of bungs and covers and also a spare pre-packed drag chute. This brought a bit of moaning from Harry and Von, saying I was being a bit of an old woman, but I had checked the forecast for the weekend, and there was a sniff of snow. I didn't fancy re-packing the chute myself in the cold and wet so stuck to my guns.

The flight up to Aalborg was spectacular. I have always loved seeing another fighter in close proximity while flying, and with the weather being absolutely clear as a bell, Harry's jet looked amazing. It was a piece of old piss picking Aalborg out, and we blasted through initials with Harry moving into close formation for a proper fighter break into the circuit. There was plenty of snow about, but the runways and taxiways were a deep glossy black. Following another landing we could definitely walk away from (I was getting good at this by now), I dumped the chute after exiting the runway and parked up for shut down.

The three 19 Squadron jets broke into the circuit just as we were crewing out. I set to, opening up the baggage pod and pulled our bags clear along with all the bungs, covers, and the spare chute. A vehicle turned up with our discarded chutes, and I folded mine up small and stuffed it into the baggage pod, and Harry did the same with his. This was a whole lot easier than repacking it at the top of a rickety step ladder into the chute housing just below the fin. Popping the pre-packed chute in there was a doddle, and we started covering the jets up and completing the turnaround by checking the fluids and pressures. The 19 Squadron guys gave us a bit of shit about putting the covers and bungs in place, but despite it taking a bit of time, the four of us were in a minibus being driven down to our hotel in town while the Fighting Dolphins were struggling to pack and load their chutes having not bothered to bring spares.

The hotel was excellent, and we settled in for a liquid lunch followed by a couple of hours of combat kip before meeting in the bar again at 1900 to plan our conquest of this renowned party town. Out of the ten of us, Harry was the most likely to chat up some unsuspecting local girl. He was quite short and ordinary looking, but he had a charm and confidence about him that never failed to succeed. Before we even left the hotel, he had sweet-talked a couple of Swedish girls who were visiting town. Believe me, if he could have bottled his charm, he would have made a fortune—he was that good.

Anyway, the girls tagged along as we headed out into what turned out to be a really disappointing night. The place was dead, with every bar all but empty. Bearing in mind we had started drinking at lunchtime, we had a fair bit of speed on and nowhere to play. The girls suggested a nightclub they knew and off we staggered. I was not a big nightclub fan and usually only went in to get a beer once the bars had closed, but even I had to admit this one was special—three floors with various Europop music, huge bars, and—don't quote me on this—but I am pretty sure it was Roxette playing in the ground floor bar. Actually, it could have been Elvis Presley for all I knew as we were all pretty shitfaced at this point. I think we were set for an even bigger night until there was a bit of a kerfuffle near Harry, and then we saw a couple of cops leading the Swedish girls away in handcuffs. They had been caught pick-pocketing from handbags in the club. OCB sobered up sharpish after that, and we were ordered back to the hotel. We could barely move on the streets as the place had exploded into life. Note to self—start drinking much later the following night, best laid plans and all that.

Saturday was a disaster, with the four of us barely making it out of our beds before 2 p.m. Von burst into my room to find me lying on my side, watching the TV on my bedside table. I had turned the TV onto its side to make watching it easier. Von told me to get dressed as we were going to the hotel sauna to sweat out the booze. This was a first for me. I had never been to a sauna before, and bearing in mind this was Scandinavia, I was bricking it thinking about what I might see. Harry was already in there sweating like an alcoholic pig, and I was glad to see that he and Von were keeping their boxer shorts on.

We sat there in the mist, sweating out a serious bender's worth of alcohol when the door opened and OCB strode in without a stitch on. He had a reputation of being 'well proportioned', and hell's bells, it showed. It was almost like he needed to sit the thing on the bench next to him it was so big. We all chatted a bit in an awkward way until he got up and poured a bucket of cold water over his head before heading off, telling us he would catch us later in the bar. The three of us looked at each other in silence and then I swear to God we spontaneously broke into a round of applause.

One epic night was enough for us and so Saturday was relatively quiet and Sunday even gentler as we were due airborne early on Monday, which brought a shitload of ice and snow, but our jets were nicely covered up from it (well done me). We blasted off into the ice blue clear air while the 19 boys were waiting on de-icing equipment before they could mount up. So, my first Ranger was behind me, and my work-up was about to go ballistic during the final stretch to me getting that Op badge on my sleeve and throwing up my op pot.

Well 'Ard, Well Cold

I was right in the thick of it now and flying regularly with our QWI leader as he started to assess me closely to see if I was worth the op badge. As with the OCU course, the last two phases were air combat and then 2 ATAF SOPs; these were the operational trips where I would man low-level CAPs working with our NATO colleagues as part of a mixed fighter force operation (MFFO) that would be our tasking in wartime. I would have to show that I could perform well enough as a fighter pilot, but also that I could plan, brief, lead, and debrief these trips to a high-enough standard. As I said earlier, the QWIL was a cool guy and easily the sharpest nav on the squadron. This made it even more important for me to impress him.

Unfortunately, the weather in December in Northern Germany was forecast to be pretty punk for the month, so the QWIL came up with a plan for us to deploy to Leuchars for a couple of nights chasing better weather. We only had one more crew available to come with us, so the QWIP on 19 Squadron and a suitable nav made up the numbers for us to be able to do the 2 *v.* 1 air combat phase. The last time I had seen the 19 Squadron QWIP, Sherlock, he had been jousting at the Clutch beer call, so I knew he would be good value. It was a wicked night as we took off from Wildenrath and we trailed Sherlock on the radar closing in and out practicing VIDs on the way in preparation for my upcoming Phase 3 VID check ride (lights out at night).

Up above 30,000 feet on the way to Leuchars, the QWIL asked me to turn the heating up on the cabin conditioning. I had to admit that it did feel a bit chilly, but I had been working so hard on the VIDs, I hadn't really noticed it. Now, with nothing too taxing to do (other than fly in formation at night), the cold had started to seep into my bones. We were both in full immersion suits with bunny suits and thermals underneath, but it seemed to be getting even colder. It didn't take us long to work out that the cabin conditioning was bust, and no matter what we did, it wouldn't reset. Therefore, we were pretty much at the temperature of the outside world, which at 35,000 feet or so was flaming well freezing. Worse still, having crewed in with the rain pelting down, my immersion suit was wet and the water on it started to freeze.

As we descended into the clear night on the approach to Leuchars, both the QWIL and I found that our legs were stuck to the sides of the footwells—not a huge problem for him, but a mare for me as I would need free movement on the rudder for landing. My teeth were chattering as I spoke on the radio to call finals, then a firm landing (well it was at night) and taxi onto the OCU line. Apparently, we looked blue to the other guys as we made our way to the mess. Our jet was definitely bust, but over a beer in the bar, we decided to tough it out so we could complete my 2 *v.* 1 combat work-up. It was odd being back in the bar at Leuchars wearing the red and yellow colours of a front-line unit, having stood there as student a mere five months before.

The next day was one of the busiest I have ever had in my whole RAF career. Three 2 *v.* 1 ACM trips with lots of G, and complicated manoeuvring and weaponeering, left my body and brain like mush. The QWIL and I were in the icebox for each trip, but during the action parts of the sortie, I was sweating buckets. Sherlock thought we would have a bit of self-deprecating fun and chose a formation callsign of Wellard for us to fly as on the first day. As Germany crews, we had an unofficial nickname of Ronne 'Well-ards' throughout the RAF, so he played up to it. It was even funnier when the next day we flew as Stillard and then headed home on day three as Flaccid formation.

Back to the flying though. The first trip was pure visual manoeuvring with us all starting line abreast with the bandit on the outside edge of the formation. As fighters, we turned hard towards him as he broke towards us. This left us line astern as fighters, and once the leader passed the bandit head on, he plugged the burners in and zoomed up out of plane as I merged as close as I dare with the bandit myself. The rules stated that we had to maintain a 1,000-foot bubble around each of us that no one could infringe. That was a safety rule that instructors watched closely back in training. Although the rules still applied to us, this was the front-line and the idea was to 'dust off' the bandit head-on so he focused completely on you as you turned to fight him. Hopefully, he would lose sight of your partner who could then re-enter the fight unseen and shoot the bandit to shit. Once this happened, we would keep the fight going until I could separate and re-enter for the kill. Therefore, I saw both sides of the fight on each split. Free and engaged tactics were a staple of fighting as a pair of fighters and something that had to become second nature to me.

I keep telling you that I loved doggers, and my aggression and enthusiasm made a good impression on the QWIL and I breezed through the first trip. Trip two saw us separating away from the bandit and running a full 50-mile intercept. This time, the technique involved the fighters flying in line abreast by 3–4 miles with a big height split. We would aim to bracket the bandit, so they had to look on both sides of the cockpit to get and maintain tally on us both. The leader would aim to dust him off, and I would hook into him from on high (out of the sun if possible) or from low if it was a dull grey sea, to engage and tie him up. Being the engaged fighter meant fighting as hard as you could and also coordinating the free fighter's re-entry using standard communication procedures.

The whole thing looked like a miles-wide giant dance in the sky, but a dance where people were trying to kill each other. To be fair, I have been to nightclubs like that. I got the chance to lead the last sortie as the final check of my competence. The last trip went really well, but I was completely knackered at the end of the day and frozen stiff. That evening was a bit of a mini-celebration with the six of us renewing our acquaintance with the Bulaka, where we failed miserably to get thrown out of.

The other guys took pity on us for the transit back home the next day, and we swapped jets, leaving the icebox to Cliff and his nav. I think they were worried that another trip would have seen us with hypothermia. One more flight saw Christmas arrive, so I had about three weeks on the ground as the station almost shut down apart from supporting Battle Flight, which I wasn't yet qualified to sit. I couldn't wait to start flying again after new year, and it was straight into the last bit of my operational work-up.

I was regularly leading pairs of aircraft out into the low-level system and coordinating whatever random MFF that pitched up on our CAP. It was amazing how all of this stuff was starting to come naturally, and things like recovering to the airfield, flying in close and tactical formations, flying circuits, and landings were just a part of my life now, whereas most of them used to be things that flummoxed me (or tried to kill me) just a few short months ago. After a couple of these trips, I was then leading four-ships with probably another four F16s hanging out on the wing, all of us intercepting and shooting whichever idiot bomber pilot tried to fly through our CAP. Interspersed with these trips, I found myself on the night wave getting ready for a couple of op checks, which I did with Lifford on the same trip.

A Dream Come True

It was a pretty intense sortie as the other aircraft in the formation launched ahead of us and headed off into the night to be our target. In the meantime, I had set up my aircraft as if it was on Battle Flight, and Lifford was going to check I could launch in the five-minute limit set by 2 ATAF and NATO. My heart was thumping as I waited, and then on a shout from Lifford, I bolted into the HAS, scooping up my life jacket and leaping into the cockpit for a fast start. I screwed up just about every switch selection as I fumbled the jet into some semblance of order. I am sure this particular Phantom was thinking, 'What the hell is he doing?' but somehow, we made the five minutes with a bit to spare and roared off to intercept our bandit.

The second part of the check ride was my phase three VID check. Lifford intercepted the target, who then went lights out. I followed the dot on my radar screen and flew Lifford's instructions as accurately as I could. This took real, cold-hard concentration to do, and I was sweating cobs and constantly wiping it from my eyes. We were in and out of cloud, so I asked Lifford to position us above the bandit to try and break out the silhouette against the little bit of light from the towns below. I flew the aircraft to a position 45 degrees off the tail with him 10 degrees down on the radar. Lifford called the exact position and then said, 'My instruments'.

At this point, I froze on the controls to hold exactly what I had in terms of altitude, speed, and heading, and then looked out of the window. I saw bugger all because it was dark and we were between layers of cloud that allowed neither the moon nor the lights of the towns to illuminate our target. I broke us away and we set up the procedure again. Following lots more sweating and hyperventilating, I looked out and saw the distinctive shape of a Phantom and made the identification—a couple more of these and I had done enough to pass my Phase 3 VID check. I was one more major step closer to being operational, and less than a month later, I was walking out to the HAS with the QWIL for my op check. In that intervening month, I had completed another day and night dual check, an instrument rating test, flown Bungle back to Leuchars for the weekend so he could see his family, and flown my final phase of four-ship lead work-ups with the QWIL.

My sortie briefing (a big part of my op check) had gone really well, and everything progressed smoothly out to the runway. We lined up staggered as two pairs on the end of the runway and I led my Number 2 in a pairs take-off followed ten seconds later by Numbers 3 and 4. The noise on the ground during a four-ship launch was something to behold, and I only wish I had had the capacity to marvel how cool this moment was. However, I was that proverbial one-armed paper hanger and needed everything I had to make the trip work. QWIL was going to be busy on the radar, so it was down to me to navigate in the standard north German murk; do all the comm; watch my Number 2's 6 o'clock for bandits; and then coordinate our formation with the four F16s MFF. Also, there was a shitload of targets to intercept and shoot, followed by organising everybody back onto CAP.

To this day, I can barely remember what happened as it was so bloody busy. QWIL told me I had passed the sortie during the transit home, so all the pressure was off me for the formation recovery. It was the happiest I had ever been in an aeroplane. I hadn't flown a single minute in control of an aircraft before joining the RAF, but here I was, operational on a front-line fighter squadron, four years and one month after taking my first ever flight in a Chipmunk—a dream come true.

The debrief went well and there were lots of handshakes and back slaps as QWIL announced I was now operational. I could now wear that op patch on my arm, just as soon as I successfully downed my op pot. Op pots were consumed on a Friday in the squadron crew room just before happy hour in the mess. My op check had been on the Thursday so the very next afternoon, the Boss handed me my op pot, and everyone watched as I got stuck in. the first mouthful of freezing cold Dort was refreshing, and I fell into the time-honoured trap of thinking 'This isn't so bad' and got to chugging. The beer then hit my stomach and all sorts of alarms went off in my body; my initial euphoria and confidence evaporated into a painful marathon of gulping and wincing. The pot was not allowed to leave my lips unless I was puking, which happened twice during the seven minutes it took me to down the beer and the egg at the bottom. Luckily, my squadron mates encouraged me with all manner of advice—none of it useful—and cheered whenever it looked like I was upping the pace.

So, just on seven minutes, my nightmare was over, and the Boss slapped the Velcro patch on my arm and shook my hand. The beer hadn't buzzed me yet, so I knew the thrill I felt was all down to the badge. I was now a fully-fledged fighter pilot, and I was flying the best jet in the world. I have no idea what happened in Happy Hour other than the squadron showing me off to 19 and then allocating a couple of guys to make sure I got to bed and saw out the night safely.

Beyond the Wall

The following weekend turned out to be epic. Ginge, who had been posted in from Treble One, decided that he was going to marry his long-time girlfriend, and so a stag night was planned. Now, given that most regular happy hours at Wildenrath were epic, a stag night needed to be something special. So, a trip to Berlin was planned. Berlin was the epicentre of the Cold War, and with the wall coming down in big chunks each day, we only had a short period to see it still segregated before complete unification. The writing was on the wall (so to speak) for the Phantom, and we knew its days were numbered once the wall fell, so what better place to go and have a hoolie? Tensions were still running high between East and West, and we had to get official permission to travel. There were only two ways for service personnel to get into Berlin—fly or military train through East Germany. We took the train.

The weekend started early Saturday morning in front of the mess as about fifteen hungover guys from 92 plus a few of our mates from 19 drank a shot of Apfelkorn to begin the journey. We loaded our bags up with beer and corn and made our way to the railway station at Mönchengladbach. We had to catch a train to some arbitrary station in the middle of nowhere, where we would meet the military train. I had no idea where we were headed so latched onto the best man, who had booked it all—good job, too, as the ticket seller at MG was so slow that four of us missed the first train out as German trains run exactly to time. They certainly weren't going to wait for four semi-drunk Brits.

The four of us got the next train out with no hope of meeting the military train so drank away our sorrows through a bottle of corn. Our Berlin extravaganza was over before it had started. I was pretty buzzed when we arrived at God knows where to find the other guys sitting on their bags on the platform. This called for a reunion drink, of course, and shortly after, the drab green military train pulled in and we filed on. The train was like something out of James Bond—old-style railway carriages with compartments and a proper dining car.

It was a long old journey, so there was plenty of time for drinking games such as 'spin the puree'. Ginge had brought a half-used tube of tomato puree that stood up at both ends with the middle pressed in. This meant you could put it on a table and it would spin freely. Whoever it pointed to after spinning had to yam their Apfelkorn. Jesus, that puree had it in for me. Just when I thought I was going to keel over, the train staff announced that dinner was served. I staggered through to the dining car and ate a three-course dinner with wine and after-dinner liqueurs.

Dinner was timed such that it was served while the train was stationary at the border to East Germany. The staff insisted that the curtains were open so that the Soviet border guards would see the decadent Westerners eating, drinking, and being merry—or, in my case, shitfaced. In other words, your life is shit mate and we are partying. The Soviet guards looked bloody miserable standing there in full uniform with their big peaked hats. The ones in the towers behind the machine guns looked miserable too, and rubbing their faces in it with beef medallions probably wasn't helping. It was completely bizarre crossing through the border and going 'behind enemy lines', but we forgot all of that as we arrived in Berlin.

We were staying at the Hotel Berlin, and I was sharing a room with Harry. It was that typically odd German set up with a double bed but two single duvets. I figured Harry would probably trap off with a nice German girl and I would have the room to myself on at least one of the nights so no problem there. After a quick shower followed by the aircrew mantra of 'Testicles, spectacles, wallet and watch,' we were assembling in the bar for our first night out.

The bar in the hotel had a big, white grand piano, and while the pianist took a break, Ginge sat down and started to play 'I Don't Like Mondays', to which we all started singing. The pianist came rushing back and Ginge started playing faster and faster as the guy got closer until he slammed the lid down and gave Ginge a huge mouthful in German. So that was us thrown out of the bar, and we made our way into town to find KLO. It was a weird place, a toilet-themed pub with shitters all over the shop and toilet-shaped seats.

This was the end of the road for Tug. The puree had done such a number on me that I headed straight to the loo (the proper one) and never made it out again—at least not under my own steam. After quite a while, the guys noticed I was missing, and Bouncer found me fast asleep on one of the toilets. Being the good mate that he was, he bundled me in a cab and took me back to the hotel. Reception wouldn't let me have my key as I was too drunk, so Bouncer put me to bed in his own room with clear instructions what to do if I was going to throw up, which I instantly forgot and crashed out. Bouncer headed back to the group for the rest of the night out. I have heard that Berlin is an amazing place to party. I wouldn't know—it was 6 p.m. and I was fast asleep.

The next morning, I was remarkably fresh. It's amazing what fifteen hours of sleep will do for you. I thanked Bouncer profusely for saving my life (he looked a bit poorly I have to say) and wandered down to reception to get my key. Once I got into the room, I saw that Harry was missing so figured he had trapped off with a local girl, true to form. A couple of minutes later, there was a banging on the door. I opened it to find Harry standing there in his clothes from the night before, minus his trousers that were neatly folded over his arm. 'Where the fuck were you last night? Reception wouldn't let me have the key so I was banging on the door for you to open up.'

'I was in Bouncer's room. They wouldn't give me the key either.' Harry strode past me and lay down. 'Two questions, Harry. First, why are you carrying your trousers? And second, where did you sleep last night?' Harry had no response for the trouser question, but his answer to the second question was downright bizarre. After trying in vain to wake up the empty room, he just sat down outside the door and fell asleep. A little while later, a very nice German guy called Michael walked past and woke him up. On hearing Harry's story, Michael insisted on him sharing his room for the night. So, Harry had shared a room with a friendly German stranger while very shitfaced. He had woken in the morning with little recollection of what had happened, next to a random man in the same bed. After a couple of embarrassing 'hellos', he had quickly dressed and bid Michael goodbye. Of course, Harry did not receive any banter at all about this.

On Sunday, we did Berlin. The huge Brandenburg Gate was still obscured in the foreground by the wall and checkpoints, but a little further down, we found a person-sized hole in the wall and zipped through for a photo in No Man's Land. We only had a few seconds before a van full of armed guards sped towards us, and we slipped back through to the West. It was a sobering thought to see all the molehills in No Man's Land, knowing they were the remnants of the landmines that had been dug up and removed.

We were all keen to get through to East Berlin, and that meant going through the famous Checkpoint Charlie. It took about an hour to get through, but it was worth it. We were able to wander freely around East Berlin, and the contrast with West Berlin was stark. West Berlin looked like any other European city that I had been to, but the east side of the city was bland and grey. The cars (Trabants and Wartburgs) looked like they were from ancient history, and lots of the old buildings still had tons of bullet holes in them from the Second World War. All in all, it was a little depressing, so we had a beer to cheer us up, bought some Russian soldier furry hats, and headed back to the West for a second night out—or, in my case, a first night out.

Everyone was a little subdued following the first night madness, and the whole thing was a quiet affair. The only thing of note was when three of us jumped into a cab and asked for the Europa Centre. The cabbie said, 'You don't want me to take you to the Europa Centre.' We instantly thought he was just being difficult as we were British so insisted he take us. He shrugged and pulled away, only to stop immediately on the other side of the road. 'The Europa Centre,' he announced a bit more theatrically than was strictly necessary. We grudgingly paid him and left with him laughing his head off.

It was a load of weary broken men that arrived back at the mess the next day. The train journey was extremely quiet and I am sure someone threw Ginge's puree tube out of the window somewhere behind the Iron Curtain. Once I got back to my room, I set my two pieces of Berlin Wall that I had bought on top of my chest of drawers next to my two CDs. Now, I realise, that these may have been two arbitrary bits of concrete the seller had found in his back yard and painted them up just to fleece tourists like me. I was too hungover to care though. I like to think they are genuine.

This Means War! Er, Again

As an operational pilot, I was declared by the squadron to NATO, and the very next week, we went to war—sort of. Every year, the station was subjected to a NATO-assessed tactical evaluation (TACEVAL). This was not the sort of TACEVAL where they turned up with a few beers demanding a bacon sandwich. Over a period of about four days, we would be tested on our ability to operate under wartime conditions. Before TACEVAL arrived, the station would prepare by practicing by itself on two exercises titled MINEVAL and MAXEVAL.

I had barely got my op badge on my sleeve, when the station hooter sounded the alert at about 4 a.m. on a Tuesday morning. We all rushed into the hard on the squadron, and it was game on. I absolutely lucked in as I was crewed with Bungle for the exercise, and for the next few days, we did everything together. It is worth describing what 'going to war' looked like in the middle of the Cold War. On arriving at the squadron, carrying all our nuclear, biological and chemical (NBC) protection kit, we changed into a charcoal-lined inner that went under our flying suit, then hung around in the filtered atmosphere of the planning, briefing and ops areas.

Messing was done centrally as the whole of the station went onto war footing, and our food was provided in hot lockers (more commonly known as 'hot locks') delivered to the squadron. Hot locks were big insulated boxes that had boiling water in a compartment in the bottom to keep the food warm. First thing in the morning, the hot lock would arrive with paper bags containing egg banjos. An egg banjo is the greatest egg and bacon sandwich you will ever see, but even after just one day on exercise, it becomes the food of the gods. As soon as morning brief was over, each crew would be assigned an aeroplane, and we would don our respirators and tin hats (later, Kevlar versions) and head off to the HAS. We would need to keep our eyes open for anti-personnel mines on the way—not real ones of course, but the NATO examining staff would liberally throw them around the HAS site to simulate them being dropped by Soviet aircraft during air raids, which were simulated numerous times during exercise.

Once inside the HAS, we would put the jet on alert and then retire to the fumigated 'Wendy House' in the HAS with our three ground crew and wait for our tasking. Some of the sorties we flew were pre-planned in order to get some training value from the flights themselves, whereas others were just random scrambles where the first one to the runway had the lead of whoever else turned up, including the guys from 19. After landing, we would be allocated a HAS to return to and once the aircraft was refuelled and 're-armed' (our ground crew were tested on their duties also, which included loading and unloading weapons), we put the aircraft back on alert. The whole thing was coordinated by the NRL on each squadron, who acted as a warlord.

Apparently, during this particular TACEVAL, the examining staff had simulated that 19 Squadron's HAS site had been cut off, so all their jets would have to come to us. This freaked the NRL out a bit and gave him an impossible task to coordinate a whole station's worth of jets, and he had a bit of a meltdown. As things got more and more stressful, he went bananas and threatened to have the ops clerk shot for mutiny or some such when she tried to tell him one particular HAS was already full with two jets and one in the revetment. I think the NRL though she was an official 'inject' in the exercise and was putting it on. Anyway, that aside, when things started to break down, the examining staff were calling each other to get to 92 Squadron to watch his meltdown, the bastards. What they should have done was back off the pressure and let him sort it out, but they just kept loading him up with more and more injects. We could hear the stress in his voice on the radio, and to this day, I still think the NATO staff were dickheads to do that. They were mostly has-beens who had probably never been that good on the front-line themselves. No doubt they have dined out on the stories for the rest of their insignificant lives.

Bungle and I had a brilliant three days of flying three times a day, including one trip where we were part of an epic eight-ship fighter sweep all around northern and central Germany. At about 6 p.m. each night, the day shift was stood down and the night flyers took over. We headed back to the hard, where we threw dinner down and had a quick shower to get the grime from the charcoal suit and the sweat from flying off before heading to bed.

There are a couple of things here that my colleagues will shudder at the thought of, if they ever read this, but I have to tell you about. First, dinner during exercise always included a sort of suet-style dumpling that was roundly known as 'baby's heads' because it looked like a row of baby's heads in a meaty gloop—a picture I will never get out of my mind.

Secondly, when I say 'heading to bed', I meant heading to the 'Submarine'. The Sub was right in the middle of the hard and had about thirty metal bunks on two levels. Each bunk was separated from its neighbour by a wall of chicken wire. Up to thirty snoring, farting men were expected to get a decent night's sleep before being back on alert at about 6 a.m. The first two nights, I was buzzed by the flying so slept very little. On the third night, I was struggling with fatigue so I asked the doctors for some temazepam to help me sleep. In those days, they could diagnose the stuff and it was an accepted part of TACEVAL. I popped my pills and settled down in my sleeping bag (NATO issue, sleeping for the use of, etc.) and was just dropping off when SENGO sneezed through the chicken wire onto the back of my neck and then snored and farted his way through the next few hours. That was me buggered then!

Temazepam doesn't necessarily put you to sleep, but it aids you in getting to sleep if you are already tired. I laid awake most of the night, listening to SENGO's trumpet solo and wearily dragged my knackered arse out to the HAS for day four. Bungle and I had flow nine trips in three days, and with the drugs still in my bloodstream, I climbed up into the cockpit at about 5.50 a.m. and carried out the comms check. Three hours later, Bungle woke me up to tell me the exercise was finally over without anyone launching on the last morning. Apparently, after checking the comms, Bungle and the ground crew had watched as my head fell forwards onto the radar repeater scope and I had just zonked out. They didn't have the heart to wake me. Lord knows what would have happened if we had been launched. All in all, it brought it home to me how bloody difficult this war business was going to be.

Darth Vader

One saving grace from the exercise was that I wasn't chosen to be tested on AR5 drills. The AR5 still gives me nightmares. It was a piece of flying kit designed to keep us safe in the NBC environment and was the most horrific bit of bondage kit you could ever dream up—a black rubber hood, inflated and vented by a handbag-sized fan, went over your head coming down to your upper chest. Inside this was a rubber neck seal that enclosed your head into an incorporated aircraft oxygen mask and visor. On top of this, you would put your flying helmet and then walk to the aircraft where you could plug into the onboard ventilation system replacing the handbag. It was so bloody horrid that only navs tended to fly in it on TACEVAL and, rarely, the odd pilot in a twin-sticker with a QFI in the back for safety, just in case something should go wrong. Just donning and doffing the AR5 was a fully choreographed event in itself and took in the region of thirty minutes for each drill.

Donning began in the hard, where we put our charcoal-lined suit on over our long johns, put rubber booties over our socks, then secured an S10 respirator on our faces before stepping through the airlock. On the other side were the vapour and liquid hazard areas where our safety equipment specialists (Squippers) were waiting for us with the dreaded black hood. All you could hear was the noise of the fans inflating the hoods of you and your nav. Around the walls at waist height was a guttering that would be filled with Fuller's earth in wartime to soak up any dangerous liquids on our bodies from outside, but during peace, it had bits of polystyrene for us to pretend that we were dousing ourselves in the real thing. The drill was to put Fuller's earth all over your hands and your respirator, take a deep breath, close your eyes, and remove the S10. The Squippers would then put you in the AR5. Once sealed into it, you could open your eyes and move on. By then, you looked and sounded just like Darth Vader.

After more Fuller's earth, it was on with the tight-fitting rubber gloves that were sealed with strong black speed tape around the wrists. You were already sweating quarts at this point, but you had only just begun. Next up was the flying suit, made doubly hard by the fact you were connected to the fan through an oxygen hose. Once that was on, it was out of the booties and into flying boots. The Squippers had to help with the laces as the rubber gloves made your hands useless for delicate tasks. Rubber booties went back on over your boots with lots of Fuller's earth again. G-pants, flying gloves, and life jacket came next. Last but not least was the flying helmet (which was a mare trying to fit on over a rubber hood I can tell you).

Once the helmet was secured, the AR5 oxygen mask was connected to the flying helmet and that was you, stuck in an enclosed rubber mask under all of your flying kit. There was a set procedure for entering the aircraft involving removing the booties and then connecting to the aircraft oxygen supply. Once that was done, you were free of the handbag and could strap in.

Doffing was the same procedure in reverse and took just as long as donning, with even more Fuller's earth as we had been exposed to the outside NBC environment. Sweat would pool above the neck seal, and when the AR5 was finally removed, at least half a pint of it would stream out. A smaller, but equally disturbing amount of sweat would spill out from each rubber glove. All in all, it was a revolting sweatfest and your long johns would be sodden. This particular TACEVAL, OCB was chosen to fly in the AR5 and Sod's law dictated that was the day they simulated Wildenrath was under attack. Their jet had to divert to Bruggen and he had to take his AR5 off after shutting down (cue lots of sweat) and then put it back on again for the next flight back to Wildenrath (yuck). I only had to do the AR5 drill twice in two years on 92 Squadron. Unfortunately, one of those times was to fly in it—more of that later.

Eyes like a Shithouse Rat

As I had become op at the end of February, the March Battle Flight programme had already been written so I missed the duty for another month. I was on the programme for April though, and couldn't wait. There were a couple of currency things to do before I could sit Battle Flight, so I found myself tanking from Victors and VC 10s, luckily without monstering the basket, and also practicing live missile-firing procedures. At any time, Battle Flight could be scrambled to fly across to the air-to-air ranges just south of RAF Valley and fire a real missile against the radio-controlled Jindivik target aircraft flown from Aberporth on the west coast of Wales.

I would need to know the procedures inside out as just making a fool of myself with live weapons would not be the worst thing that could happen. I practiced the profile a couple of times on my next trips and then after a night close formation flight and another flight with a taxiway take-off, I was deemed ready to go in the shed. Interspersed with these trips were the usual 2 ATAF SOP flights raging around at low-level and one really hard sortie that had everyone on their toes.

It was Scooby's annual tactical check (TAC CX) and he had organised four jets from 19 Squadron to join his four-ship for a big CAPEX involving MFF and lots of targets. I was op now so trusted to take part in this extravaganza. If the MFF pitched up, we were looking at twelve–sixteen fighters on CAP with God knows how many bombers to shoot at. Eight Phantoms lurching into the German gloom looked rock hard with each jet smoking as the pilots cancelled their afterburner following the gear and flap coming up.

As we entered the low-level play area in good order, Scooby came on the radio with a re-tasking. This put a thought bubble over each cockpit, and he then announced we were going to man a kill zone. Kill zone was in our SUPPLAN SOPs and was a box of airspace with a reference point transmitted as a latitude/longitude and an orientation. The lat/long gave the CAP position and a box extended a number of miles away from it in the direction of the orientation. The dimensions of a kill zone are probably still classified (I really should check, I know), but trust me when I say it is a big wodge of airspace laterally, longitudinally, and vertically. Kill zones would be promulgated during war time to counter large-scale Soviet raids that may pass between the SAM engagement zones. Any aircraft in the box, with a hot vector towards the CAP, was declared immediately hostile, and we could shoot at will.

It goes without saying that returning friendly aircraft needed to avoid a kill zone at all costs, but that included the fighters manning the kill zone themselves. If I entered the kill zone to shoot down an enemy aircraft, I would then have to exit it at 90 degrees to the orientation to get outside of the box so I could return to CAP, otherwise I would look hostile and could be shot down by one of our own. This was the first time a lot of us had done a kill zone and it showed. The navs in particular were working extremely hard to get the nav kit sorted and still run the radar. I can't remember pulling the trigger more than on that sortie, there were so many targets.

The only guy who seemed to be taking it all in his stride was Scooby. Then again, he was the only one who knew what was going to happen, so he looked as cool as a cucumber. The clever bugger had turned his own TAC CX into a TAC CX for everybody else in the formation, including the 19 Squadron boys. We were all beaming in the debrief as it had been an awesome trip despite the hard work. Scooby had managed the whole thing brilliantly despite the usual shitty German weather. As one of the older pilots in our formation had remarked in the debrief, 'You need eyes like a shithouse rat in weather like that.'

Battle Flight

Here it was then. The day had finally arrived—my first day on Battle Flight. I don't mind admitting that I didn't sleep a wink the night before, I was so excited. This led to me arriving for duty in the early morning mist at about 6 a.m. The outgoing crew were still asleep, so I just wandered around outside the HAS, soaking up the atmosphere.

Across the taxiway, I could just make out the 19 Squadron Battle Flight HAS. Each day, both squadrons would generate one aircraft, fully armed for Battle Flight, with the duty squadron at the time providing a spare aircraft also. The duty squadron was shared on a rota and would take the role of QRA 1 (quick reaction alert) and Q3, with the other squadron providing Q2. This meant providing aircraft and crews. If a scramble message came through or the hooter went off, both Q1 and Q2 would come to cockpit readiness and check in with the engines running by calling 'Battle Stations engines running!' If Q1 was serviceable, it would launch and Q2 would be stood down. On my first Battle Flight duty, I was to be Q1. At twenty-four years old, I was the first line of defence for Central Europe, so I had better get my shit together.

I kicked my heels for an hour or so and had a cuppa while chatting to the RAF police dog-handler who was patrolling the site. That brought it home to me how serious this was. I was crewed with the NRL for my first duty. He was older and much more experienced, and would keep me calm (no chance). The off-going crew woke up and we completed the handover briefing. Then it was a case of checking the jet, another cup of tea, and settle down onto the sofa waiting for the hooter, which didn't go off. I couldn't sit still at all. I bounced around the shed constantly going out to check the jet while the NRL sat calmly doing the paperwork that squadron leaders had to do.

At about 11 a.m., he had had enough and sighed heavily. 'Tug, you need to sit down and relax otherwise you are going to burn out.' He

Faith, *Hope*, *Charity*, or even *Desperation* in the Falkland Islands shelter.

A beautiful morning in Cyprus.

Refuelling from a C-130 in the Falkland Islands.

Last Phanton trip with Bobby—in a 74 Squadron FGR2.

Me in my beautiful Blue Zulu.

Me taxiing in at Wildenrath.

Checking the gunsight on 56 Squadron with Klaxon.

Concentrating while crewing in.

My first Snakebite confirms my posting to 92 Squadron.

Fancy dress in the Falkland Islands with Sly—must be a toga then!

Posing with Jimmy at Limoges Airshow.

Close formation take-off with me on the wing.

Flying in close.

The 92 Squadron ops building.

Van Morrison—legendary car and sometimes bed for the night.

Blue Zulu in Delta Disperal, ready to fly.

Blue Zulu just showing off.

Above: Me tanking from a Tristar.

Below: Flying back from Aalborg.

Recovering to Akrotiri.

The legendary Pig and Tape.

Right: First week on 92 Squadron in front of the squadron nameplate.

Below: Ops building in Akrotiri, Cyprus.

The moon over my Phantom, QRA Akrotiri.

Searching for another waterfall in Iceland.

Clean jet ready for doggers.

That bloody tube on QRA in the Falkland Islands.

Above: Final Phantom trip—filling up my immersion suit with water.

Right: Fiftieth anniversary of the Battle of Britain parade.

Shaking hands with OC 56 Squadron after my last Phantom trip.

Hanging out at Valley, waiting for a missile shot.

had seen it all before with young pilots, I guess. It didn't help that in the kitchen, there was a huge cartoon-style mural on the wall of a Phantom caricature threatening a Russian aircraft with the following phrase underneath that mimicked a famous Pepsi commercial at the time: 'It's a nothin doin', hooter soundin', stomach churnin', dinner droppin', tea spillin', doors openin', engine turnin', runway thrashin', reheat blastin', action called Scramble!'

Anyway, I finally forced myself to sit down and read the paper before the excitement of lunch arriving. Each day on Battle Flight, we were given a menu from the mess, and our food was delivered in a hot lock. You learn very quickly that curries, chillies, and stews/casseroles travel really well in a hot lock, but everything else comes out soggy.

Life on Battle Flight is pretty boring once the excitement wears off, but from time to time, we would have visitors from the station school children, visiting senior officers, or even friends and family. These visits were brilliant as they broke the monotony and also gave us a chance to talk about the aircraft and Battle Flight in general. We would request a 'doors check', so the hooter would go off and the HAS doors would open which looked pretty cool, especially with a fully armed Phantom lurking behind them. The funny thing though was that whenever it was a school visit, the kids always raved about the fire engines and rarely mentioned the Phantom.

Nothing like that was on the cards for me today though, so it was crappy Forces TV interspersed with bouts of stress willing the hooter to go off. Eventually, 11 p.m. came around, and I went to bed dressed in flying suit, G-pants, and boots. I think I finally got off to sleep at about 2 a.m. and was wide awake drinking tea again at 6 a.m. Reluctantly, I handed the jet over to the next crew and went back to the mess for breakfast before having the rest of the day off.

The very next day was Sunday, 22 April 1990, and I was back on Battle Flight with Bouncer. The excitement was still there, but I was nowhere near as stressed this time—until the hooter went off that is, and my world turned upside down with my first ever live scramble. After that momentous event, I was walking a little bit taller and a little bit wider—a proper fighter pilot at last. That turned out to be the one and only Battle Flight scramble I ever had at Wildenrath. I was brought to cockpit readiness a few times, but all the other scrambles happened for me in the Falkland Islands and in Cyprus.

Harry's First Crash

Being an op pilot put me in the mix with everyone else on the squadron. The nature of the job in Germany demanded that we were four-ship leaders after our TAC CX and could lead up to sixteen on CAP. Any more would be unmanageable in the airspace. I was just another pilot now, so attention turned to the other convexees, to get them through their work-up. One of the new navs, Edge, had just arrived and I was trusted to fly his first trip on 92. This was a big deal for me as I had to brief him on all the HAS site procedures much as Jimmy had done on my first sortie about six months previously.

I was meticulous in showing Edge everything, and we had a very pleasant NAVEX around Germany without any incident. It was just another day on the squadron. At about the time Edge and I were enjoying a grand day out including flying over the famous Möhne, Edersee, and Sorpe dams, a few of the other guys had deployed to Valley to conduct our annual live missile shoot. That day, the weather at Valley had been poor visibility, and the missile shoot had been cancelled. Harry was leading the four-ship as primary shooter and tried to bring them back to the airfield for a visual formation break. I guess the clue that it was unfit for that was when three and four in the formation split off for instrument approaches, but Harry stuck with it.

By all accounts, his landing was 'firm', having struggled to keep sight of the runway downwind in the murk. On touchdown, both his mainwheel tyres burst and he buzzcut his way down the runway on the rims in a hail of sparks before coming to an ungainly halt. The flying rubber from the tyres had damaged both ailerons, both flaps and the speed brakes, and both engines had to be dropped for checks. Also, the runway needed emergency repairs so the station commander at Valley was a bit narked.

Bouncer and I were detailed to fly a spare aircraft into Valley to replace Harry's and were told to take landaway kit and hang around to see if we could get a live firing. Valley ATC were a bit chippy with us when we called them up the day after the runway repairs were completed. I suppose the last thing they needed was another Phantom crashing into the ground on their shiny new tarmac, but we landed anyway and taxied into the Strike Command Air-to-Air Missile Establishment (STCAAME) dispersal to meet the rest of the guys.

Harry looked miserable as sin—been there, done that so I felt for him. Bouncer and I were formally in-briefed by the STCAAME staff and we drifted into the missile practice camp (MPC) way of life of lounging around waiting for the weather to clear in the range. It was sunny and warm at Valley, but the visibility was poor, so we settled on some deckchairs and watched the Hawks doing their circuits. It was only a couple of years ago that had been me, but I was a world away from that now. I marvelled at how much I had crammed in since then—wings; fired a gun; dropped some bombs at TWU; done air combat; tanking; got my op badge; and live scramble. The list was endless.

The next couple of days, I flew three MPC profiles. One was as secondary shooter (the primary was fully serviceable so I didn't get to shoot – damn!) and two as photoshoot where I saw a Sparrow III come off the primary and whoosh downrange, and also a Sidewinder piss off the rail at Mach 3—that was something. The following day started slowly with strong winds at Aberporth preventing the Jindivik from launching. The Jindy was a small aircraft-sized remote-controlled drone that flew out of Aberporth airfield and was controlled from the ground there. It would carry a radar enhanced target and a flare pack so that we could target it with either missile depending on the profile. It had limited wind and weather limits, and that day, the wind was too strong. The deckchairs came out and we assumed the position.

There was a bit of noise then as four Phantoms from 56 Squadron arrived in the circuit. They had been flying some low-level in the brilliant Welsh countryside and dropped in for a refuel. I had about 250 hours on the Phantom at this point, but I was still fascinated by how it looked so I watched them as they landed. Then things got exciting. As one of them landed, there was a huge bang and both mainwheel tyres burst. Cue lots of sparks and lots of 'Oooohs!' from us. Then things got really exciting as the nav ejected from the rear cockpit. Apparently, the ATC tower controller had seen the sparks and had called 'You are on fire!' The nav had thought 'screw this' and left at speed accordingly.

This was the first time I had seen a live ejection and it was gobsmacking. There was an almighty bang as the seat gun fired and then a short whoosh as its rocket pack took it up to about 300 feet before the parachute deployed just in time to break the crump into the ground. It was all over in a few seconds and looked horribly violent. The pilot stuck with the aircraft and it came to a screeching halt just on the intersection of the runways. That meant all the Hawks had to divert to the relief landing ground at Mona. The station commander was apoplectic. His newly laid runway was cut to ribbons again, and he was on the warpath.

He made a bit of a dick of himself threatening to bill the squadron for the damage and saying some unsavoury things about our jet and the fleet in general, about how unprofessional we were. I think (and hope) he still has nightmares about Phantoms destroying his precious runway. All our Boss could say at the time was 'I hope the nav wasn't Iron because he is posted to us next month!'

We later found out in the bar that it was Iron. We were grounded the next day as the runway was repaired again. The initial investigation into Harry's tyre drama had discovered an anomaly in the structure of the tyres and this led to them checking Iron's tyres with the same findings. It looked like a bad batch of tyres and we could all see the relief on Harry's face—been there, done that, Harry!

The next day, we sloped off back to Wildenrath looking like a bunch of rather naughty boys who had broken the runway they had been playing with. I didn't get to shoot, but there would be other chances for me and we were sick of the station commander scowling at us, so it was probably best that we went home.

Number One Tip Top Officers' Mess

My life was one long round of low-level four-ships, happy hours, Battle Flight, and parties, and I couldn't have been happier. There was another dining-in night where I sang about the departing guests again (badly this time as I had broken my own unofficial rule of not drinking too much if performing), which had a crowd-pleasing chorus. I was really on top of the world. To cap it all off, I was asked to go on a Ranger to Cyprus for the weekend.

Every year or two, each fighter squadron deployed to RAF Akrotiri for armament practice camp. APC was the air-to-air gunnery detachment, and every crew had to make the NATO minimum score for air-to-air gunnery by shooting at a banner towed by a Canberra aircraft. These dets were legendary, but I had just missed the last one. Although this wasn't APC, I would still get to see all of the places and things that I had heard of, such as 'Animal House' (the block of rooms fighter squadrons always stayed in), Chris's Kebab House, Limassol, and a whole host of other things. I couldn't wait. I was crewed with Von, who hadn't been there before either, and we were being led by Doc and Jimbo.

We thundered off early morning and flew for a couple of hours into Sigonella in Sicily. Sig was an Italian Air Force base, but also had a big US Navy installation where we could refuel. Odd thing though—we refuelled through the hot pits. This entailed shutting only one engine down and taxiing in between a load of pipework. While the engine was still running, we were plugged in and refuelled. My bizarreatron hit maximum when I saw one of the US Navy ground crew climb up on Doc's wing and swipe a Shell Amex card to pay for two jet's worth of gas. The whole event took about twenty minutes, and we were off again to Akrotiri.

After another two hours, we could pick out Akrotiri on the brown slab of land in the beautiful blue Med. All told, five hours was the longest I had ever spent strapped to an aircraft ejection seat, but I barely noticed it as we broke into the circuit. I was at a stage now where I had the capacity to look around at the scenery while flying in the circuit. I just wanted to take it all in, and the view of the beaches and the beautiful blue sea was stunning.

Less than a year ago, I would have been fighting the big ugly bastard of a jet around the circuit, probably 200 feet high and dangerously slow. Now I was ahead of the game and loving it all. I squeaked it onto the runway and shut down on the pan. I could see the ops building that the fighter squadrons used during APC and all the squadron badges and colours were plastered on the side of the building and on the concrete pathways. Jimbo announced that the bar was about to close after lunch, so he and Von would go and secure some drinks while Doc and I put the jets to bed. 'Jug of brandy sour, Doc?' asked Jimbo.

'Sounds good,' said Doc.

'How about you, Tug?'

'Yes, I'll try a brandy sour from the jug if there's enough to go around.'

'No, Tug. We all have a jug each.' It was going to be that kind of weekend then, and it was. The mess at Akrotiri was brilliant—a huge dining room and beautiful Colonial-style bar with a big patio. Brandy sour was *de rigueur*, and my first jug went down without touching the sides. We lugged our bags to our accommodation block—the famous 'Animal House'. This was where the fighter squadrons lived on APC. The rooms were functional with big, old air-conditioning units that your buddies would fill with talcum powder when you weren't looking so you got covered when you turned the unit on.

The most important bit on the block was the fire bell on the wall outside. This wasn't because we were worried about fires though. No, it acted beautifully as the bottle opener. A quick shower and change saw us ready for a couple of sharpeners in the bar before heading down to Chris's Kebab House on the strip just down the road from the main gate. A Cypriot kebab at Chris's was another rite of passage for a fighter crew, and this was going to pop another cherry for me. It all begins with a huge welcome from the staff and bottles of Thisbe and Pink Lady wine accompanied by nosebags and the Tahini bowser—pita bread with chopped cabbage and a vat full of tahini.

Up next is the squeaky cheese (halloumi) followed by sheftalia (a lamb kebab sausage thing). I think this might be the point where the Kokinelli shows up. Kokinelli is a wicked, fortified red wine with the alcohol content of George Best's liver. That pretty much saw me off for the night. Apparently, I ate my way through a giant pork chop and then a Cypriot racing chicken, but I don't really remember much once the Kokinelli started.

We all staggered into the mess for breakfast the next day, and I met another legend from the fighter world—George. He had been a waiter in the mess for decades and was somewhat flamboyant. 'Gentlemens! Welcome to the number one tip top Officers' Mess! *Efharisto!*' He recognised Jimbo and Doc and made a big show of introducing himself to Von and I, pulling our chairs out for us and taking our order. Drunk food is the same the world over, but the mess breakfast (and, as I was about to find out, every meal) had the freshest fruit and salads I have ever seen.

The rest of the weekend was just brilliant—Limassol, wind surfing (or trying to) on the private beach at Akrotiri, and lots of brandy sour and Kokinelli made this the best weekend since I started flying the Phantom. Sunday night was a bit quieter, but we were still four weary Cobras who climbed into the cockpit and blasted off into the early morning blue. A refuel through Sig should have seen us home, but strong headwinds meant a quick splash and dash in Lahr in southern Germany. There were two beautiful F18 Hornets on the pan as we arrived in Lahr that were probably only about a year old. My jet was at least thirty-five and was pissing oil and fuel out like some sort of incontinent pensioner. All told, I was over six hours in the cockpit and after the heavy weekend, I slept the sleep of the dead that night.

I Get One Over the Beast—Almost!

Cyprus was a huge fighter pilot venue ticked off, and the very next month, I ticked off another—Decimomannu. Deci was an Italian air base on the southern end of Sardinia close to Cagliari. It housed a couple of squadrons of Italian Air Force F-104 Starfighters—talk about a rocket ship! It was also nice to think that there was a fighter out there that was as old as ours and that we could out turn in air combat.

The reason we deployed to Deci every year was to conduct air combat training against dissimilar types. The US, Germany, Italy, and ourselves paid for the upkeep of an instrumented range over the sea to the west of Deci. Whenever we flew in the ACMI (air combat manoeuvring instrumentation) range, we would carry a pod about the size of a Sidewinder, and that would download our flight and weapons data to three stations on the ground—or, more precisely, on the surface of the Med. This data was then used to reconstruct the flight on a big cinema screen in the debrief cabin. It would show each aircraft flying along in its formation, engaging in combat with 'enemy' aircraft from the other end of the range. The reconstruction could be shown as a large-scale God's eye view that could be zoomed in to individual fights if necessary. There was also a sideways view to show the height profile of the mission, but the coolest thing was that they could select any of the cockpits to get a pilot's eye view. This was especially cool during a guns kill.

Oh, I forgot to mention. When you pulled the trigger for a shot, a missile would fly out from your aircraft, and if it was a successful shot, it would put a coffin around the target and he would be kill removed from the fight. There was almost a party atmosphere as a missile closed on an aircraft with shouts of 'ooooooooh!' and people humming the theme from *Jaws*. I get ahead of myself though.

In the two weeks prior to Deci, we got into the swing of flying clean aeroplanes again with no external fuel tanks. I had forgotten how slick the jet was, and that first take-off had me whooping in delight again. I tried my best during the couple of ACM trips I had, but mostly I was shot to shit by the much more experienced guys on the squadron. Normal service continued with my monthly emergency simulators too.

The Beast and I had settled into a comfortable relationship where I think he saw me as a pet project, and I would readily ask his advice on all sorts of things, but mostly tactics. We would regularly banter each other—me about how old he was and how shit his simulator was, and him about anything he wanted to, really. His knowledge, skill, and reputation were so vast that I was merely a speck of dust on the horizon, so an easy target for him. Then the day came when it was my turn to get the upper hand—an opportunity fell into my lap to finally get one over the Beast.

He wasn't getting any younger, and the twenty or so steps up to the sim cockpits must have been a drag five or six times a day. He trudged up behind us and waited for us to strap in. I had Bouncer in the boot. Once he had removed the safety strut from the canopy, he handed me my headset. We didn't wear helmets in the sim. Instead, we wore ATC-style headphones that had a boom microphone attached to one of the earpieces. The boom could be adjusted by swinging it up and down and a little bit in and out. As I put my headset on, I noticed there was no microphone. Rather than tell him straight away, I let him walk all the way down to the bottom of the steps and then shouted for him to come back up. I can't tell you how much pleasure I got from watching him huff and puff his way up those steps and then ask, 'What is it, young man?' in a breathless voice.

'There's no microphone on this headset, Beast,' I said with total satisfaction in my voice. My moment of euphoria lasted a mere second as the Beast reached up to the top of my headset and pulled the boom down from where the last guy had pushed it. 'Oh shit!' was all I could think.

The Beast gave me a withering look and said, 'This is going to be an interesting sim, young man,' and almost skipped back down the steps with a smile on his face. Bouncer was unsympathetic as he knew we were going to get a hard time as a crew. 'You dickhead, Tug!' was all that came out and to be honest, I deserved a lot more. To be fair, the Beast was great with us. Either he admired my pluck at taking a shot at the title, or he thought that I was so destroyed by it that nothing he could do could make me feel any worse. Anyway, the story got round and I took a bit of banter for it.

Deci

I subsequently went to Deci a lot of times in my career, and it is by far and away my favourite detachment. It was always warm and sunny with mostly clear skies; we were flying clean jets that handled like rockets; we were flying against all sorts of other aeroplanes; but most importantly, Deci was the place where I thought we bonded more closely as a fighter squadron than anywhere else on the planet.

Every trip was doggers, so it induced a bit of friendly competition and a whole lot of support from your buddies in the formation (so long as they weren't arseholes of which no one on 92 Squadron was—not so with the other fighter squadrons). I arrived with a few other guys and all of our ground crew in the back of a Hercules. This was like spending six hours in a washing machine with a heavy metal band, and we would try and alleviate the boredom by reading, sleeping, or playing cards. Cards can be tricky when you can't hear a word people are saying, so over the years, I have become quite adept at playing silent crib and gin rummy.

The jets arrived a couple of hours later and we all assembled in the RAF liaison offices for an in-briefing. Each nation that used Deci had liaison personnel permanently based there to conduct admin and coordination. One of ours was a squadron leader called Bogs. This aircrew liaison post was usually filled by a guy at the end of his career to give him a tour in the sunshine as a pat on the back (not to mention extra cash from overseas allowances) or to a guy whose career was down the toilet and was going no further. Bogs had previously been a Phantom nav, but not a very good one by all accounts. Therefore, he fell into the latter category.

The in-brief was the same each time—don't get drunk; no stupid flypasts; if you go off base, don't forget your Italian base pass, or 'Baysa-Passa' as it was always referred to; and don't, under any circumstances, damage the patio furniture at the accommodation block. On his arrival in post, Bogs had secured funding for some very nice wooden loungers, tables, and chairs for the patio outside the unofficial bar at the block, which was known as the Pig and Tape. The usual sequence of events would be as follows:

Fighter squadron arrives. Fighter squadron gets in-briefed. First night madness in Pig and Tape. Furniture gets burned. Bogs goes mad. Everyone pays £20 to buy new furniture. Fighter squadron leaves. New fighter squadron arrives, etc. *ad infinitum*. I don't think Bogs ever got the idea of getting cheaper plastic furniture, or maybe he did and he was just saving us all from a horrible death inhaling toxic plastic fumes because it would surely have been burnt.

The rooms in the block were functional with a big metal roller Venetian blind on the full-length window. There was no air-conditioning (this is 1990, remember), so I used to sleep on top of the bed with my desk fan on all night to keep cool.

It was stretching it a bit to call the Pig and Tape a bar. It was just the end ground-floor room fitted with patio doors and two enormous chest freezers. One was for the resident fighter squadron, and the other for the resident bomber squadron who would deploy to Deci to practice bombing on the range at Capo Frasca—sad bastards. We were flying like hooligans doing doggers against rapidly dynamic moving targets that were actually trying to shoot us down, and they were hurling 3-kg practice bombs at the ground all day.

The first flying day at Deci, I was programmed for two 2 *v*. 1 trips with the QWIL in the back. Everyone did a couple of looseners in-house like this to get in the swing of things before doing dissimilar air combat training (DACT) against whoever else was there and wanted a fight. As I got out of bed at 5.30 a.m., I went through the preparation of shit, shower, and shave, and just before leaving my room for work, I pulled up my roller blind with a graunch and headed out the door. In the corridor, I was met by a very angry middle-aged man in a dressing gown and slippers. It was one of the flight commanders from the bomber squadron who fixed me with an aggressive stare and said through gritted teeth, 'There is an unwritten rule here that you don't pull your blind up before 0700 because of the noise it makes!'

I was so flummoxed that I heard myself say, 'Where's that written down, Sir?' which seemed to throw him a little and he stropped back into his room. Still being a mere flying officer, I had no idea if I was in the shit or not, so I decided to go and see the Boss and do a bit of *mea culpa*. 'It's okay, Tug. I know who you mean and he is a bit of a stroker so just ignore him.' On reflection, stroker pretty much summed him up. I mean, who the hell takes a dressing gown and slippers on detachment?

These first couple of trips were a hoot, but only lasted about forty minutes each. That included ten minutes each way to the range, bookending twenty minutes of raging around in full burner and pulling up to 6 G. I got back into the habit of fighting while talking to my leader or wingman, depending on which position I was in. We used tactical callsigns to help the ground controllers recognise us during the fight, so each time I took a shot, it would be 'Tug, Fox 2 Tug.' My voice gave away my excitement whenever I got a guns kill. 'Tug! Guns kill! Tug!' leading the QWIL to coolly ask me to calm down a bit, although he seemed to be doing it with a bit of a chuckle.

Recovering to Deci was a bit of an art form. There were two official recovery points—Alpha South to the south end of the airfield was relatively close to Deci and was used if we were on the northern runway (which we predominantly were). If the wind changed and they switched to the southerly runway, we would have to come in through Alpha North, which was a bloody long way away and considering we were always a bit short of gas after ACM, we would often be economical with the truth about our true position on recovery. The radio would sound a little like this:

'Deci approach, this is Razor formation for recovery.'

Approach would answer in an outrageous Italian accent: 'Rrrrayyzor! How many sheeps are you?'

'Razor is a four-ship.'

'Hokayy Rrrrayyzor you report Alpha North.'

'Razor is Alpha North,' we would say with fingers crossed.

'Rrrayyzor contact theee towerrr.'

As I was always told. There are lies, damn lies, and Alpha North. Airspace was a little tight at Deci, and we invariably had a last-minute 90-degree turn onto the run in from initials. There wasn't enough time to go from an easily manoeuvrable tactical formation like arrow to close echelon for the break into the circuit. Therefore, we would be called into echelon prior to the 90-degree turn and manoeuvre like that. If I am in echelon starboard and my leader turns left, I have to climb while on his wing to maintain the turn in formation with him. He can only bank gently, otherwise I don't have the time to stay up on his wing and will lose formation on him. If there are aircraft outside of me in echelon, they would have to climb even higher and have no chance of staying in formation. Cue the flat turn.

We were not specifically taught flat turns on the Hawk but witnessed the technique required a little from line astern formation. Rather than stay up on the leader's wing while he turns, you bank at the same rate and effectively slip in under his fuselage to match his angle of bank. You keep matching his angle of bank and use power to stay scarily close to his dirty oily underside. It means he can use lots of bank and put it on or take it off a bit more rapidly than he could if we were in echelon. When he rolls out, you are miraculously back in echelon. That was all well and good as a two-ship, but my first go at it was as a three-ship and I was the poor sap in the middle. I am not sure if the QWIL's arsehole was spasming, doing 5p/50p, but I am damn sure mine was. It looked awesome though.

It all got a bit bullish in the Pig and Tape that first night with everyone recounting the shots they had taken and bantering each other about the fights to come in the next two weeks. We hit the sack relatively early as we all wanted to be fresh for day two, when we were taking on the US Air Force's finest—the F15 Eagles.

USAF F15 guys were an acquired taste. They were all shaped like upside-down triangles with slim waists, muscly chests, wraparound shades, and wraparound teeth—pleasant enough to your face when briefing, but you got the impression they thought of themselves as higher beings that were gracing us with their presence. They were flying the undoubted 'King of the Hill' and all of their top students through training were posted to the F15. They were extremely disciplined and anal in their approach. Put all of that together and you could see why we just wanted to kick their asses.

The F15 itself is enormous for a single-seat fighter—think of a tennis court and fill it full of metal, and that is an F15—massive engines and highly manoeuvrable with belt-fed missiles. We stood no chance against them, or so you would think. I had not seen one up close before so was just thrilled to be sharing the same piece of airspace with them. QWIL had other ideas though and came up with a plan to screw them over. Normally, a pair of fighters would operate line abreast in battle formation to have both radars and all of the missiles pointing at the enemy as we attacked them. The F15 radar got longer pick-ups than ours, and their Sparrow missiles had longer range and were faster than our Skyflash. When you are out-sticked like that, you have to come up with some sort of pre-merge tactic to confuse your enemy and then get into them like a sneaky bastard.

QWIL had us head in from the north at high level with our wingman about 10 miles behind. Once the fight was on, the radar warning receiver (RWR) lit up like a Christmas tree, so we knew the F15s had us. I turned back through 180 degrees directly towards our Number 2, and as he passed us, I rolled onto our back and went vertically downwards for about 15,000 feet before pulling out and facing up to the F15s. We were now doing about 1.3 Mach and were out of the F15's radar scan. Number 2 turned tail sharpish and ran away bravely at 1.4, and we pitched up into the Eagles where I shot one with a Sidewinder.

'Tug. Fox 2. Tug,' I said calmly and then eased in behind the second one and gunned him. We knocked the fight off and set up for one more. I have no idea what happened on the second fight because I was too busy roaring and swearing about the first. Anyway, it is only the first fight that counts. They shot us to shit on the second one, but who cares? They were already dead. Always win the first fight—it is the only one that matters.

The Most Fun with My Trousers On!

I was unbearable in the Pig and Tape that night, I can tell you, as was everyone else on 92 as we had royally dicked the F15 squadron all round. God I was loving Deci! The next day was the most fun I have had with my trousers on—two trips to introduce me to 1 *v.* 1 *v.* 1 ACT, meaning three aircraft, all fighting as individuals. Everyone was your enemy, so no one was your friend.

We started at three separate points in the range, and at the call of 'fight's on,' we raced to the centre point called the 'bullseye' as we had to get within 5 miles of it before our weapons became live. The ground controller would call our positions from bullseye in rotation and we would have to mentally build a picture of where the other two aircraft were. If anyone was killed, they were given a vector to remove them from the fight, and thirty seconds later, they were regenerated and could join the fight again. All sorts of tactics and shenanigans came into play, with some crews hanging out at the edge of the range to let the other two fight it out, then rage into the bullseye and sneak into the fight when the others weren't looking.

I admit I once followed a kill-removed aircraft at a discrete distance so that as soon as he was regenerated, he turned around to get a face full of my missile. This happened a fair bit to be honest, and we regularly heard calls from the ground controller of 'Jack, you are live… Jack, you are dead, bug out north.' It happened to me plenty of times as well. The strange thing was that 1 *v.* 1 *v.* 1 was never going to be a scenario for real, but it helped us to develop our mental processing to build air picture and was also brilliant for in-cockpit coordination of who saw what and whether to prosecute an attack or break defensively. I bloody loved it, and the sortie in the afternoon was even better.

QWIL and I led the second sortie and he briefed it up. We were going to do a full sortie of just visual fights using a Mercedes split to set them up. I would lead us all to the bullseye and call 'Outwards turn, go!' I would fly straight ahead, and the other two would turn out through 120 degrees to form the spokes of the Mercedes badge. We had to hold our headings but could change altitude.

If I was leading, it was my prerogative which way to orientate the formation. I may head straight into sun so that at the outwards turn, I could climb up into it making it tricky for the others to see me when we turned in, or if it was hazy over the sea, I might hit the deck and wallow around in the murk for a while. After we had separated for a few miles, I would call, 'Inwards turn for combat, go!' and the fight would be on.

An added factor to this mission was that the QWIL made us draw secret weapons loads from a hat, so you only knew what weapons you had (it may be one Skyflash and one Sidewinder per fight or even guns only). Your loadout would determine your tactics. If I was the leader and had a Skyflash, I would always cheat and turn in way before calling the inwards turn, just to have the best chance of using that longer-range shot. If I was gun only, I would not bother turning in and just hit the deck, letting the other two fight it out and then try and pitch up into their bellies where they couldn't see us. I wished these trips could last forever. Everyone was beaming after 1 *v*. 1 *v*. 1, even if you had got your tail shot off time and again.

I moved onto bigger missions including two of us *v*. two F15s sweeping for three German F4Fs acting as bombers. We had to sidestep the F15s to get to the bombers. I had never seen so many pieces of metal raging around the sky at the same time. It was like a scene from the Battle of Britain. The most bizarre trip though was when I briefed up a flight between two of us and three Italian Starfighters. The F104 had stubby little wings, which meant it was shit at turning, but by God it could motor. Their tactics consisted of going very fast (and I mean very) into the merge, and then keep going, unless they could get an easy shot. We got tally on two of them at 27 miles.

The usual would have been ten on a good day, but their engines were so smoky it was easy. The leader was the only one that had selected afterburner to clean up his smoke and must have hit the merge at about 1.8. We took some head-on shots—the Sidewinder seeker was going mental with the heat from his afterburner. Normally, a fighter would cancel their afterburner at about 10 miles to cool the jet pipes and deny these kinds of shots, but he didn't care. He was obviously on a mission to go as fast as he could and dare us to turn in behind him and try to catch him. We ignored him as he blew through and we shot the rear two. The leader went straight back to Deci on a fuel priority, recovery after only fifteen minutes airborne. As we had to try and match them for speed (getting about 1.4), we only managed a thirty-minute trip ourselves.

Shut Up, Bobby, or I'm Going to Punch You!

The local restaurants made a fortune out of us, and it was almost the law that we had to visit specific ones each time we went to Deci, such as the Lorelei. These evenings out always went the same way—a couple of sharpeners in the Pig and Tape; thirty men then jumping into minibuses to the chosen venue; lots of wine while spending an aeon ordering the food; eat drink and get merrier; throw some lira to whoever was sober enough to pay the bill; with a huge tip as, no doubt, we had been too loud; then the owner would bring out his vast collection of digestifs and sit with us a while.

Whereas Cyprus had its Kokinelli, Deci was known for a whole range of paint-stripping yammers—Fernet-Branca, Pétrus, and Grappa. Some of the bottles looked like he had filled them himself, while other had bits of twig and the scrapings of the garage floor in them. Back to Deci afterwards for a coffee and a flaming sambuca in the Italian officers' club would see the night off—unless it was the weekend, in which case we would burn Bogs' furniture and drink until dawn.

This particular weekend was something special. Just as Ginge had decided to marry his long-term girlfriend, so did his best mate, the Kid. They had spent a long time together at Leuchars before coming to 92 and were joined at the hip. It was time for another stag night, and this time, it was going to be Rome. We were most of the way there in Sardinia, so it was a quick hop over on a scheduled flight into Rome and a bus into town. There were about twenty of us that hauled up to an outside terrace café in a beautiful piazza somewhere in the centre of the city for a mid-morning beer, which turned into a four-hour food and drink extravaganza.

Mindful of my early bath in Berlin, I was pacing myself this time, as I was a bit of a classics geek and really wanted to see a bit of the Eternal City. A couple of the duty adults thought it best if we take a bit of a breather and go and find the hotel before hitting the town in the evening. We piled into a few taxis, and someone in ours made the mistake of saying to our driver, 'There's an extra twenty in it for you if you beat the others to the hotel,' not thinking for one second the driver would understand. I can now confirm that the fastest car in the world is a Fiat 128 taxi. At least I had sobered up by the time we got to the hotel, having sweated all of the beer out through my skin.

The hotel we were in was characterful. By that I mean I am sure it was rented by the hour. Bobby drew the short straw and ended up sharing a room with me. The room needed refurbishing to bring it up to the standard of basic, but we were the only ones to have a shower *en suite*. Shower is a fancy term for a water pipe over a hole in the floor and a manky plastic curtain. There was a nice balcony, though, looking out onto a classic Roman tenement street scene.

The evening's entertainment passed without incident apart from the Kid parking his pizza on the pavement, but I was chuffed I made it through to the end of the night like everyone else. The next day, I was looking forward to a bit of sightseeing before the evening flight back to Cagliari. Sunday began badly though. As I woke slowly, I was dimly aware of the sound of running water and as my sight came into focus, I saw a picture I have never been able to cauterise from my mind. In the corner of our room stood a big, naked, hairy-arsed man covered in soap suds. 'What the f…?!' I shouted, waking up Bobby.

The man in the shower turned around, not improving the view at all, and we finally recognised Stan W. 'Hope you don't mind lads, but you have the only room with a shower.'

'For the love of God, pull the curtain round!' I wailed. The next half hour saw a procession of semi-naked hungover pilots and navs trudge into our room for a soaking.

Rome was spectacular, and in only one day, we managed to see the Trevi Fountain, the Spanish Steps, and the Forum, as well as tours of the Colosseum and Vatican City. We even managed to fit in an altercation with a couple of guys who tried to steal my wallet (until Lurch punched one out), so covered all of the touristy ticks. Everyone was a little subdued on the bus back to the airport, everyone except Bobby. I absolutely love Bobby, but he is a bit full on and has no concept of either personal space or when to keep quiet. While everyone else settled down for a rest, Bobby was in full transmit mode, sitting next to me. I was desperate for a quick kip, but he just kept talking to me. Then he told a shit joke that I didn't respond to, and that kicked off a sequence we still talk about today.

'You didn't laugh at my joke, Tug.'

'No, Bob.'

'Why not?'

'I'm just a bit tired.'

'You want me to shut up then?'

'Please.'

'Ok, I'll shut up then. I mean I don't have to speak if you don't want me to? I can just sit here and look out of the window. You get some sleep if you need to. I'll leave you in peace. Everyone else seems to be sleeping anyway so no problem. I just thought that …'

'Shut up, Bobby, or I am going to punch you!' That did the trick. Looking back, I feel awful about saying it, but it was either that or kill him. Being as thick-skinned as he was, it was forgotten the next day, and the two of us flew a lot together in the second week and had an absolute hoot. He had a real knack of winding up the F15 guys in briefings and debriefings, which all added to the fighter crew bonding process.

At the end of another hard week, our engineers fitted the Fletchers back onto the jets and we transited back to Wildenrath as four-ships. In only eight days, I had flown sixteen trips and lost count of the number of times I had pulled the trigger (and pulled all manner of missiles out of my tail). I had turned myself inside-out pulling G and become even firmer friends with my squadron mates having shared flights, fights, and outrageous nights in the Pig and Tape being a proper fighter pilot. My love affair with my aeroplane became deeper and deeper. Without the bulky fuel tanks on board, it was as naked as the day it rolled off the production line and danced its mesmerising dance around the skies of the beautiful blue Med. Like I said, I bloody love Deci!

Barry Smallcock

A bit of bother had been brewing while we were away in Deci between the 19 Squadron guys who lived in the mess and OC Catering Flight (a position known universally around the RAF as OC Chips). Mess rules had been 'adjusted' such that you could not use the dining room if you were in a flying suit. That was all well and good, and we were all used to changing into jacket and tie for dinner, but it meant we would have to eat breakfast in civvies or blues and then change into flying suit to go to the squadron, which was ludicrous when you consider that the Blunties (anyone who wasn't aircrew) could eat in their blues and then just go to work as normal.

The main issue was that crews coming off Battle Flight didn't have time to change before breakfast service finished. OC Chips had got the backing of the PMC (president of the mess committee), who was OC Ops at the time. OC Ops was a nav but hadn't sat Battle Flight in years and was a bit out of it in our eyes. The argument was based around whether flying suits were standard working dress or not. It all came to a head when some of us were reported to OC Chips by some Blunty snitch, and this resulted in a pow-wow headed by the PMC.

It was supposed to be a discussion where we could make our case, but turned into an all-round patronising bollocking. It was mooted that we might choose to live out of the mess in local rented accommodation, and OC Chips snorted as the PMC said, 'I very much doubt that!' Within a month, about twelve of us from both squadrons had moved into various towns and villages. The bar takings in the mess crashed, and it turned into a bit of a ghost town during the week with Friday happy hour being the only time it was buzzing, but not as often.

I moved into a house with Plop and Fatty in Heinsberg. At the same time, I changed the big black Datsun for a stunning metallic green Porsche 924. I needed something more reliable now that I was driving to work every day, but true to form, this was not it. It was a bastard to start, and a few weeks later, I discovered it wasn't that good at stopping either. Each day on arriving at the main gate to Wildenrath, my ID was checked and then my car was checked for bombs. We travelled into work and back in civilian clothes because of the IRA threat. I had to stop the car, turn the engine off, and then open the bonnet and boot so the guards could give it a thorough investigation.

One morning, the guard asked me to stop the engine after I had opened the bonnet. I had the ignition key in my hand, but the engine was still running. He gave me a withering look that said, 'You really should be driving something better than this, Sir.' The only way I could stop the car was to stall it, but that left all the electrics live. It was almost impossible to find a garage that would take it on. The local guy wouldn't touch a Porsche 924 as they were too much trouble, and the Porsche dealer didn't want to as 'it wasn't a proper Porsche'.

It took two weeks to find a VW mechanic that took pity on me and patched it up. So, for two weeks, wherever I went, I had to stall it on and then unhook the battery to stop it from going flat. Amazing that my thirty-five-year-old aeroplane was in better shape than my five-year-old car. Living out was okay, but not a patch on being in the mess, but it was the principle of the thing. Dining-in nights and happy hours would see us all booking rooms in the mess for the night, and it was a bit like old times again.

One particular dining-in sticks in the memory. It was a stag night so no spouses and was just after we had voted with our feet. The PMC was a bit chippy with all the junior officers that had dared to move out, so throughout the dinner, he was throwing bollockings about which made the environment a bit more inflammatory. To cap it all, the guest of honour was not a well-liked man. He was a previous Phantom pilot called Barry Hallcock and was serving up at HQ as wing commander air defence. He had demanded to be dined out from the only RAF fighter base in Germany.

The PMC got up to introduce him and started to tell the story of how he got his nickname which was Mozzy. Apparently, years before when he had been a squadron leader, he used to answer the phone so quickly the 'squadron leader' bit sounded like the buzz of a mosquito, and he became known as 'Mozzy' Hallcock. We all knew this story, but the PMC was revelling in telling it. There was a lot of low-level grumbling as everyone hated Mozzy, but when it came to the big reveal, the PMC said, 'And that's why to this day he is known as …' At this point, Lordy, one of the navs from 19 shouted, 'Barry Smallcock!'

The place erupted in howls and cheers and the PMC, who knew he had lost control, threw Lordy out and sat down fuming. Mozzy then proceeded to give a forty-five-minute state-of-the-nation speech that had us begging for an early death. He was offensively boring. Yes, there were a lot of things going on in the world—half rumours and facts about the future demise of the Phantom—but when all is said and done, all we wanted to do at a dining-in night was get shitfaced and hear a funny speech or two. No such luck on the latter that night, I can tell you.

Bang! Whoosh!

Pretending to shoot missiles every day at Deci set me up quite nicely for the following month when I did it for real. This is one of the biggest and most important moments for a fighter pilot, and I was excited and bricking it in equal measure. No. 92's last MPC had ended early and in some ignominy following Harry's 'crash' and Iron's ejection. I guess we probably had some missiles left over that needed firing before they went out of date, so in early August, we deployed back to Valley to see them off.

I am not sure if they had sent the station commander away on leave, but there were no angry mobs with pitchforks as we arrived so we settled into the classic MPC lifestyle again of lounging around and waiting. It was a bit like being on Battle Flight waiting for the hooter, but more relaxed. The weather cleared pretty sharpish, and we launched with us as photo-chase. It seemed almost unreal as I watched a Sparrow III serenely detach from the underside of the shooter's jet, drop a few feet, then rage off into the distance at high speed with flames coming out of its tail. The acceleration was breath-taking and I could barely believe what I was watching—what a privilege to see something like that.

That afternoon was supposed to be even better for Iron and me as we were primary shooter. The weather was hot and hazy, and the Jindy was coming out of the sun. That would have been fine, but we were doing a boresight shot, which meant I had to see the Jindy and keep it in the gunsight. The Jindivik is tiny and a bastard to get eyes on, even when it is putting out flares. We started the run and Iron got it straight away on radar. He locked it up and conducted the intercept calling range and bearing to me all the way down. As soon as I got tally, he would break the lock and select boresight on the radar. I then had to visually track the Jindy and keep it in the boresight to keep the radar energy on it so the Sparrow can track—great plan but I'd be buggered if I could see it.

The range got down to about 8 miles, and if I didn't see it soon, our closing velocity would mean there wouldn't be enough time to get the missile off. No joy. I finally saw the target as it passed off the left wing. The whole exercise was knocked off and I led us all back to Valley.

I can't tell you how deflated I was on the way back. Iron was trying to cheer me up, but I knew I was in for some 'Blind Pugh' banter. Bantering a fighter pilot about his eyesight is like challenging the size of his manhood. Luckily, neither the secondary shooter or the photo-chase had seen the Jindy at all so I felt a little better. The weather the following day was forecast to be dogshit, so the Boss led the drinking and singing in the bar, which helped me drown my sorrows a bit. When something goes awry in flying, you can only put it right on the next trip. With us not flying the next day, my salvation was going to be a long time coming. I might as well get drunk then, and I did.

Horror of horrors—the weather was gin-clear as we ate breakfast the next day, and Iron and I were slotted in as primary shooter again with the same boresight profile. There are so many things that can go wrong and stop you from taking the shot—unserviceable aircraft on start-up; missiles not tuning to the radar frequency; poor weather; traffic in the range; Jindivik broken; or radar failure airborne. Not one of them happened, and so, a weary and hungover crew got radar contact and then visual on the target in time for the pilot to call, 'Firing. Firing. Now!' over the radio and pulling the trigger.

Time slowed down. I heard and felt a loud bang as the Sparrow was ejected from the aircraft, followed by a long whoosh! I just glued my eyes on the Jindy and came left harder and harder to visually track it in the boresight. We were pulling a good 4–5 G as it whizzed down our left-hand side and I knocked it off and pulled up. Our Sparrow had a telemetry pack in it rather than a warhead, so I wasn't expecting to see an explosion. I was expecting to see something though, like a missile going past the target at high speed. It was then that the photo-chase called, 'Yeah, it tracked for about a second then nosedived into the sea.' Bollocks!

The disappointment of that news was far outweighed by the whole experience though. Once again, the Phantom had given me something I had only dreamed of as a kid, and yet, it was just another part of my life now. We flew back to Wildenrath that afternoon and carried on as if nothing special had happened. The shear-wafer connection between the aircraft and the missile had pride of place in my bedroom though.

My Hat and the Queen

I have always loved history; I just love real life stories. As such, whenever I joined a squadron, I always made a point of reading the squadron history and finding out about those who have worn my colours previously. No. 92 Squadron had a rich story since forming in 1917 at Colney Heath. It was the highest-scoring squadron of the Second World War, and in the 1960s, it was the Fighter Command official aerobatic team flying sixteen blue-painted Hunters called the 'Blue Diamonds'. We had some famous names from the Battle of Britain, including Brian Kingcombe, Bob Stanford-Tuck, and Geoff Wellum.

The thing about history though, is that all of us add to it every day, so everyone who had worn the red and yellow was a famous name in my eyes. No. 92 Squadron had a lot of battle honours, and these were displayed on the squadron standard. I got to see the standard regularly as pretty much as soon as I arrived on the squadron, I was 'volunteered' to be the squadron standard bearer. A squadron standard consists of a black pole topped with a beautiful silver eagle. Attached to the pole is a large heavy silk flag, light blue in colour, which is inlaid with lots of gold thread, depicting the squadron crest and motto, as well as those battle honours. As the standard bearer, it was my job to ensure the standard was on display at every dining-in night, and also to show it off at formal parades. I thought it was a real honour, but had no idea how much of my time it was going to take up.

In just two years on 92, I paraded two or three times for the usual formal visits, but then got sideswiped by two other huge events. The first was the squadron being awarded a brand-new standard (the old one was fifty years old so we were entitled to a new one). There was a big parade at Wildenrath in front of the commander-in-chief of RAF Germany, including a fancy lunch and a Diamond 9 flypast.

However, this was nothing compared to September 1990 and the fiftieth anniversary of the Battle of Britain. This was the big one—the largest flypast over London since the end of the Second World War and a huge parade in front of Buckingham Palace and Her Majesty, the Queen. Each Battle of Britain squadron still active got to parade its standard, supported by a full flight of airmen and airwomen. Obviously, with an event this size, it wasn't going to be a case of rocking up and marching about in front of Buckingham Palace. No, there was lots of practicing of rocking up and marching about to be done first.

I and my 19 Squadron colleague packed up our standards and best uniforms and decamped to RAF Uxbridge for the week before the parade. Uxbridge was the home of the Queen's Colour Squadron of the RAF regiment. These were the smartest soldiers in the UK military and were world-renowned for their discipline and prowess at drill. Their main job was ceremonial and included guarding royal palaces and parading the colour for the Royal Air Force. All of us standard bearers were sent there to sharpen up our drill and smartness. At the same time, Edge was sent to RAF Halton to drill with all the troops as he would be leading our flight.

We began with a dress uniform inspection. I thought mine looked pretty good, but the squadron leader on the Colour Squadron thought otherwise. My shoes needed a good bit more bulling, but he was absolutely horrified by the state of my hat. It was immediately banned from the parade, leaving me only one option—get into London at some point and buy a new one. Our programme didn't have any slack in it, so the squadron leader Joe'd one of his flight lieutenants to lend me one for the big day. I could tell he wasn't happy, and having had a good look at my own titfer, I couldn't blame him if he thought I was going to ruin his.

Next up was lots of practice of unfurling, carrying, and marching with the standard. I was escorted by our squadron's warrant officer, a couple of the ground crew NCOs, and one of the ground crew airmen during all of this. We got used to being shouted at again as we marched around the Uxbridge parade square. It was all a bit like being back in officer training. Just when we thought we were getting it sorted, the Colour Squadron guys would come out and practice and we got a reminder of how shit we were!

The final bit of our first two days was practicing the royal salute. When this was called, we would remove the standard from our sling, hold it out to the right, and let it out horizontally. Then we would drag it along the ground in front of us—£80,000 of standard dragged on the floor. Having got our personal drill down as standard parties, we then travelled to Halton for a day to practice with the full parade. This was especially poignant for me as I was parading on the same ground as my dad had marched on forty years previously when he had joined the RAF as an apprentice armourer.

The final two days saw us rising at about 2.30 a.m. to be bussed into Central London for our final practices *in situ*. The whole shebang, including the RAF massed bands, formed up (in the dark I might add) on Horse Guard's Parade, and then we marched down the Mall to Buckingham Palace. Once the parade was done, we marched back to dismiss. The formality of it was amazing. There is a set procedure for unfurling the standard, and also for securing it back in its leather sheath afterwards. The parade forms in a certain way, then has to march in time and manoeuvre correctly. It's no wonder we needed all that practice.

The event on the day went very smoothly, and as we stood in front of the queen, with tens of thousands of spectators watching us, I was absolutely beaming, right up until the Diamond 16 of Phantoms flew overhead and I instantly wished I was in one of the cockpits. The standard bearers got their reward later as we displayed the standards in the law courts at a reception hosted by Princess Margaret and had VIP seating on the banks of the Thames to watch an amazing firework display. It was a bit odd walking across the street in our mess dress, but what a night! Just for the record, I smuggled my own hat onto the bus on the day and swapped it out with the pristine parade standard one I had been lent. I very much doubt the queen saw how tattered it looked anyway, but it made me feel so much better wearing it. I loved that hat.

Movers—or Not!

Around the time that I had been shooting my live missile, Saddam Hussein had invaded Kuwait and set in motion the events that that would culminate in the First Gulf War. Almost immediately, the United States formed a coalition of forces and deployed aircraft into the region. Saudi Arabia requested defensive air support and the RAF sent some Tornado F3s into Dhahran. The UK had just sold the F3 to the Royal Saudi Air Force, so it was politically sound to send an RAF F3 Squadron into theatre. I don't know if it is completely true, but I believe there was a bit of hand-wringing at high levels as the Phantom was more capable at that time (the F3 had lots of performance issues in hot climates).

Anyway, the upshot was that six Phantoms from Wildenrath were deployed to provide QRA duties out of Akrotiri, to defend the Forward Air Head supply route into Saudi. Ten crews went out on the first wave, and the station chose the ten most experienced crews split between the two squadrons. I don't know if they expected the whole thing to kick off straight away, and that's why the most experienced guys went out, but nothing could have been further from the truth. I had 300 hours on type by then so wasn't going to make either the first or second cut, so I turned my attention to a deployment I was next in the slot for—the Falkland Islands.

I remembered watching the Falklands conflict on TV in 1982. I was in the sixth form at school, and only eight years later, here I was, packing my kit for my six weeks as one of the QRA crews down there. After the war was over, the RAF based 23 Squadron down in Port Stanley. The runway had been bombed by the Vulcans, and a temporary runway had been installed with cables, much like an aircraft carrier. Over the years, the commitment had reduced to just four aircraft and five crews; they had also moved to a purpose-built aerodrome called Mount Pleasant Airfield (MPA). The crews were provided by each fighter squadron still in service with the Phantom—92, 19, 74, 56, and the OCU.

The squadron was now only a flight designated 1435 Flt, which was a famous number having been instrumental in the defence of Malta during the Second World War. In those desperate days, the flight had three Gloster Gladiators named *Faith*, *Hope*, and *Charity*. Our Phantoms were given those names, and the fourth jet was called *Desperation*—an apt name given the look on the faces of our ground crew who served for four to six months down south, rather than only six weeks like us.

The flight was run by a squadron leader on a four-month rotation, shared by all the squadrons. I was crewed with Bouncer for the duration of the det, and he had just been made an authoriser. The incumbent Boss was a nav from the OCU called Nemo. Apparently, he was a great guy with a good reputation. All good then? Not quite, but more of that later.

It is a bit of an expedition getting to the Falklands. Essentially, you fly forever to the far end of the earth, and then go for another few hours and there it is. The only way there for us was by Tristar out of Brize Norton, so Bouncer and I lugged our flying kit and a bag full of civvies over to 60 Squadron, and those boys helpfully ferried us over to Brize in an Andover, saving us a monster drive through Germany and France and the south of the UK. The Falklands experience then began in earnest with a depressing night in the Gateway 'Hotel' at Brize—shitty room, shitty food, shitty everything.

The next morning, we were in the hands of the movers—never have a group of people been so badly named. The empire they had built was designed to make your last day in the UK for six weeks or four months as miserable as possible and show you that you were nothing but a speck of shit on the bottom of the RAF's collective shoe. After checking our bags in and going through what passed for security in those days, we joined all the other passengers in a large waiting hall. In itself, this was okay, but being the RAF, we had to go through at least one more level of faffing about. Passengers were called in alphabetical order to have passports and boarding cards checked once again before boarding. The movers would call one letter at a time and would make sure all of the 'A's had passed through before starting the 'B's. Woe betide anyone who stood up too soon.

I bade Bouncer farewell as he was in the top half of the alphabet. After what seemed like an age later, there were three of us left in the hall— myself, a young girl called Young (coincidentally), and a guy who must have been called Zebadee or Zorba because he was made to wait until Ms Young had gone through the check. On getting through this check, I found myself in an almost identical hall with everyone else again. Finally, we boarded the Tristar, in alphabetical order again, and lumbered off on an eight-hour trek to Ascension Island.

As officers, we were up in the 'business class' end, which was nothing more than a wider seat, but as there was no entertainment on board other than the paperbacks I had brought with me, I wandered down the back of the Tristar (which was half empty) and found four clear seats. By lifting up the armrests, I was able to lie flat and get some sleep. We arrived in Ascension about midnight and trudged off the aircraft into an enclosure that had a small café/bar. We weren't allowed outside the fence (something to do with customs and immigration) so threw a couple of beers down and got back on the big, white bird for another eight hours to the Falklands.

It's About Bloody Time You Got Here!

Hours later, our first clue that we were close was an announcement from the captain that we were about to be intercepted by two Phantoms. Shortly afterwards, a fully armed Phantom turned up on the left wing mirrored by another on the right. The next day, I would probably be escorting the Tristar out of MPA. I looked in absolute wonder at the jets. I had seen the Phantom this close up plenty of times, but I was usually working my ass off flying in formation. Here though, I could just stare out of the window and take it all in. Dear God, it looked awesome—mean bearing, bristling with weapons, and two aircrew who looked incredibly cool in their dark-visored flying helmets. I could see the Falkland Island's crest painted just aft of the radome and the large letter designator on the tail.

Today, it was *Hope* and *Desperation* escorting us. The jets then went belly up to the Tristar to show off all the weapons as lots of passengers clicked away with their cameras. Then there were plenty of 'oohs' and 'aahs' as both of them popped a couple of flares before lighting the burners and spearing off in front of us. The roar from the burners was huge even from inside the Tristar, and I couldn't help but smile to myself. The captain announced that there was a message from the lead Phantom that read, 'To Tug and Bouncer. It's about bloody time you got here!' It was obviously from the incumbent 92 crew, who we were replacing, and would be heading home the next day.

Arrival at MPA began with a briefing (of course it did; this is the military after all) in the arrivals building. A RAF policeman proceeded to scare the shit out of everyone by telling us all about the many things that could kill us in the Falklands if we weren't careful, chief among them being the landmines. The Argentinians had mined everywhere it seemed, and they were a very real threat to our safety. The minefields were carefully wired off and marked with handy signs with skull and crossbones on them. That was the only bit of the brief anyone took notice of. After two eight-hour flights, all we wanted to do was find our rooms and kip. The 56 Squadron crew met us once we had escaped the briefing and took us to our rooms in the accommodation block.

The block was massive, and I mean massive—so big it was called the 'Death Star'. Running through the middle from one end to the other was a wide concrete-floored corridor called 'Coronation Street'. End to end, it was rumoured to be 1 mile long, and all the accommodation areas, gym, sports hall, messes, and shops came off it to both sides. All of the aircrew were on one corridor near the officers' mess. We each had a standard prefab-style bedroom with communal shower and toilet block, but the end two rooms on one side had been knocked together to make a bar. This was the famous 'Goose' I had heard so much about—the scene of many late-night drunken adventures.

The Goose was a private 1435 Flt bar that was definitely licensed, or unlicensed, depending on who was in charge of MPA at the time, and also if they had actually ever been invited to the Goose. In its long history, the Goose had been closed down a number of times, usually by some bell end of a Blunty and on one occasion, by some bitter old gimmer who had previously been chopped from a fighter OCU. For now though, it was open for business. It was full of old sofas; a small kitchen area (which was where all the beer fridges were); and was packed with bits of shot down Argentinian Pucaras and Skyhawks. I remember a low walled corner section covered by the outboard part of a Phantom wing that had crashed some years before.

Orange Llamas? My Arse!

Once we had dumped our bags, we changed into flying suits and got a lift to the HAS site for some more specific in-briefs. We met the Boss and the other crews. Nemo was a bit offish with us and muttered something about Germany crews that I didn't quite catch. He then went on to pre-bollock us about fatigue usage on the aircraft. He was tracking the amount of fatigue that each crew used up, and then plotting a 'Wall of Shame'. I could imagine this would be a big deal if the F4 was going to stay in service a lot longer, but we all knew its days were numbered. Nemo had a bug up his arse about it, and it looked like the crew we were replacing had extended their line all along the Wall of Shame and out into the corridor.

So, Bouncer and I were now the 92 crew. We knew the 19 Squadron crew, and they were good young guys like us. The 74 crew were older and much more experienced, but very cool with it. Will Phillips was the OCU pilot flying with Nemo and seemed pretty happy. The 56 crew were a couple of knobbers—not a bad average though for five crews, I guess. The HAS site had lots of shelters should the island's air capability need reinforcing, with the four closest to the Q shed being the ones that housed the jets. Nemo had an office up in the newer briefing and office facility across the taxiway where the engineers were mostly housed.

The main activity though took place in and around the Q shed. The shed itself was nestled between the Q1 and Q2 shelters down in a dip at the end of a very steep 50-m ramp. There was a crew room and a couple of bedrooms for the aircrew, and that was mirrored for the ground crew. A big communal kitchen, showers and toilets, and an ops room set up completed the facilities. Q sheds are the same the world over—functional, but a bit grubby and smelling of sweat (after flying) and dirty rubbery smells from the immersion suits.

Readiness was ten minutes, which seemed a little pedestrian coming off five minutes on Battle Flight, but we would need an extra twenty–thirty seconds to do up our immersion suits and then twenty more to run to the jet. The life jackets and helmets were hanging up in the corridor and the more mellow of crews would even take their 'goon bag' off altogether and hang them up, and just walk around in long johns, bunny suit, and internal G suit—not very fetching, and something I was never relaxed enough to do. I spent all my time on Q in the Falklands wearing my goon bag, albeit shrugged off to my waist and then held there by tying the sleeves in a knot. I seem to remember that readiness went down to fifteen minutes overnight so I would take it off and then fit a rubber bung in the hole for the anti-G hose, so I could bin my G-pants completely. The thinking was that we would be pulling minimal G at night so wouldn't need them.

If Q2 was launched, it was a case of zipping up the immersion suit and putting on the life jacket while sprinting up the steep ramp (which believe me was like the north face of the Eiger in full kit) to get to the Q2 shelter. However, if it was Q1, you would bolt out of the Q shed, turn sharp left, and run uphill for about 80–100 m through 'the Tube'. This was a black corrugated tube that went through the ground up to the Q1 shelter. We ran further than Q2, but this shelter was the closest to the runway, giving us a quicker launch time. I still have nightmares about that bloody tube—its dark maw swallowing me whole while blasting 40 knots of wind in my face as I struggle uphill in all my kit, but I'm getting ahead of myself.

The flight ran a well-proven ten-day schedule during which each crew did two days of Q1, Q2, fly crew, duty crew, and stand down. It was only the days off that were consecutive, giving us a chance to get away from MPA to visit Stanley, one of the radar sites, stay with some of the locals, or just stay in the Death Star and get shitfaced and sleep it off. Q1 and Q2 flew once each day with the fly crew flying twice, making two pairs per day. Our first full day, we were fly crew so should have got two trips, but one of the jets was down in the afternoon so I got just the one familiarisation trip in the morning, and what a trip.

Will Phillips briefed it all up and was flying with the 19 Squadron nav as Nemo had meetings up at HQ that day. It was going to be a standard famil where we would get airborne and conduct a fiery cross (explained later) and then a full Navex of the islands with Will and Bouncer showing me all the main landmarks. The Navex would include a measles (explained later also) at the radar site on Mount Alice. We would then tank from the resident C130, do a couple of intercepts against each other, then finish with some circuit practice back at MPA.

During the brief, Will dropped in that we would go across to Beaver Island at the south-west tip of West Falkland and try to find the orange llamas. Now I knew a spoof when I heard one, and I snorted a bit before saying, 'orange llamas? My arse!' Will looked up smiling and asked if I had heard of the orange llamas. 'Come off it, Will, I'm not a student anymore.' All three of them started in on me trying to convince me, but you have to be up a lot earlier in the morning to catch me out.

Crewing in was a new experience. The shelters were light and airy, unlike the drab low-slung Germany HASs. The jet was fully armed so there were extra checks to go through before we were ready to taxi out behind Will to the runway. I lined up alongside him, and he gave the wind-up signal. Once the engines were stabilised at 80 per cent and we were holding on the brakes, I gave a thumbs up and Will tapped the front of his helmet and released the brakes as he nodded his head forwards. I let my brakes off and pushed to full mil to keep formation as we rolled. Another head nod and we were rocked outboard into burner. I barely registered the kick in my arse concentrating too much on my references, and before long, we gracefully lifted into the clear Falklands air. Once the gear and flaps were up, Will cleared me off to my own pre-determined point to set up for the fiery cross.

MPA was defended by RAF Regiment Rapier missile batteries. We were able to give them some realistic training by attacking the airfield from a number of pre-planned directions. These were known as 'fiery cross', and Will had planned for two separate directions at the same time. The rules were not below 250 feet and not above 500 knots. Yeah right! Bouncer had pre-briefed me that everyone blew the crap out of the airfield during a fiery cross and actually, that would be much better training for the Rapier crews.

I came in from the north behind Mount Kent to dick the airfield, while Will went south to attack the harbour area. We could hear the Rapiers lock us on the RWR as we blasted over the Q shed, shaking up Q1. We joined up to the east of MPA and had a good look at Port Stanley before joining the circuit for a practice approach. We weren't allowed to touch down at Stanley but made a low approach to see what it would look like if we had to divert there in the future (the plan would be to put a cable into Stanley, much as they had done after 1982).

There then followed the most amazing Navex I have ever done. Lots of famous names flashed by underneath us—Tumbledown, Goose Green, San Carlos Water, Falkland Sound, and A4 Alley. I was dimly aware that we were punting around about 100–150 feet. This was the lowest I had flown in my life, but it seemed normal. It was institutionalised that everybody broke the low-flying rules in the Falklands, including the C130.

Next, I knew, we were approaching Alice and calling for a 'measles'. Each of the radar sites (Alice, Byron, and Kent) were made up of ISO container blocks that sufficed as accommodation and messing and all the radar kit. They all sat atop prominent pieces of high ground to provide early warning of approaching enemy aircraft. The radar aerials and such were supported by lots of high-tension guy cables. As you approached for a flypast and got low enough, the guy cables interlinked and formed 'dots' that looked like measles. I didn't see them as I was too gobsmacked at how low Will was dusting off everyone stood outside on the hill top. We blasted Alice a couple of times and then went in search of the tanker—phew! This trip was full on and non-stop (like every trip in the Falklands as I was about to find out). This would be my first time tanking from a C130, and my first time tanking at low level.

We intercepted the Herc and dropped in behind. The weather was gin-clear, and he trailed his wing hoses and settled at about 2,000 feet. Will went behind the left, leaving me the right. The basket looked huge and was rock solid in the airflow, and Bouncer talked me in first go—awesome! The C130 was immediately my favourite tanker. As we guzzled down the gas, the Herc guys came easy left and we all gracefully came back north over Falkland Sound. Had I not been overstressing my oxygen flow indicator, I might even have said I was cool and relaxed. I mean, look at us—plugged in at low level, turning left, and holding a beautiful looking formation. It was almost like I knew what I was doing in the jet.

Gone (mostly) were the days of worrying about being chopped and having it all taken away from me. I was just living my dream. Although we had both filled to full, we spewed all of that fuel out in a twenty-minute thrash doing intercepts and going supersonic. A quick circuit got us on deck and straight into the shed as Q2 that night—back into the old routine of lounging on the sofa in full kit, eating crappy food, and watching crappy videos. It was a real athlete's lifestyle again. Oh, and by the way, we didn't see any orange llamas, so I felt vindicated at calling everyone a bullshitter and seeing through their spoof. The TV was turned off at about 8 p.m., and the radio tuned to BFBS to listen to 'darts on the radio' from Port Stanley, I shit you not!

Ok, Tug, Down You Go

One of the jets always seemed to be unserviceable the first two weeks we were there, so the flying came in fits and starts for Bouncer and I. This meant lots of downtime, so lots of sport, lots more bar, and the chance for some outings. First chance we got, Bouncer commandeered a Land Rover and showed me the sights of Port Stanley. The drive there was a one-hour slidey shingle adventure, and we were viciously buzzed a couple of times by the 19 Squadron boys who were fly crew that day.

By the way, it looked ace. The numerous skull and crossbones signs reminded us of the dangers of the minefields, and it was sobering to think that just eight years before, we would have been driving through a war zone.

Our very next flight saw us airborne as a singleton running intercepts against, and also tanking from, the Herc. It was nice to have a free and easy trip where we could do what we wanted and go anywhere we chose. Bouncer showed me around some of the areas I hadn't seen on the first trip, and we found ourselves over the billiard table landscape of Lafonia. 'Ok, Tug, down you go,' I heard from the back and I set the RADALT to very, very low and descended.

We had discussed this before getting airborne—Lafonia was another rite of passage for young fighter crews to do some ultra-low flying—horribly illegal, but no one to witness it. I bottled out at about 50 feet I think. There was a flimsy argument that during the next war, we would need to be skilful enough to fly this low, but that was just bullshit. All the time, Bouncer was shouting 'Lower! Faster!' but he respected that I had reached my limit and didn't press me for more. He must have flown with some monsters in the Falklands before me if that wasn't low enough!

I pulled up to about 80 feet and thought I was going to have a nosebleed, it looked so high. We did the usual sprint up Falkland Sound with the burners in, trying to raise up rooster tails from the water, and generally larked around a bit. We beat up MPA a few times on recovery to 'help train the Rapier crews', and that was that—another trip ticked off; a bit more Q; and lots more bar—all part of Falklands life.

Speaking of ticked off, Nemo maintained his quiet hostility towards us and got a chance to vent at us over a minor incident. We were sitting Q1 when the telebrief crackled, calling us to cockpit. Off we shot, goon bags pulled up over our heads, life jackets on, and grabbed the helmet. We burst out of the door and up that flaming tube. Once we had jumped in, I plugged my comms in to hear Bouncer breathlessly call, 'Battle Stations. Engines off!' This was the call we used in Germany, 'engines running' if we had started up.

My hands were hovering, just waiting to gun the jet into life. We were told to hold and then fifteen minutes later, with lots of two-way comm giving us the picture of a possible intruder approaching from the west, we were ordered to stand down after it turned away from the islands. I reset my cockpit, and we strolled back down the tube to the Q shed where all the crews had gathered. Before we could get some of our kit off, Nemo barked at us to get in the crew room and proceeded to dress us down in public for using the wrong comm. 'It's cockpit ready. Engines off, not battle stations. You're not in Germany now!'

'Don't I bloody know it!' I thought. I couldn't get my head around why Nemo was being such a dick. Under pressure, as we were when being scrambled, surely we would default to our natural reactions and comm? Also, did it really matter anyway? The GCI controller at Kent had understood us perfectly. Ah well. We put it down to Nemo being a bit hormonal (he was only halfway through his four-month stint) and thought no more about it. Then, a couple of trips later, we gave him something to really rail on us.

'Chute Gone'

It was another brilliant trip that included escorting the Tristar into MPA. We intercepted it about 80 miles out and checked there were no senior officers on board with the captain. Once we got the okay, we joined on the right wing and went through our standard moves. This included showing the weapons, popping flares, and slipping underneath the Tristar's belly to covertly pop up on the left-hand side and try to surprise the passengers. I would pop the probe out as it is always cool to see things move on the aeroplane. We ended with a barrel roll over the top and lit the burners to scoot away as they made their final approach into MPA.

The weather was closing in and there was a stonking crosswind. Once the Timmy was down and out of the way, I plonked us on the deck and pulled the chute handle. Bouncer called 'Good chute,' and we slowed down to taxi speed at the far end of the runway. ATC told us we could drop the chute on the runway, so I put the handle down and the wind down the runway should have been enough to pull it away from the aircraft as usual. Bouncer called 'Chute gone,' as he couldn't see it anymore in his mirrors.

I turned 180 degrees at the end of the runway to see a big billowing chute go under the wing, and the next thing that happened was we came to a juddering halt as it wrapped itself around the right main wheel. We were well and truly stuck so had to shut down right there on the end of the runway. Cue much embarrassment as we were surrounded by fire crews and our own ground crew, who between them, cut the chute away, and towed us back to the HAS site. I was expecting a belt-load of banter, but instead, the 74 guys said that the Boss wanted to see us in his office right away.

Bouncer and I stood to attention in front of his desk while Nemo tore us a new arsehole each about how unprofessional we were. I wasn't having that so protested about how we were convinced the chute had gone, but he was having none of it. He then put the seal on it for me. His newly arrived pilot (Will's replacement) had been on duty in the tower, and he had told Nemo that we had deliberately held onto the chute and turned into it on purpose or some shit like that. This was the first time I had seen a fighter pilot dob in one of his colleagues, and it stank.

We shuffled off suitably bollocked, and I added Nemo and Snitcher (as his pilot was now known) to my list of 'dickheads I have met in the air force'. We had some sympathy from the other guys, especially when we got the report that the chute jaws had seized on us, but we were definitely top of the shit pile for the rest of our deployment.

Our next two-day stand down saw us desperate to get away from Snitcher and Nemo, especially as they expected us to socialise as normal with them in the Goose. The saving grace was that the 56 Squadron crew had changed out and I met Grim for the first time. He was an older back-seater but with a wicked sense of youth and enthusiasm—something I would witness first-hand about a year later.

Bouncer had organised us a lift on the Bristow's Sea King out to Alice for a night stop. Bristow's had a contract to supply all the settlements and radar sites in the Falklands, doing a great job of ferrying people, animals, and stuff around. They dropped us off on the cliff top, and we were greeted by the GCI controllers we had been talking to on the radio each time we flew. We were greeted as if we were the first human beings they had ever seen. It wasn't until we had spent about an hour there that I got the impression of how remote these poor bastards and their engineers were. It was no wonder they looked a bit feral and acted a bit wibble. They were brilliant hosts though and showed us to our bunks in the ISO container that passed for accommodation.

We dumped out kit and headed to the 'dining room' for a spot of dinner and then hit the makeshift bar with our hosts. As I was a new guy, I was asked if I had seen the famous Falklands video. Looking at the reprobates around me, I was expecting to see some sort of dodgy porn film, but what I actually saw was even more horrifying from a Phantom pilot's point of view. Two Phantoms were doing a flypast at Alice and were being filmed by one of the guys on the cliff top. The jets had 'dirtied up' so gear, flaps, and hooks down and I think they even had the probes out too. The first jet flew over at very low height while cleaning up, but the second one had everyone diving for cover as his hook almost seemed to hit the cameraman in the face.

That itself would not be unusual given some of the flypasts that went on down south, apart from the jet being in wing rock the whole way through. Wing rock in the Phantom was an indicator of imminent stall so it was about to fall out of the sky. As they go over Alice, they stay in wing rock and sink down the far side of the cliff, before struggling back into a shallow climb. The pilot did not even select afterburner to try and recover. I must have watched the clip ten times over that first night, and each time, I was even more astounded. Having overloaded on aviation pornography, the Boss at Alice pulled out his liar dice and the evening ended badly for me. I had never played liar dice before, but figured it couldn't be much different from poker dice—wrong. Each time I lost, which was a lot, I had to drink a shot of some kind of wild, homemade hooch. Even when I thought I was winning, the veterans of the game surreptitiously added their own extra dice to the cup to screw me over. All in all, they did a number on me and I retired that night very hurt indeed.

Breakfast took some effort to keep down, and then our new best friends, who we loved above anyone else (apparently my words from the night before), took us on an expedition down the mountainside in some tracked vehicles to visit an old, abandoned whaling station. There were penguins of all types everywhere and to see them like that in the wild was a real thrill. I had seen lots of penguins from the air on my few trips so far, and the 'sport' at the time was to low-fly over the beach where they would stand in big clusters and watch them look up and then fall over backwards like a set of dominoes as we went over the top—hardly PC, but that was the Falklands—the land that time didn't give a shit about.

It only took an hour to get downhill, but about three hours to get back up and we only just made it in time to grab our bags and pile into the back of a Chinook for the trip back to MPA and our Q2 duty that started at 6 p.m. that night. To this day, I remember very little about that night at Alice. What I do remember, though, is that those guys looked after us like we were royalty, and when any of them turned up at MPA for a night, we reciprocated in the Goose.

Rat and Terrier

We had another couple of great trips doing low-level intercepts. Bouncer and I practically lived in the low-level arena day to day, so his radar handling skills down there were shit hot, and we more than held our own against the UK-based crews, who just didn't get that kind of practice back home. There was a tricky day where we were fragged to fly with Snitcher and Nemo. Nemo briefed up a rat and terrier exercise where we would launch first and set up a CAP wherever we chose, and they would take-off and try to sneak past us unseen to a finish point over on West Falkland. We had no idea what route they would take, and they also planned to do it all silent with no comm to ATC, which meant we would have no idea when they were getting airborne. I'm sure they were trying to put the young German upstarts in their place, but they didn't know that I was more than happy to cheat at any time if it meant getting my own back on anyone I held a grudge against.

Straight after the brief, I called a mate in ATC and then our buddies at Alice and Kent, asking them to keep quiet about what they saw on their radar pictures. As soon as we cleared out of sight, I blasted us up to 25,000 feet and hung around in the overhead of MPA. We were nicely above a thin cloud layer or two, but we were able to see them get airborne and immediately turn east away from where our CAP was supposed to be. Obviously, they were going to kill some time to get us fretful that we had missed them coming through the CAP. I shadowed them all the way out to Stanley and as they went way north of the town, they turned to head west. I rolled on my back and Tirpitzed straight into their six and gunned the living shit out of them. I cannot tell you how awesome it felt calling 'Guns!' on Snitcher and having him break hard to the left to finally get sight of us.

I knocked it off and we briefed a five-minute hiatus to reset the CAP. Again, I went unseen and zoomed up to roll off the top at about 25,000 feet. The five-minute hiatus was bullshit as Snitcher and Nemo turned in after only two as I knew they would (you can't kid a kidder). I let them wang about at low level for a bit to get sweaty and then dropped in again to gun them. Four times this happened, which just goes to show the lengths I will go to for revenge. We kept our dignity in the debrief and made up some shit about CAPing in just the right place and gaining unseen entries to the fight. I don't know if Nemo questioned his own prowess on the radar, but to be honest, I didn't really care. The Cobras were on top and flying high—25,000 feet high to be precise.

Another Germany Fuck Up

All our fun came to a grinding halt that night as Bouncer and I took to the skies in the inky black of the Falklands' winter night. It was blacker than Satan's arsehole with little or no cultural lighting and a thick overcast layer blocking the moon and stars. It was mad being up at this time, and even madder that we tanked from the C130. Of course, we couldn't rely on the Argentinians to attack only in the daylight, so it made sense I suppose to practice some intercepts at night. The weather clamped in quickly during the flight, and I was mightily relieved to take an instrument approach from ATC and plonk it down just as the snow started to come down hard. The Herc just got in behind us and flying was off for a few days.

We only had five more trips including a Q scramble, and my first Falklands det was done. For our final trip, we escorted the Tristar that was due to take us home the next day and brought in the new 92 crew to replace us. Once we landed and debriefed, we packed up our flying kit into the Q3 Land Rover and drove back to the Death Star to pack up for the following day. We parked up outside the back door to our block and lugged our flying kit up to our rooms to secure it in our kitbags.

No more than fifteen minutes later, we went back to the Rover to find that RAF police flight had crook-locked it, even though it had a huge Dayglo Q3 sign in the windscreen. A quick call to police flight told us there was a station standing order 'forbidding the parking of vehicles anywhere other than in the official parking slots, Sir'. Our explanations fell on deaf ears, and to release the Rover, they would need to contact our commanding officer—oh bollocks. My final afternoon in the Falklands ended with another stand-up bollocking from Nemo. His first comment of 'another Germany fuck up!' led me to think he had some sort of Germany envy or inferiority complex going on, but the reasons behind it were immaterial. We gave him and Snitcher the big ignore in the bar that night and I bid farewell to the Falklands, looking forward to getting back to normality.

On dets like the Falklands, we would hand carry our F5000s with us. The 5000 was our confidential report on our flying performance. Every year, we would receive a F1369 (said as 13-69) that detailed our performance as officers in Her Majesty's Air Force, and also an insert to our 5000. The 1369 gave our flight commander, Boss, and station commander a chance to appraise us and our suitability for promotion;

it also gave us a chance to ask for our preferences for our next tour.

I always asked for the following in order: US fast jet exchange; another Phantom tour; and tactics instructor on the Hawk, although I might have put Red Arrows down my first year. Then I discovered that the Reds was basically a Harrier mafia in those days and therefore mostly knobheads and were unlikely to choose a one-tour average Phantom pilot. Also, the more time I spent as a front-line fighter pilot, the less I fancied staring out of the same window doing close formation every day for three years.

The 5000 had every course report in it from the start of flying training and a yearly report from then on. As a young aviator, I had never seen my 5000 as it was confidential and locked away in the flight commander's cabinet. However, this was my first chance to see it, so I slit the sealed envelope and had a look. There were no surprises through training really. I was an average performer with potential apparently (I liked that bit) and a bloody hard worker (I particularly liked that bit).

I then read the latest bit, which was an insert from Nemo. The bastard had stitched us both up left right and centre. He called us unprofessional, which was rich looking at how he and his pilots operated, and the heights they were flying around at, and all sorts of other unsavoury things such as lazy and gash. In my albeit limited career so far, I had never been considered lazy or gash so I was pretty badly stung, as was Bouncer. The first thing I did on getting back to 92, was fess up to OCB that I had read my 5000 (he expected that anyway) and argued my case against what Nemo had written. 'Don't worry, Tug,' he said. 'No-one gives a damn about Falklands reports. He only saw you for five or six weeks so it means nothing.'

I was still a bit pissed about it, but happier to be back on solid footing with the people who mattered. Also, I was able to tell the story of how we had gunned Snitcher and Nemo into oblivion, which cheered up the 92 crew, who we had replaced in the Falklands and who had felt Nemo's tongue-lashing time and again over the fatigue they had used.

Back to Cyprus

The First Gulf War seemed to be approaching at a snail's pace with political demands and counter demands flashing around at world leader level. The initial deployment of ten Phantom crews had been replaced by another ten crews, and these were now due home too. It became apparent that there weren't enough aircrew or ground crew to sustain this commitment, so the decision was made to reduce down to four jets and five crews, just like the Falklands. The next group of crews were due to fly out just a week or so after my return from the Falklands, so I obviously was not on the list.

However, one of the 92 pilots on the list was having some family issues, so I volunteered for his slot. I had no sooner washed and dried my pants from the Falklands det, when I found myself on a transport to Cyprus for the next two months. This would turn out to be the best two months of my life on the Phantom.

I had already been to Cyprus on the Ranger so felt comfortable on arrival. The first-night kebab at Chris's, Brandy sours, and Animal House all had a familiar feel to it. Once we were in-briefed, it was a quick famil flight and then straight onto the Q schedule I had got used to down south. It helped that we knew every crew really well, being from 92 and 19, but I have to say, everybody was a good guy.

The Boss was a flight commander from 19 called Gimmer, and he was crewed with their newest pilot, Hughie. No. 19 had also sent a second tourist pilot, BB, and crewed him with Guvnor, who was their newest nav. There was a mixed crew with Harry from 92 in the front and Mandela from 19 in the boot. We had sent Doc out initially, but he was replaced by Oz from 19 shortly afterwards, meaning another mixed crew with Senna from 92 in the back. Then there was me. I lucked in big time as I was crewed with Bungle.

It seemed that everyone had something to offer, and we quickly gelled into a tight knit, raucous, banter-fuelled group that I have never seen before or since. Gimmer was as mellow as you like and was a calming influence on Hughie, who still had a lot of youthful mischief in him. Doc (then Oz) and BB were experienced pilots and good fonts of knowledge, although BB freaked us all out by claiming, rather matter of fact, that he would happily eat anything his head or face produced—just try mentally listing those things now and you will see how horrified we were. Bungle was the perfect nav for me. I already knew how good he was, so knew he would spur me on to being as good as I could be. He had also seen it all before and was relaxed and sanguine, which was the perfect foil for my sometimes 'angry young man' persona in the air.

Just Call Me Pop Boy!

Gimmer doled out secondary duties on the first day with deputy boss going to Bungle, and various other jobs such as flying programmer, recce officer, entertainments, security, intel etc., being shared around. I was made QRA officer, which pleased me no end as I loved Q and was happy to sort all the procedures and liaise with ATC over Q priorities and procedures. Hughie waited patiently for a job, and it seemed like Gimmer had forgotten him. After a long pause, Gimmer looked at him and said, 'Hughie, can you sort out the beers and soft drinks for here and back at Animal House please?' Once Gimmer had walked out, Hughie looked at us and said, 'Soft drinks?! Why not just call me Pop Boy?' So, we did, and it is still what I call him today.

My shakedown trip was with Mandela, and we went over the beautifully blue Med for a day tactics trip. We got used to talking to the radar folks on Mount Olympus (known as Oli Radar) and had a good look at the features in the local area. The first trip in a new locale is always a steep learning curve as the procedures all seem different, and of course, we were working with a combined 92/19 ground crew force as well. The crew room and ops buildings were an unusual environment too with the crew room being upstairs; this is where we hung out on Q also. The weather was usually beautiful during the day for flying and a bit chilly in the evenings. It was nothing to complain about though—two weeks ago, I had been freezing my nuts off in the Falklands snow, and now I seemed to be in paradise.

Bungle and I took to the skies the next day for more of the same, then we were into stand down crew over the weekend. Bungle wanted to show me the sights, so we spent a night up in the Troodos Mountains visiting the guys and girls at Oli Radar and then took the long and winding drive up to see Makarios's Tomb. Culture ticked off for a bit, we returned to Akrotiri and went straight into fly crew on the Monday. We had two absolutely brilliant, fun day-tactics trips and honed our crew skills for QRA. The second trip of the day, we dumped the jet into the approach end cable after a request from ATC for airfield training. I always loved taking the cable.

Although it was nowhere near as violent as I imagined a carrier landing to be, I think it gave us a taste of what it must be like. The Phantom was born for the carrier so it was more than happy. I added 'hook down' to my pre-landing checks and flew a decent pattern around finals. There was a big clunk just before touchdown as the hook shoe banged onto the runway, and then what seemed like an age before it caught the cable and slung me headfirst towards the instrument panel.

Very quickly, the programme started to get routine just like the Falklands, so Oz suggested we have a spot-landing competition. The middle point of the numbers on the threshold would be the spot and the caravan controller would mark how long or short our mainwheels were from the spot. We could have as many practice circuits as we liked, and then had to declare which approach we wanted officially scoring before touchdown. Therefore, we would be scored on one pass only.

I had no chance as there were three pilots more experienced than me, so I didn't feel any pressure at all. At the end of our next trip, Bungle and I had saved enough gas for four attempts. The first three were all decent circuits, but I couldn't tell if they were any good for the spot. I declared to ATC that this was my scored attempt and came in to land. I thought it looked okay on landing, but we didn't give it another thought as we taxied in. I had my mind on getting back onto Q as I signed the auth sheets when there was a call from ATC to the ops desk. By all accounts, our mainwheels were bang on the spot and no one else had got close over the last couple of days. I was absolutely gobsmacked. Perhaps I did have a bit of skill after all? If ever they decided to save the bloodshed and contest the next war by organising a spot-landing competition between us and the Russians, then I was your man.

Top Gun Gunned

Routine hit our personal lives away from the jet too. Every meal in the mess was accompanied by George's effusive 'Welcome Gentlemens! This is number one tip top dinner at Officers' Mess. *Efharisto*!' Almost every night we weren't on Q started with a jug of brandy sour, and the weekends saw us at the beach at Akrotiri or downtown Limassol. Anything that broke the routine was most welcome. We tried the station cinema and watched an interesting version of Julia Roberts in *Pretty Woman*. The film was shown on four separate reels, but the projectionist played them in the order one, three, two, four, which we rather felt spoiled the character development somewhat.

BB and Guvnor went off on one of their down days to get motorbike licences. This was a notorious bit of Cypriot culture. Guvnor had never ridden a motorbike in his life, so BB hired a couple of mopeds and taught him how to ride in about thirty minutes. They turned up at the test centre in a clatter of bits and the examiner told them to ride about 100 yards up the road, then turn round and come back. BB went first and passed, and as Guvnor set off, the examiner went inside to write up the paperwork for both licences. This was handy as Guvnor fell off completely while turning around at the end of the road. Brand-new licences in hand, they sped off around the local area. The amazing thing was, that flimsy piece of paper could be swapped for a full motorbike licence in the UK—shocking!

Next up for us was an amazing trip against an aircraft I had only ever dreamed about seeing—the F14 Tomcat. The US Navy had a full carrier battle group deployed in the Gulf ready for the war. Actually, for all I knew, they might have had two or three. Anyway, the USS *Saratoga* was steaming through the Med to set up off the western edge of the Middle East and was looking for some affiliation training to sharpen up their Tomcat crews. Bungle and I were leading our pair, and I took a ship-to-shore telephone brief to go over rules of engagement, weapons loads, contact frequencies, set-ups, and rendezvous points.

It was at that point that they casually announced there would be four of them rather than the two we were expecting. We were seriously outgunned by just two of them as their performance and manoeuvrability were in a different class to us. Still, what an opportunity to fight against a jet I had seen in the film *Top Gun* just a few years ago while still flying a puny Jet Provost in training. We agreed that they would take their long-range Phoenix active missile shots, but they wouldn't count as they wanted to get in some visual merges for air combat training. That suited us as it gave us a chance, not having to sidestep their long stick. I thought back to the trip the QWIL had briefed against the F15s in Deci and thought we would try something similar, with maybe a bit of cheating as well on the first fight.

I briefed up our pair, which had Oz and Senna as the number two. The plan was that Oz would be up high just below the contrails at the start point, and I would start on the deck about 20 miles in front of the start (only a minor cheat). At 'fight's on', Oz would press in supersonic and then turn tail at about 30 miles to get the Tomcats following him. Normally in this situation, they would expect the move we made against the F15s and would no doubt be looking low. Bungle would then lock them up, and I would start climbing to give them a big fat target to look at. I was then hoping that being 20 miles closer than they expected would draw all four Tomcats down into the fight, desperate to get a kill on me, and thinking they had stymied our plan. At this point, Oz would be turning back in at high level and should have his pick of the targets to swoop in on.

An added extra to the trip was the fact that we would be getting airborne from the taxiway parallel to the runway. Again, this was to give training to ATC at Akrotiri as they would need to block off all of the entries to the taxiway. The last thing we wanted was a Land Rover to drive out in front of us during take-off, so it was a check of all the various entryway traffic lights and the general procedure. It was imaginatively called 'Operation Block Off', and we lined up on what looked like a very narrow taxiway, with Oz on the main runway. I used as much of the taxiway as I could by lining up right on the end, and then we were cleared for take-off.

Holy shit, the tower looked incredibly close as we blasted past it, as did the various vehicles parked up to watch the spectacle (Block Off was tannoyed around the station and had obviously attracted a crowd). It was all over in an instant and off we scorched out to meet the legendary Tomcat.

Not a single one of them had tally on me as the sea was a murky grey that day, but all four of them committed low to find us. They were spread over an area of about 5 miles, and I had the glorious sight of four aeroplanes just off to my right and high. I selected the Sidewinder and got a growl on the rear right guy, mashed the SEAM button to get a solid tone and as soon as I passed the leaders, thereby making the merge happen, I took the shot and called the kill. We still had about 10,000 feet of separation so I plugged the burners in and pitched up into the rear left. All hell broke loose then.

Two huge lumps of metal swung their wings forwards and were on me in an instant. My plan pretty much assumed that we would be shot in order to get Oz in unseen, but having got one kill I didn't expect, I was keen to get another. The Tomcat I was on was popping flares like they were going out of fashion, so I just pressed in and selected the gun. I was amazed how big the F14 looked in the gunsight and was so enthralled by it that I had no idea what the hell else was going on in the fight.

Bungle was popping chaff and flares as Tomcats 1 and 2 queued up behind us to take their shots. I called 'Guns!' on my bandit and heard a loud and clear 'FOX 2! FOX 2!' from Oz as he pumped Sidewinders into

1 and 2 from behind. I knocked the whole fight off, and after everyone checked their gas, we found that we didn't have enough for another set. God, you have to love that afterburner. We all said our thanks and goodbyes over the radio, then headed back to Akrotiri while the Tomcats went back to the Saratoga.

I was absolutely buzzing again and added a few knots to my break speed for the circuit, while simultaneously taking quite a few feet off the break height. Big smiley faces greeted me in the debrief, and we came to the conclusion that we must have taken out three of them before I was killed and we knocked it off. The guy I was gunning probably got away with it as we guessed I was shot to shit before pulling the trigger. I managed a telephone debrief with their leader, and he confirmed our suspicions. By all accounts, I was a missile pin cushion as Tomcats 1 and 2 pumped every last weapon they had into me before my guns kill. He readily agreed that they had been suckered in and needed a lot more work-up before the whole shebang kicked off in Iraq. He finished up by saying they had had a blast too, and it was great to fly against a vintage aeroplane—always banter from a position of disadvantage, I guess?

The Stroker in the Tiny Car

The next couple of days saw everyone having a go at the Tomcats, and it was obvious that they were sharpening up fast. As Saratoga arrived in the Med, USS *John F Kennedy* handed over and steamed out. The quality and sharpness of their crews was a world away from their colleagues on Saratoga, and it just went to show how a proper war footing can affect performance. The JFK boys were all over us like a rash, and none of our wacky tactics had any effect on them as they shot us from all angles.

One particular day though, a F18 Hornet from JFK diverted in to Akrotiri. The USN pilot had missed a couple of approaches back onto deck so had the embarrassment of diverting into us for gas. Senna and I met him at the jet, and he looked pretty shaken as he had almost landed on vapour. We got him into the crew room and got some food and drink into him while Gimmer organised his refuel. It was looking like he might need to stop over for the night, so those of us not on Q planned to take him down the strip to Chris's for a kebab and a few beers in exchange for a good crawl over his aircraft in the morning.

Out of nowhere, a small RAF MT Metro screeched up outside and OC Ops from Akrotiri squeezed out and demanded to speak with the Hornet pilot. OC Ops was a fat ex-Herc nav who I think had a bit of a thing against fast jet crews. His sleepy hollow posting in the sun had been rudely interrupted by the build up to the Gulf War and he had been forced to act semi-operational again.

After five minutes, he blustered out and the white-faced Hornet pilot told us he had just been bawled out for daring to land at Akrotiri when the Status of Forces Agreement did not allow for it, and he had been told in no uncertain terms that he was to fuel up and sod off before he caused a diplomatic incident. Apparently, it would have been less trouble all around if he had just run out of fuel and ejected into the Med. That put OC Ops at the top of our all new knobhead list, and we drove our new comrade out to his F18, waving him off while apologising profusely for the stroker in the tiny car.

'Toasties Ready!'

Saddam Hussein started firing Scud missiles into Israel, and each time a launch was observed, we were brought to cockpit ready on Q just in case Cyprus turned out to be the target and we would need to launch for survival. Tensions in the region were rising markedly, and we saw a big increase in traffic in the Med. Bungle and I were airborne as Q1 in early December on a normal training mission when Oli Radar tasked us to intercept an unknown aircraft in the area. Bungle got an early contact of a relatively slow mover at 28,000 feet, and we set up for a stern intercept from slightly below the target.

I got tally quite early and a warning from Bungle that they were slow speed as he got the Q camera out from the casing. It was an easy ident of an E2 surveillance aeroplane—twin prop with a mushroom-like radar mid-fuselage and an odd tailplane set up. The blue star on the side nailed it as Israeli. We were still quite heavy with gas, and with all the weapons on board, it took a bit of effort to fly slow enough for Bungle to get the photos. It was pointless trying to formate on them as I was already hanging on the compressor blades, so I did a series of slow flypasts and repositions until they turned away from Cyprus with a wave to us. That incident brought us an intelligence debrief on landing and a nice black and white photo of the E2 for my logbook. These moments of pure excitement were offset by the absolutely ordinary experiences of being on det.

There was a small snack bar behind the ops building run by a squat, wide Cypriot chap who had an enormous hooter. Pop Boy and I had got into the habit of a mid-morning cheese and onion toastie, but no matter how often we went there, we could not engage him in any conversation, not even to find out his name. Obviously, he became known as Bignose (thank you, *Monty Python's Life of Brian* again), and he made a small fortune from us as we became almost addicted to those toasties. All good things come to an end though, and this was no exception. Bignose would put the toasties in the machine, and we would head back to ops to await his shout of 'toasties ready!'

For some reason, Pop Boy went out early one day and saw Bignose holding each nostril closed in turn and blowing out the contents of the other before shouting 'toasties ready!' It still turns my stomach knowing he then handled our food, and cheese and onion toasties bring me out in a cold sweat even to this day.

6666—What Does That Mean?

As we got into December, we got permission to go down to fifteen-minute readiness overnight as Q1 and I think sixty minutes for Q2. This allowed us to head back to the mess for dinner in the evening and even grab a quick shower before heading back to the line to sit Q. The Q3 crew would drive us in the Sherpa van, and we would leave it parked right in front of the mess, full of our g-pants and life jackets, just in case we got a scramble code on the QRA pager. A page of '9999' on the LED readout would mean a scramble and a five-minute drive from hell in the Sherpa straight to the jets for launch. We were just glad to have proper food each night rather than Hot Locks, and the chances of a night launch were probably slim.

The big event in the mess in December was always the Christmas draw. It was a chance to dress up in dinner jackets with squadron cummerbunds and bow ties and enjoy a lavish function in the mess with great food, lots of drink, and the chance to win all sorts of expensive raffle prizes. A couple of crews from Wildenrath flew out to sit Q for us, which was a nice touch, so we could all go to the draw. They also said not to take over Q the next day until about lunchtime.

My memories of that night are sketchy at best, but I do remember not winning a stinking thing. I also recall Bungle waking me up, telling me it was about 6.30 a.m. and we needed to get ready for Q1. 'Late start, Bungle,' I managed to croak out through my dry mouth.

'Fair point, Tug,' he replied, 'but you are still in your DJ, and if you look carefully, you'll see that you have been sleeping in the storm drain.' I slowly stood up to find that I was level with Bungle's ankles and peering over the wall of the huge storm channel outside the mess. I can only guess I took a tumble into it (minor cuts and bruises bore that theory out) on my way back to Animal House and decided to stay put and get some kip.

I was nowhere near fit enough for Q, so thank God we had a few hours to recover before the late handover. Bungle had a less than gentle recovery programme for me, which started with driving me to the beach and forcing me to swim in the December cool Med. That got my attention, I can tell you. Then came a huge drunk food breakfast with lots and lots of liquids. The swim sobered me up in an instant, and we took over Q, praying for a quiet day.

Christmas was also approaching, and it must have been tough for Gimmer and Bungle, who had children at home. The rest of us were either married with no kids or singlies like me. Q had been a little quiet of late, but that was about to change. We had just sat down to eat dinner one night in the mess (we were Q1 with Oz and Senna as Q2) when the pager bleeped. Pop Boy held it as Q3 pilot and designated driver. We were out of our seats and bolting for the door, when Pop Boy shouted, 'It's okay lads, its 6666.'

We calmed down a bit and asked what '6666' meant, but Pop Boy couldn't find it in the decode list. 'Hold on,' I said and snatched the pager from his hand. When I turned the pager the right way up, the 6666 miraculously became 9999, meaning scramble! We raced to the Sherpa, and Pop Boy drove like a maniac while we kitted up in the back. He screeched to a halt next to the jet where our ground crew already had the Houchin going.

As soon as we checked in at cockpit with Oli Radar, we were told to scramble and given a vector to an unknown aircraft getting too close for comfort. My first ever practice scramble about a year ago had been at night, and I had managed to screw up most of the switches, so even though my blood was pumping, I was a lot calmer this time, and we fast taxied in good order—canopies down, vent knob in (welcome to the learning curve, Tug!) pins out, flaps down, jettison safety ready, and boom, we were off. There was no stopping on the runway, just taxi on and keep moving as I smoothly moved the throttles to full Mil, rocked them outboard, and slammed to full burner. After a quick check on the nozzle gauges to see the burner light, it was a boot up the arse again and away we went.

As soon as we were airborne, I pulled the gear and flaps up while turning towards the target. I stopped the climb at about 15,000 feet as our target was mooching about at low level. The night was black as a black thing and the Med was full of big nasty thunderstorms. Bungle was chatting with Oli and called the contact to them. He then called, 'Judy, Judy,' to silence them and ran a picture-perfect stern against a manoeuvring target. Our RWR kept lighting up, but we couldn't get any solid information from it. Nevertheless, I was starting to get a little pissed that we were being tickled by what could be a hostile radar. I armed us up and we were popping chaff out whenever we got a light on the RWR.

Bungle set up the VID for me and talked me in. There was a little bit of moonlight, so we chatted about that and decided to try and come in from below. We carefully brief set the RADALT at 100 feet and any alarm from it would be an immediate pull up. Bungle had the target at 1,000 feet, and I closed in to 300 yards. When I looked out, all I could see was black. They had no lights on, so I went back on instruments and overshot to set up again as the target was pretty slow too.

The second VID was smooth enough down to 300 yards, but this time, Bungle used the night scope to try and get the ident. Bear in mind here that this was 1991 and night vision goggles were a long way off. The night scope was a cumbersome camera-sized bit of kit attached to a small axe handle and it was shit. So, around we went again for another try. While doing our third approach, OLI had launched Q2 with Oz and Senna. We heard them checking in but tuned them out for now while we conducted another VID from below.

Bungle warned me that they were descending, and we were glued to the altimeter as they descended through 800 feet. We constantly cross-checked altimeters as they continued to drag us down below 500 feet. It was still pitch black, and I saw the RADALT light come on and go full burner to climb away and to the left. I was absolutely furious that these clowns were happy to force us into the sea, and now wanted to pump a missile up their arse and see how they liked that. Bungle calmed me down, and shortly afterwards, Q2 called us to a tactical frequency. Bungle gave a debrief of the events so far, and Oz came up with a plan. They would run a VID and try their night scope, but at the same time, Oz wanted me to fly close formation on him. If he and Senna got no sight at 300 yards, he would call '3, 2, 1' and then select burner and pull up to see if we could make the ident from the light of his reheat. What?! You are kidding me!

I didn't think for one second it would work, as it sounded so outrageous, but we were out of ideas so gave it a go. Oz and Senna kept tabs on the bogey while we ran a VID on them, so that I could join in close formation. As I have said before, close formation at night seemed like a step towards madness to me, but here I was in echelon on Oz's wing as they ran the intercept. I have to say, it was a beautiful piece of flying by Oz. He was intercepting a target that definitely did not want to be intercepted, but his movements were so smooth and empathetic that I had no problem staying in close. Senna's radar work must have been tip top too. After a few minutes, they called that they were stabilised at 300 yards, and then that Senna's night scope gave no ident.

The next thing I heard was '3, 2, 1', and the whole of the Med seemed to light up as Oz's afterburners lit. There was an immense roar as he pulled up and I locked my arms to hold us in the same piece of sky while Bungle looked down on the bogey. 'Got it!' he shouted and then calmly reported to Oli that it was an Electra—an Israeli intelligence-gathering aircraft. We were getting close to the 'Take me home Willy' light coming on, so it was straight line back to Akrotiri for us, leaving Q2 to shadow the Electra.

The night seemed to have got even blacker as we transited back. I had one eye on the fuel and knew we needed to get it in off the first approach otherwise we would be poorly placed. I was calling that we would be fuel priority and would need radar pick up for PAR, when something otherworldly happened. On the outside of the canopy in the F4, we had a 6-inch length of string 'nailed' so that it lay up the front window. It was supposed to help us assess drift when we were strafing (yeah right). Anyway, it started to glow electric blue, and a river of electric blue rain water was snaking its way all over the top of the canopy from the end of the string. Both Bungle and I had the same blue light dancing inside the canopy above the coaming. I had seen St Elmo's fire once before in a Jet Provost, but given the difficult trip we had just had, and the come down from the adrenaline, this time, it took my breath away. It was so beautiful.

Had I been a sharp and professional aviator, I would have remembered from my ground school lectures on meteorology that St Elmo's Fire is a 'weather phenomenon in which luminous plasma is created by a corona discharge from a sharp or pointed object in a strong electric field in the atmosphere (such as those generated by thunderstorms)'. Thank you, Wikipedia, for stopping me from digging my old Met books out. 'Thunderstorms' is the key word, of course. Unfortunately, right there and then, I was just me and not a sharp and professional aviator, and as such I completely forgot that St Elmo's Fire is a good indicator of an increased risk of lightning strike. So, when we did get struck by lightning shortly afterwards, I fair near shat myself.

We went momentarily from complete darkness to bright light as the lightning arced onto the right wing, and then back to the inky black. The only way I can describe the feeling of shock is to compare it to how you feel in the instant when a big stone cracks your windscreen on the motorway. I was glad to get down that night and get back into the crew room. Once Oz and Senna got back on deck, we discussed that outrageous burner plan all night—what a great idea and I was gobsmacked that it had worked. After much patting on the back, we had finally worked out our adrenaline and got a few hours' sleep on Q before handing over the next day.

We had to tell the story over and over again but didn't mind at all. Talking about flying is almost as good as flying sometimes, and reliving the experience would help me to develop into a better aviator. We were just getting ready to go off Q onto our stand down when an official car drew up with a flag on the front. Out got an old RAF guy in a blue beret, and he wandered in and introduced himself as the commander of British Forces Cyprus. He had heard about the scramble and wanted to come down from HQ at Episkopi himself to meet us and hear the story first-hand. He seemed to think it was a cool tale and ended up thanking us for what we had done. He then shook our hands and said that if we needed anything while we were on the island, we were to contact him personally—what a refreshing change from some of the senior officers we had come across (OC Ops, for example), who just saw us as an annoyance with our loud aeroplanes launching at all times of the day and night.

I Flew with Santa!

Gimmer had not flown for a little while, so he bumped Bungle out of my back seat and took his place for one trip. He was very relaxed and a joy to fly with, and it struck me that this was the first different nav I had flown with in over a month. I had got so used to flying with Bungle that I had almost forgotten what it was like to fly with someone else. That's not what made this trip unusual though; it was what happened while we were taxiing in.

It was 21 December so just before Christmas. As we cleared the runway after landing, Gimmer said, 'I'm just going off intercom for a bit, Tug. Keep her slow and steady if you would.' I was a bit flummoxed but let it pass, and as I got close to the ATC Tower, I got ready to wave to the controllers as usual. Today, it looked like there were tons of them waving through the big windows, and as I waved back, I caught a glimpse from the corner of my eye. I turned around to see Gimmer standing to attention on the right wing, saluting the tower with a Santa hat on his head. I was speechless and just laughed my head off. I heard, 'Back on intercom, Tug,' as if nothing had happened. Thank God I was due for stand down for a couple of days—life was getting way too bizarre for comfort.

Bungle told me we were off to do some more culture, and we bundled into the car and headed off to Paphos. I am a bit of a classics nerd, so when Bungle took me to the Tomb of the Kings and we saw the Greek and Roman mosaics, I was in seventh heaven. We followed this with the freshest seafood lunch in the small fishing harbour of the town. In those days, Paphos was not the drink-fuelled stag and hen night toilet it has the propensity to be now. It was quiet, relatively untouched, and just what we needed after our mad trip a couple of nights before and my experience with Santa.

'Negative, Tower! This Is Q1 Scrambling'

We were back on Q2 for Christmas Day, opening the few cards and pressies sent out by the squadrons and the station at Wildenrath. I felt a bit bad for Bungle and Gimmer, who were missing Christmas with their kids, and then felt bad for myself as the mess refused to send out any food for us for some reason. They were running a skeleton staff over

Christmas and so couldn't or wouldn't sort out a Christmas lunch for us. Word got around and a couple of the ATC controllers brought us some pizza from a local restaurant, which was a nice touch for which we were extremely grateful.

This was my first (but not by any means my last) experience of being on duty on an important event, but that is Q—every hour of every day, and someone has to do it. Christmas passed in isolation on Q as if it was just another day. On Boxing Day, we were Q3, which made me duty driver, and then next it was Q1. As Q1, we would fly with the fly crew in the morning, then they would fly with Q2 in the afternoon. It was a fun trip in the morning, but the gas didn't seem to last long as we were fully armed up and weighed down with all the missiles and the gun pod. After debriefing, we settled down for our usual packed lunch and a relaxing afternoon in the sunshine waiting for a scramble message that probably wouldn't happen, until it did.

The call came through to the ops desk, and Gimmer set off the air horn, which got me and Bungle running towards the jet at the same time as the ground crew. I wrestled with my life jacket as I ran, my helmet and inner cap already firmly on my head. Oli passed the scramble message as soon as we checked in, and I went through what was becoming a remarkably familiar routine. In no time at all, we were taxiing out to the runway. I switched to the tower frequency and called, 'Tower, this is Q1 scrambling for runway 27. Take-off immediate.'

All was as advertised, until tower replied, 'Q1 hold short of the runway. I have a C130 approaching finals for runway 09.'

I was stunned. We were Q1 scrambling for God's sake. Canopy, vent knob, pins, and jettison safety all done, we were only 50 yards from the runway. 'Negative, tower! This is Q1 scrambling. Break off the C130. Take-off runway 27 immediate!'

'Q1, you will hold! I say again I have a C130 on finals for 09.'

That was it. I had had enough. 'Tower. Q1 scrambling. Operation Block Off Immediate!'

We turned left onto the taxiway as tower said, 'Er, say again Q1.'

'Operation Block Off now! Q1 rolling!' Onto the parallel taxiway, with burners in, off we roared airborne just past the tower in opposition to a very confused and worried Hercules who was about 50 yards to our right as we passed him. There was some kerfuffle on the radio, but we switched to Oli almost straight away and Bungle got his head into the scope. The contact looked as though it had originated from the Israel area again but faded from Oli's radar, so we patrolled the area for an hour or so with no luck before turning back for Akrotiri.

The debrief with tower was going to be interesting, especially with me being the QRA officer. We guessed the tower controller was new in theatre so didn't know the significance of QRA (not sure how, but we were willing to give him the benefit of the doubt). That was before we got down and back to the squadron, where OC Ops was waiting for us in his nerdy little car. He looked even more pumped up and indignant than usual, but we gave him the big ignore until we had signed in and held an intel debrief over the phone to Oli Radar. Then he started in on us—how dangerous and unprofessional we had been; how disrespectful to his tower controller; and who did we think we were, etc.

Bungle was always great at calming me down, but he let me have my head a little on this one. 'We were Q1, Sir. And that made us the most important aircraft in the area when that hooter went off.' Cue much blustering, sweating, and purple-faced gurning as the wing commander tried to face down the adrenaline-fuelled flying officer. 'And if you had ever been on Q in your life, Sir, you would realise that and we wouldn't be having this conversation.'

It was at this point that Gimmer stepped in and saved my smug overload from causing my inevitable court martial. He asked if the wing commander would like him to contact Commander British Forces Cyprus to discuss Flying Officer Wilson's actions given that Flying Officer Wilson had just led the night scramble a couple of days before that had been mentioned in Commander British Forces Cyprus's monthly report. So, OC Ops left quietly, and we all had a bit of a back-slapping session to celebrate seeing the old duffer off.

As I settled back down onto Q, it struck me what a confident, bolshy, little git I had turned into—compare me now to how I had felt on that first Phantom trip only about 380 hours ago in my logbook. I would like to say with hindsight that I mentally admonished myself to be on my guard and watch for arrogance creeping in, but that would be bullshit. I was loving myself right now—I loved Cyprus; I loved flying with Bungle; I loved being on Q; I loved my squadron buddies; and I absolutely adored my aeroplane.

Harry's Second Crash

Life continued with the usual round of trips being beaten up by the F14s. I think the JFK guys were pissed about going home and missing the big hoo-hah, so they were taking it out on us. We hosted a half squadron of Canadian Hornets for a night on their way into Saudi Arabia, trading them a night at Chris's (where one of them fell asleep on his giant pork chop) for a look around their jet the next day before they departed. They also taught us three very funny bar songs, one of which was so disgusting it turned our stomachs.

New Years' Day 1991 arrived with another early morning swim and another day on QRA—routine, routine, routine. I was Q3 and duty driver on 8 January and popped into the mess to run a couple of errands. One of the Akrotiri ops guys collared me and said, 'You might want to head back to the squadron, Tug. We just heard one of your jets has gone in.'

The words hit me like a steam train, so I rushed to the Sherpa and sped like an idiot back to the flight line. Gimmer looked white as a sheet. Harry and Mandela's jet had gone down in the sea, but there was sketchy news about how and why. The resident search and rescue squadron had launched with a Wessex to mount a rescue, but we weren't sure if the boys had made it out. News then started filtering back from Oz and Senna that there was a least one dinghy in the water, and then two, thank God! The Wessex picked up both guys and flew them directly to the military hospital (TPMH) near to Akrotiri, and all we could do was wait for news on how they were.

Standard practice was to take notes on timings and to impound the authorisation sheets and any other documents related to flying, so we cracked on with all of that while we waited. Poor Oz and Senna were bombarded with questions after they got down, and slowly, the details came out. When launching as a pair, the Number 2 would carry out a full radar and weapons check, which would take about twenty–thirty seconds. They would then call the leader to jink right or left. The leader would turn hard in one direction through about 90 degrees, then reverse back into the Number 2's 6 o'clock for their own checks. Bearing in mind that the jets would be heavy straight after take-off, and being fully loaded with fuel and weapons, that reversal manoeuvre at relatively slow speed needed a bit of respect.

The angle of attack would build rapidly at slow speed, meaning the ailerons would become dangerous to use and the jet would have to be turned with rudder alone. Apparently, Harry's jet had departed during the reversal, and the two guys had only just got out in time. Being airborne and watching that sort of thing happen must have been a huge shock, and so Oz and Senna did a great job as on-scene commander, coordinating the rescue until the Wessex arrived, and then getting safely back on deck. All told, Harry and Mandela were extremely lucky, escaping with some compression fractures in the spine and a few bumps and bruises. We all breathed a sigh of relief, but we were now down to only four crews to cover the Q programme, meaning we were into day on, day off Q. We weren't too far from the end of our deployment, so OCB, who was the next det commander, and Doc flew in early with a replacement jet.

It's A Prowler!

Our replacements were due out in about a week or so, and we started to look forward to heading back to Germany and normality. Just before that, I flew with OCB as a famil for him. It was an amazing trip involving us simulating an attack on a British Destroyer steaming through the Med. I have to admit, we were pretty low over the top of it and my break back into the circuit was 'tasty'. OCB seemed okay with it all so I obviously hadn't gone completely feral, and it looked like my ability was matching my ambition for once.

My final mission in Cyprus was with Senna, and we were holding airborne Q flying against Doc and Guvnor. We had just separated out by 50 miles to start the first intercept, when Oli Radar gave us an airborne tasking to intercept an intruder. I rocked the throttles outboard and snapped us through 180 degrees to face up to the threat. Oli continued giving us vectors until Senna called 'Judy, Judy!' and we flew a perfect stern to roll out 1.5 miles behind at 10,000 feet. Straight away, it looked like an A6 Intruder, but not quite. Oli were pressing us for an ident, but we were stalling a bit as we closed in—we didn't want to make fools of ourselves and so called it 'friendly and American'.

The next thing we heard was Doc shouting, 'We will be there in twenty seconds!' We really should have been much better and quicker at recce, but finally, we came to the conclusion it must be a Prowler (the electronic warfare version of the A6).

Then Senna said, 'It's definitely a Prowler, Tug. The RWR has just melted into my lap!'

Just as we were about to call it in, Doc and Guvnor roared past doing about 1.4 Mach with Doc shouting, 'it's a Prowler!' The Prowler is a very important asset, and having an unseen F4 flash past at high speed spoiled the overall atmosphere of friendship and non-aggression that Senna and I had cultivated with them. Shortly afterwards, Oli announced that we had four high-speed targets inbound. Guessing that these were going to be four angry F14s, we waved a final goodbye to the Prowler and made our way back with Doc in tow. Once the wheels touched down vaguely near the threshold of the runway, my Cyprus was officially over. Our replacements took the jet off our hands and put it back on Q.

We had a couple of down days to pack and force down a last kebab and a criminal amount of Kokinelli and brandy sour, then it was an evening check-in for the C130 home. There wasn't enough space in the back of the Herc (which turned out to be a blessing), so BB and I had to sit up front on the bunks in the cockpit. It meant I was able to sleep in the dark throughout the tedium of the flight.

We arrived at Wildenrath at O-dark-hundred and watched the young co-pilot land about a third of the way down the runway. After much stamping on the brakes and thrust reverse, he wrestled it to a halt just before the end of the runway. Unfortunately, BB and I were plugged into the intercom and we heard the co-pilot say to the captain, 'Blimey! I didn't think we were going to make it there!' which didn't fill us full of confidence, and we couldn't wait to get off the aircraft in case he crashed on the taxi back in.

We stepped off the Herc on the visiting aircraft pan, and I went flying onto my arse on a big patch of ice. I was just about to start ranting about how I could have broken my neck when the mover announced to everyone that while we had been airborne on the way back from Cyprus, the first wave of Tornado GR1s had gone in and bombed targets in Iraq. My sore arse paled into insignificance at that news. My best friend was based at Tabuk in Saudi Arabia and no doubt would have been part of those first raids.

My life for the next few weeks consisted of flying, Battle Flight, and watching BFBS to get news of the war. Tornado GR1s were getting shot down and watching the crews paraded on TV by the Iraqis made us feel ill. It was weird to be conducting a normal life while our mates were in harm's way. One particular day, we had been tasked to do some affil against the Mirage F1s out of Reims. The plan was to fight a 2 *v.* 2 in French airspace (which was notoriously difficult to operate in), land at Reims for lunch, and then another 2 *v.* 2 to come home.

The Mirage F1 was optimised for high-level intercepts so the first two guys didn't come below 40,000 feet apart from take-off and landing. This was all a bit shit as we didn't get the chance to turn and burn with them. Lunch was in their officers' club, and we were hosted really well. I was a bit shocked to see some of their guys drinking wine (which we politely declined). I was even more shocked to see that two of the guys drinking wine turned out to be the two we were flying against for the second trip—*vive la difference* and all that.

The Man with a Van

Announcements were coming thick and fast while Germany was pressing ahead with reunification. There was going to be yet another defence review, and the main news for us was that the German Air Force was going to be allowed to police its own airspace. Wildenrath was to be closed, and the first squadron to go would be 92. I was absolutely gutted as was everyone else on base. How dare they fold my squadron with all its amazing history?

That was bad enough, but it meant all sorts of changes in our personal lives too. Shortly after the announcement, I met my poster for the first time. The fast jet poster was an ex-fast jet aviator doing a ground tour that 'would be good for his career' and usually came straight after promotion to squadron leader. As a student, and also as a young pilot so far on the front line, I had never once contacted him, just taking what was sent my way and dealing with it. The older, married guys had a lot more invested, so they would badger him constantly to find out what career plan the RAF had for them (usually no plan). The poor bastard spent all his life fielding phone calls from irate aircrew, and then trying to fight fires in manning.

All of us were given an interview slot, and being a 'W', I was pretty much last. He looked like he had been machine-gunned by the time I saw him, but all I noticed was the massive zit on the side of his nose. It was enormous and I couldn't take my eyes off it. I was given the opportunity to state what I wanted to do after 92 folded, and I asked to be transferred over to 19 for the final twelve months of the Phantom. My argument was sound—I had only spent two years in Germany; I was fully operational and up to speed; it would be mad to post me back to the UK where I would need to qualify in a different environment, etc. 'You're going to 56,' he said and shut my file.

'Yes, Sir,' I said then threw up a nifty salute before walking out. So, my posting was to the Firebirds at Wattisham in Suffolk. Myself, Bobby, and Lurch were headed to 56, and Bungle, Harry, Von, Fatty, and Plop would go to the Tiger Squadron—No. 74.

There was all manner of stuff to be sorted out, but at least we had a few months of notice. First on the agenda was a car. We were entitled to buy tax-free cars on a government scheme. I had never been able to afford a new car before so took the opportunity and put my order in. It meant selling my Porsche (which I did quickly), but I was now without a car while my new one was being built.

Massey stepped in to help and sold me a car for DM 1000 (about £300). He had got into buying and selling second-hand cars, and I was now the proud owner of a shitty brown escort van that everyone immediately called 'Van Morrison'—not quite the fighter pilot image I was going for, but Van Morrison did me proud, never breaking down and providing me a handy 'room' for the night after happy hour. Thank God no one knew I was sleeping in the van from time to time as I would probably have had my commission stripped from me.

Darth Vader Flies

Once again, it was dual check time, and despite the fact that the world was moving away from a Cold War footing, it was decided to combine my check with a flight wearing the dreaded AR5. My protests once again fell on deaf ears, and I found myself ready to go through the full donning process. A small crowd had gathered as the AR5 procedure had a macabre feel about it, almost like I was headed to the gallows. As the hood went over my head, I was encased in my rubber tomb and breathed in like Darth Vader awakening for the first time. I was sweating gallons just with the anxiety of wearing it, but the smell of the rubber and the claustrophobic feeling sent my glands into overdrive.

The odd thing is that once I was in the cockpit, it was a lot better. I sweated like a pig anyway when flying (ah, the glamorous life of the fighter pilot), so this was no different. It was the thirty minutes of donning faff either side of the flight that was the nightmare. All told, I flew for almost two hours with the Boss in the boot. I flew as well with the AR5 on as without, and my lookout and other functions were not adversely affected. I couldn't wait to get it off afterwards though. There was an even bigger crowd there to watch my doffing procedure. The full pint of sweat that collected in the rubber neck seal always drew a few 'oohs' and 'aahs' as it spilled on the floor. I must have smelled like the Devil himself after that trip, and there was a large exclusion zone around me until I hopped in the shower and changed all my clothes.

Now that word was out that the Phantom was for the scrap heap, everybody wanted to have some sort of association with the old girl. Battle Flight was the hottest ticket in town, with visits all day long. Bungle and I even had to stage a full-on scramble for one senior navy officer, but at least it got our pictures in the paper. The station even continued with operational days where we surged four or five waves per day and a couple more at night, launching every aircraft that could fly. It certainly didn't feel like we were on a wind down.

No. 92 Squadron had been tasked to help the USAF F16 units at Ramstein evaluate their new air-to-air missile—the AMRAAM. If we fired a Skyflash or Sparrow, we would have to keep the radar locked to the target in order to support the missile all the way to impact. This would mean we needed to keep pointing at the target, which would make us vulnerable to their weapons, and we would still be getting closer to the target all the time we were supporting it. We would minimise that closure by turning hard after missile launch to put the target on the edge of the scope, but it was still a tricky situation to be in.

AMRAAM was an active missile. At a certain distance from its target after firing, AMRAAM had its own radar and could support itself, meaning the host fighter could turn around and run away. This 'fire and forget' ability would revolutionise air-to-air tactics in the near future. Actually, the F14 had had this capability for some time with the Phoenix missile, but AMRAAM was light years ahead in terms of manoeuvrability and speed. It was also awesome in close quarter combat.

I was flying with Bungle again (he must have been sick of me by now) and we punted off as a four-ship to meet up somewhere in southern German airspace with the F16s. What happened then was possibly the most boring forty-five minutes I have ever spent in a Phantom. We did about four splits, presenting them with the canned formations they had asked for, and within ten seconds of the 'fight's on' call, they had declared us all dead. We knew AMRAAM was good, but it wasn't a flaming death ray.

On the last split, we were all a bit pissed off and tried a confusion tactic, but the F16 Leader just knocked it off before we got inside 30 miles—what a complete waste of gas. This went on all week apparently, but thank God I wasn't on any more of those trips. Everyone was getting frustrated, so at the start of the second week, we were supposed to provide two targets for their four-ship but we launched three instead and sent one down to low-level to sneak in unseen. Those guys shot the shit out of them while the F16s were looking at the pretty pictures on radar.

92 MiG-Killer Squadron

We all needed a bit of a blowout and that came in the form of the QWI Pilot's annual tac check. Lola was a cool guy and had managed to cobble together nine aircraft between us and 19, so he briefed up a nine-ship sweep against eight F16s from Beauvechain in Belgium. It was an epic trip over the Ardennes region with seventeen bits of fast-moving metal all trying not to crash into each other, while aiming to get as many kills as possible. I was flying with OCB, and like every other nav, he was working like a one-armed paper hanger to make sense of the radar picture and my shouting whenever I saw an F16.

At the end of the melee, the four 92 Squadron jets landed at Beauvechain for the night and we were hosted by 349 Squadron of the Belgian Air Force. What we didn't realise was that the Belgians wanted to do another trip with us in the afternoon and finish it with a mixed-fleet flypast of F16s and F4s. I thought this was bordering on illegal without permission from HQ RAFG, but OCB shrugged his shoulders and authorised it anyway. What were they going to do to us if they found out—scrap our aeroplane?

By all accounts, our four-ship of Phantoms looked ultra-cool nestled closely in behind the box of F16s, and we celebrated not crashing and being subsequently court martialled, downtown at the Ambiorix Bar in Leuven, where all the local fighter crews drank. It was a big, big night. We were staying at a really nice hotel from what I recall, and Harry (who had fully recovered from his ejection in Cyprus) took his chances, sharing a room with me again. His bad experience in Berlin had obviously been forgotten. True to form though, he trapped off with a local girl in the bar, and I had the room to myself all night.

Breakfast was a quiet affair. Out of the eight of us, only myself and OCB made it and were on time for the bus. Don't get me wrong, I am not speaking myself up here. I only made it because I was flying with the flight commander and it would have been an uncomfortable trip home if I had been late. OCB was fuming, and as the ranking officer, he was in charge and proceeded to bollock everyone as they shuffled down to reception after he had sent me on an errand to wake everyone up.

I still hadn't found Harry, and to this day, I have never forgotten the look on OCB's face as Harry sauntered into the hotel, having been dropped off by his latest squeeze, to find everyone in flying kit, ready to board the bus. He was like the Flash going to our room and getting changed in double-quick time. We were supposed to run a 4 *v*. 4 against 349 on the way home to Wildenrath, but they had retired hurt so Lola briefed up a standard 2 *v*. 2, but no one's heart was in it. We floated past each other a couple of times with no turning or burning before tiredly making our way back home.

I just wanted to stick it on the ground and be done for the weekend, but our bastard drag chute failed on landing, so I dumped it and blasted back airborne into the circuit. This would mean a cable engagement, but because we had only floated around for the past hour, we were still fat on gas, so I had to spend another thirty minutes or so, burning off enough fuel so that we were light enough to take the cable. This did nothing for OCB's mood, and the other six guys in the formation took the sensible option of buggering off home before we landed.

A couple of weeks later, I managed to claim a bit of fleeting celebrity quite by accident. One of the by-products of German reunification was that the GAF got their hands on the East German MiG-29 Fulcrums. The Fulcrum and the Su27 Flanker had been demonstrated at various air shows by the Russians and had pretty much put the shits up the West. Russia had traditionally built crappy unsophisticated aircraft in bulk, sticking to Stalin's mantra that 'quantity has a quality all its own'. Up to this point then, we didn't really sweat about any of their aircraft, even in a Phantom.

Fulcrum and Flanker were game changers, though. They came with outrageous manoeuvrability and scary weapons. These aircraft were thought to be on a par with F15s and F18s. The GAF was just getting to grips with the MiG-29, and it became apparent very quickly that they were an ergonomic nightmare, and the workload for the single pilot was off the charts. However, it was still a very potent machine and once again, 92 Squadron was selected to take part in some trials against them. They went for it straight away, asking us to run a four-ship through their two-ship low-level CAP, up north near the Peheim mast, which was a standard CAP in northern Germany.

It was Bungle and I crewed together again, and we were Number 4, so wingman of the second pair. The weather was dogshit bad, but we managed to pick our way through to the CAP and Bungle got the MiGs straight away. You could hear the excitement in everyone's radio calls as we got closer to seeing the big, scary Russian jet. Bungle was calling the ranges down, but we had pledged not to take any head on shots to give the MiG-29s the best training we could. I could barely see the lead pair in front of us, even though we were only a couple of miles back.

Then, out of the gloom in my 2 o'clock, a big slab of dirty metal turned in front of me to get a shot on our Number 2. I was almost speechless but called it to Bungle as I selected the gun. He locked them up, and I coolly closed in, calling 'Mike-Lima 69, guns on the MiG-29, 10 miles south of the Peheim'. When I say coolly, I actually mean I bawled it out over the radio like some sort of excitable teenager. Oh wow, was I full of myself after that! The next run had us queueing up behind the MiG-29s, all trying to get guns kills and barging each other out of the way. I had been the first though. I was a minor celebrity after the debrief and for days afterwards, everyone answered the crew room phone with '92 MiG killer Squadron. How can I help you?'

Flame Out the Front—Very Bad

Less than a week later, my celebrity status increased, but for all the wrong reasons. Von and I were up against OCA doing supersonic intercepts at night. He was our target, and it was our job to intercept and identify him up at high level above 40,000 feet. Being overland in Germany, we had to maintain above 36,000 feet when supersonic to ensure we didn't blow out everybody's windows in Düsseldorf. OCA separated out by 70 miles to give us space to get up to speed and the fight was on.

I went through the Rutkowski climb profile, which I had learned on the OCU, but as I selected the burners, there was a huge bang and a 15-foot flame came out of the left-hand intake, lighting up the sky.

Rather than take you through the entire engine lecture from the OCU, I can sum up jet engine theory in one sentence—flame out the back, very good; flame out the front, very bad.

The left-hand engine had surged and the turbine temperature was off the top stop—at least 1,000 degrees. I pulled the throttles back to idle and recovered the aircraft to level flight with German air traffic shouting at us for being below 36,000 feet. This was the first time in my life that I called 'mayday', just to shut him up. With the left-hand engine at idle, the turbine was still off the top stop, which meant the surge was locked in and I had to shut the engine down.

By this time, OCA was about 50 miles from us and asked us what had happened. As soon as we told him, he said, 'Right. See you on the ground,' and switched off the frequency without offering any help. We were a bit dumbstruck but cracked on with the drills as we recovered to Wildenrath for an approach end cable engagement. It looked like I had done all of the immediate action drills properly, and Von took me through the follow-on actions from the flight reference cards.

Now, in our defence here, the FRCs were notorious for being badly written, and we were always told in our emergency sims and at the OCU that when we got to the bottom of a card, we should turn over onto the next one and do that drill if appropriate. 'If appropriate' is the key phrase, of course. So, we finished the card and Von turned over the next card, which was all about relighting the engine. I tried to relight it and it just got to 20 per cent. Then there was another bang and it seized on us. I shut it back down, and we took the cable at Wildenrath. Hurrah—what a pair of heroes bringing this sick aeroplane back home safely. I was just writing up the safety signal afterwards when OCA walked up and asked me to take him through our actions. When I got to the bit where we relit the engine, he stopped me and asked, 'You did what?'

'Tried to relight the engine, Sir, but it wouldn't relight.'

'What was the turbine temperature?'

'Oh, 1,000 degrees, Sir.'

'And you tried to relight that engine?' Note that I am not seeing the approaching steam train that is about to hit me in the face.

'Yes, Sir, but it wouldn't relight.'

'Of course it wouldn't relight, you idiot; it had cooked itself to death!'

I was a bit agape then, having gone from hero to zero in the space of a few seconds. It was at this point that one of the ground crew came in and asked us to come out to the HAS. When we got there, all I saw was a couple of guys stiff-arming the turbine blades into a hessian sack from out of the jet pipe where we had blown them during the relight. There was a similar operation going on in the left-hand intake, where it looked like the compressor blades had parted company with the spool also.

Now, I had done jet engine theory three times in my life—on the Jet Provost, the Hawk, and, most recently, on the Phantom OCU. Each time, I had been told to leave an engine well alone when the turbine had got to those temperatures and definitely don't try to relight it. However, as learn, exam, dump, go flying was my usual MO, I had forgotten all of that. When we had the initial surge, we probably lost one blade or maybe a part of a blade. By relighting, I had pretty much stripped both the compressor and the turbine spools of all of their blades. I don't know for definite, but I would guess it was about £250,000 down the drain. Guess how popular I was after that? It was a funny thing too—my next sim with the Beast seemed to be wall-to-wall engine surges.

Iceland

My last three months on 92 before it folded were a whirlwind of parties and varied flying experiences. I took part in my first Diamond 9 flypast for an official visit to Wildenrath by some arbitrary senior officer. Prior to this, I had always missed the flypasts as I was usually in the parade as the squadron standard bearer. The Boss had taken pity on me, probably following the Battle of Britain parade in London, and dicked the junior nav to take it on until the end.

What a hoot it was being in a Diamond 9—proper Red Arrows stuff, but in a mean-looking fighter jet. I flew sorties against Harriers (beat them), Tornado F3s (beat them) and F18s (okay, let's not talk about how ugly that was). I also managed to fit in a couple of Rangers too. The first was to Keflavík in Iceland. OCB had been offered a posting to the USAF F15 base there as the RAF liaison officer and was given a couple of jets to go up there and check it out for a weekend.

The station commander wanted to go as a final jolly, so he led the pair with OCB. I was asked to go in the second jet with the NRL—so, one group captain, two squadron leaders, and Flying Officer Wilson. My role was obviously going to be bag carrier and general dogsbody, but I hadn't been to Iceland before so I was just happy to be included. The plan was to transit to Kinloss in northern Scotland for a refuel, then press out over the North Sea to Keflavik. Both trips would see us struggling for gas with the second trip needing us to call Keflavik to get their latest weather while airborne and make a decision whether to press or turn around. There was a point of no return, so if the weather was dodgy, it would be squeaky bum time.

On the first leg, we dropped into RAF Linton-on-Ouse for a flypast. Linton was one of the basic flying training schools, and graduation days were very special with lots of flypasts. The station commander had briefed me 'not to go below' him. Actually, going below him was a physical impossibility as he scraped his belly along the flight line with me flying in a loose formation just a little bit higher. We had plenty of time transiting to Kinloss to let the adrenaline settle, then it was a swift refuel and a check of the weather. The weather at Kef was shit (of course it was) with poor visibility in snowstorms.

I only had a white instrument rating, meaning I had to add 200 feet to my decision height on radar talkdown. I didn't have enough hours for a green rating, which would have meant a DH of 200 feet. I was unlikely to be out of cloud at 400 feet according to the forecast, so it was looking like the NRL and I would have to go home to Wildenrath. 'Let's give it a go, Tug,' the station commander said. His logic was that the weather at Kef was notoriously changeable, and if it was okay when we called up, he was happy for me to take a stab.

We got past the point of no return without getting any radio contact with Kef. When we finally got in touch, it seemed the weather was much worse as the snowstorm had thickened. This left us poorly placed, but me in particular. The station commander's plan was to send me down first to check it out, so off we went. By this time, it was dark and the snow was lit up by my landing lamp during the talk down and seemed to be shooting into our faces. The turbulence was horrific, and the NRL and I came to an accord that I would fly down to green limits.

There was no sign of the ground at 400 feet, but a few seconds later, I saw some of the approach lights followed by a snow-strewn runway. I plonked us down firmly and let the jet slow itself down, shit scared that the brakes would make us skid. The NRL made a quick call to the others that we were down, thereby simultaneously telling them it was okay, and that the group captain was under pressure to match the flying officer's skill or blind luck (delete as appropriate). I fully expected it to be me putting both jets to bed in the snow and sleet while the senior officers did whatever senior officers did in those circumstances, but got a pleasant surprise when all four of us got pissed wet through putting on all the covers and bungs. The incumbent RAF liaison officer picked us up and took us to the US officers' club for a few beers and a bit of food before sorting us out some rooms and a vehicle for the weekend.

The next day, we explored Iceland to give OCB a taste of what was to come on his next tour. From what I could see, there was going to be lots of waterfalls. My God did we see waterfalls, and they were all spectacular. We were driving around on volcanic ash and dirt roads. Well, when I say driving, I mean rallying. The station commander wanted to drive and who were we to argue?

As soon as he got behind the wheel, his inner racing driver came out, and we skidded and slipped our way around the island searching for hot geysers and more waterfalls. The landscape was other-worldly, and there was a constant stream of steam bubbling up through the ground wherever we went in the countryside.

It was all a bit odd being on a Ranger and not being totally drunk, but food and booze were eye-wateringly expensive so we couldn't actually afford to go on a bender. For once then, I was able to appreciate everything we did without the spectre of a splitting hangover headache. Of course, we went for a swim in the Blue Lagoon and that didn't seem real either. It was snowing hard, but there we were, in the crystal-blue hot water of the natural spring, not believing the place existed.

When we took the hire car back on the Sunday evening, it looked like it had been driven through a pigsty that was inside a muddy hole and was full of shit. Once again, as the only flying officer, I was expecting to be the sad sap who had to clean it. Once again though, I was taken by surprise as the station commander picked up the jet hose and proceeded to give the car a wash down.

It struck me at this point, what a special brotherhood this aircraft engendered. Of course, there was a rank structure, but these three senior officers were no different from me. We were Phantom aircrew—a special club that only a few got to join, and a club that was going to be taken away from us in little over a year.

I wanted as many experiences in this aeroplane in the short time I had left on it, so before launching from Kef back to Kinloss, I asked if we had enough gas to go north so I could fly inside the Arctic Circle for a minute or so. It was a bit touch-and-go on fuel, but we did it anyway, and as the NRL called to me that the INAS had us north of the required latitude, I was buzzing and took a photo of the random bit of ground we were over before heading back towards Scotland. To tell the truth, the INAS could have been in the bloody Maldives for all I knew, but I like to think we were in the Arctic Circle.

TDPU

I amassed almost 100 hours in my last three months on 92 and quite a few of those trips were with Bobby. This was handy as we were both heading to 56 later that summer, and we formed a strong bond that would become unbreakable in the fire of some of the initial animosity we would face on our new squadron. My final hoo-hah was a three-ship Ranger to Cyprus for five nights. I was crewed with Von for the whole trip, and the other pilots were OCA, who was the duty adult, and Lurch.

The well-worn turn through Sig was almost a cookie-cutter for us now, as was the walk from Animal House to the mess bar and the inevitable jugs of brandy sour. As this was an extended Ranger, we flew a couple of local intercept sorties either side of the weekend and made a point of doing a few circuits at the end, to lay down some final 92 Squadron Phantom noise on the airfield. One of the jets went unserviceable on the Monday, so OCA stayed behind (being the only authoriser and air test pilot), and Von and I led the pair home.

Akrotiri mess had helpfully made us packed lunches to eat in the air, and as soon as we got to transit height on the way to Sig, I tried to put the autopilot in so I could eat. For some reason, the autopilot was in a mood and kept cutting out, forcing the aircraft to buck a little until I took control. It took about four attempts to get it settled, and once it looked stable, I opened my packed lunch. First up was a hard-boiled egg (shell on), which, with the best will in the world, is not something you can, or even should eat in a fast jet cockpit; it should be against the law.

I thought I would give the sandwich a go. The mess had cut my sandwich into about sixteen handy bitesize pieces, but had wrapped it in about three metres of clingfilm and it took me a minute or two to unwrap it. At last, I made it through the plastic and balanced my sandwich on the pocket of my g-pants while I secured the devil's boiled egg back into the box.

Right at that moment, the autopilot had a fit and bucked my bitesize sandwich pieces all over the cockpit floor. I had a small moment of 'for fuck's sake' before trying to pick it all up and salvage the least oily ones to eat on the ground at Sig. The final straw turned out to be the drink sachet. Von was already pissing himself laughing at my misfortune when I stabbed my straw into the sachet to see the orange squash spurt out over my g-pants and flying suit. Yes, I know I should have had the straw in my mouth to catch the juice, knowing about the effects of the reduced pressure in the cockpit, but I was in such a kerfuffle over the sandwich that it slipped my mind. So, lunch was a bust and I spent the rest of the trip slagging off the autopilot.

We arrived back at Wildenrath in time for disbandment party season. It seemed that every night in June had some sort of social event, with the weekends being epic and, in a couple of cases, extremely dangerous. The season kicked off with our formal end of 92 dining-in night. The mess was being refurbished (that will become relevant later), so we held the dinner at a private restaurant just over the Dutch border. In essence, we were all being dined out so the Boss made the only speech and we were all presented with a glass-bottomed tankard full of Dort. As one, we rose to our feet and downed the frothy brew in one to discover the Squadron crest etched into the glass at the bottom of the tankard.

The next night saw us hosting a tactical discussion and procedures update (TDPU). That sounds very professional until you realise that TDPU actually stands for 'thinly disguised piss up'. Basically, this was a huge boozy party at the HAS site. We had invited every fighter squadron in the European arena to come and celebrate our demise, and they turned up in droves—tons of F16s, F18s, GAF F4Fs, and even a couple of F15s pitched up for a summer's afternoon and evening of drinking and generally larking about.

Earlier in the afternoon, the Kid and I had diverted into Hopsten (German F4F base) with a single engine failure and were in danger of missing the fun. Next thing though, an Army Air Corps Gazelle helicopter pitched up to give us a lift home. As soon as we had called or emergency, Wildenrath had scrambled a chopper to 'rescue' us, and we flew home in style (slowly), arriving at the HAS site just in time for the first beer.

Even today, I am unsure what went on that night, but some of it was captured on film and I have a few hazy memories. Obviously, there was a shitload of beer and Apfelkorn as well as some classic German drunk food—lots of bratwurst in bread rolls, etc. Then things took an odd turn when Scooby turned up in his old VW Beetle, which he had painted up in 92 Squadron colours. A competition ensued where teams of three had to down a beer each in turn, climb in the Beetle, and race off around a course on the HAS site. On returning to the HAS, we all had to pile out and drink another beer. It was all timed, with the fastest team winning bugger all as far as I could tell. So, the cream of Europe's fighter crews were yamming beer down and then haring around a HAS site full of aeroplanes and people before spearing back towards a HAS chock full of more people. The madness is obvious now, but thank God this only lasted about four iterations before a Canadian F18 guy murdered the clutch (he had only ever driven automatic before) and brought the whole sorry thing to an end before someone got hurt.

What to do with a dead car then? Of course—burn it. We set about it with sledgehammers, which were only there as part of another competition to destroy and burn some pianos, and then someone set fire to the fuel and up she went. The fire section had been pre-warned and had a couple of engines on site. Once the fire really took hold, they decided enough was enough and turned the hoses on. Unfortunately, the VW Beetle had a magnesium alloy engine block and the water, fire and magnesium combo gave off a startling white light that perpetuated the fire. For some reason, we thought this was the perfect time to sing 'The Flag'. To my eternal embarrassment, I am on film, holding a sledgehammer and singing 'The Flag' to a burning car. The car eventually burned itself out and we all toddled off to bed.

The next week, I was due to fly with Bobby on the first wave of the day, and I arrived at work to see an all-blue Phantom in one of the revetments. The Boss had got permission from RAFG to paint up XV408 blue in tribute to the 92 Squadron Blue Diamonds. Before the Red Arrows came into being, some front-line squadrons would do formation aerobatics at air shows, and 92 Squadron's Hunters had been painted blue and became the 'Blue Diamonds'. As we were disbanding, it was seen as a nice thing for us to have a blue jet again. It looked bloody awesome, and the yellow cobra and red maple leaves on the tail stood out as a work of art against the blue.

I was leading the first sortie, so I asked if we could have it for its first trip in that livery. The answer was yes, and what made it even cooler was that RAFG agreed we could have our own callsign of Mike-Lima 92 for it. We were working with some Belgique F16s over the Ardennes, but got almost nothing productive done as everyone just wanted to formate on us and tell us how cool we looked.

The Night We Brought the House Down

I was starting to pack up my kit ready for my move to Wattisham, and we also had to start packing up the squadron kit and memorabilia. Once we were disbanded, all of our squadron stuff would be stored away just in case our number was resurrected at a later date. This included the squadron silver, our stuffed cobras, and our beautiful deep red leather armchairs that dominated our crew room.

Not everything warranted a place in storage, so the Boss held an auction one day of lots of things hanging around ops and the crew room. The proceeds would go into the squadron fund and fuel some of the upcoming parties. There were two things I had to have. First was the ops room wall clock. This was a cheap, shitty, plastic, battery-powered clock that has a bright yellow border round it. I was amazed that I was the only one who wanted it so got it for my opening bid of DM20. By the way, it is still on my kitchen wall nearly thirty years later as I write this.

My second target was way more popular. I was desperate to get the 92 Squadron tea mug with 'Battleflight Pilot' written on it. This was the pilot's mug that sat in the Battle Flight shed and had been used by decades' worth of Phantom pilots before me. After a few minutes of bidding, there was only me and Harry in it. Bid and counter bid went on, but my last bid of DM100 finally secured it. To this day, it is one of my most prized possessions and nobody is allowed to use it just in case it gets damaged.

The last few weeks of a disbanding squadron is an odd time. There is a ton of ceremonial stuff such as disbandment parades and the laying up of the squadron standard, formation flypasts, and parties—all of which are carried out under a cloud of resignation that everything is about to come to an end that no one wants. The RAF had decided to celebrate its participation in the Gulf War with a huge flypast over Buckingham Palace. The flypast would include every aircraft type involved in the conflict and our part (in conjunction with 19 Squadron) was to provide a four-ship of Phantoms that would join with twelve Tornado F3s for a Diamond 16 formation. This would necessitate a bit of practicing, so we deployed to RAF Coningsby in Lincolnshire for a week of flypast practice.

It was odd being in a F3 crew room knowing these guys (a lot of whom were ex-Phantom) were going to replace us and our brilliant jet. The F3 was still suffering from its bad rep of poor performance and crappy radar, but the banter was good between us and there was some gentle competition over which aircraft looked better in formation.

Our four-ship was at the back of the diamond, slotting in as a neat box when the twelve F3s had got together. I was Number 2 of our box so concentrated fully on our leader as he moved into his box position right in the middle. OCB, in my boot, kept a lookout outside of the formation and on the F3s around us. I was acutely aware of the mass of metal surrounding me as we manoeuvred about the sky. The F3 looked okay up close but nowhere near as mean or cool as our jets. I can't say I was relaxed in the formation, but I was way more competent than when I first flew formation with Coops on the OCU, and was now able to take in fully the sheer pleasure of the event.

A spare F3 was barrel-rolling around the formation, calling various aircraft numbers with advice on closing up or slackening off. This aircraft was called 'The Whip' or 'Whipper-in' and it was a great gig to get on. The Whip ensured the formation looked as good as possible. The Whip had no pressure to fly formation, got to see the formation up close, and offered helpful hints like 'Number 4: 3 feet forwards.'

Number 4 would then say 'copied' on the radio and move forwards. We all knew that in the cockpit of Number 4, the pilot would be shouting to himself, 'Screw you, whip! Try doing my fucking job! 3 feet for God's sake!' After the practice, we would split into four-ships to recover back to Coningsby, and all came into the circuit in echelon four to break and land in turn. There were at least thirty-two people in the debrief from the aircraft, plus a number of authorisers/supervisors and various hangers-on. It was all very pleasant with no major points, and we were just about to split when a video cassette was delivered to the debrief.

The formation leader had arranged for the station photographer to video our four-ship arrivals in the circuit without us knowing. His four-ship looked good, but the next one was a little 'bouncy'. The last bunch of F3s was ropey at best with Number 4 playing catch up to get into position in time for the break (and failing), and then it was our turn. We were rock solid and looked immaculate, so held the bragging rights in the bar that night.

The next practice that week went just as well, and we were looking forward to showing off over Buckingham Palace. However, on the day of the flypast, the weather closed in, and after all that, we were cancelled. As we made our way back to Wildenrath, a six-ship of Tornado GR1s had fought their way through the dodgy weather and completed a flypast over the queen. In the end, I figured this was actually the best outcome—the GR1 boys had done the lion's share of bombing in Iraq and had been shot at and lost a number of their crews, either killed or taken hostage, so they deserved to have the whole spotlight on them.

Happy hour that week in the bar was interesting to say the least. In true RAF style, Wildenrath's closure announcement had coincided with lots of infrastructure expenditure that included refurbishing the bar. The contracts had already been agreed and let, so the work went ahead regardless. The cost was nothing in comparison to the new hardened pilot briefing facility that was being built on our dispersal, that would always sit empty with no squadron to live in it. The bar had some beautiful new wood panelling including a suspended wooden ceiling. A few beers in and no one took any notice of the finer details—it was just the bar to us.

Singing broke out as normal, and culminated in one of the 19 Squadron boys climbing onto a table to sing, 'One man on the table!' This quickly escalated into two, three, four, seven, nine men on the table. Just as it looked like the table had reached full capacity, Lurch reached up to the ceiling to steady himself and found that the roof panels lifted up. The next thing I saw, he had pulled himself up into the roof space and disappeared, only to reappear over by the bar. Upside down, he poked his head through the lifted panel and shouted, 'One man on the bar!'

What happened next was carnage. Like a herd of rats, various aircrew clambered into the roof space to follow him to the bar. Unfortunately, whereas Lurch had crawled along the joists, the rats just piled across the panels. There was a huge bang; all the lights and electrics went off; and about a dozen aircrew fell from the ceiling onto the bar floor amid shattered pieces of polished wood. There was a moment of silence and then a bit of moaning and groaning started up. Someone had the wherewithal to call the med centre to get some ambulances over.

Plop had tried to arrest his descent by grabbing one of the long screws holding the roof joists in place, but his hand had slid down the screw, cutting through to the bones of his finger joints. He was lucky compared to Jaho though. Jaho was a young student pilot holding with the squadron, having completed his basic flying training. He had held for over a year waiting for a multi-engine course, and his date had just come through. He seemed to be moaning a lot more than everyone else, and when we finally found him under a pile of wood and people, it seemed that both of his wrists were pointing the wrong way—poor bastard.

OC Ops, who was still the PMC, went mental. Both squadron bosses were pretty sanguine about it and kept all the shit off us, and we divided up the repair bill between the forty or so of us that were in the bar. My last operational trip on 92 was a four-ship lead with OCB in the blue jet. It was a standard trip down at low-level, but included us pulling up in the middle to tank from a VC10. The VC10 was packed full of military and amateur photographers, all desperate to get pictures of our beautiful bird. I was presented with some of the pictures afterwards, and they were breath-taking.

No. 92 had been de-declared to NATO, so that Friday, the Boss held a post-happy hour party at his house. It was a bit of a sombre mood, and at midnight, we all removed our op badges and put them in our pockets. It was right then that a majority of us agreed to always carry that badge with us for the rest of our days. If you were called out on it and failed to present it, you would have to yam whatever you were holding—some of us still do that to this day.

2, 3, 4, 5, 6, 7, 8, 9

The final days of flying arrived for 92 Squadron in the first week of July 1991—two trips of Diamond 9 flypast practice ending with a final Diamond 9 over the top of our disbandment parade. OCA was leading the nine-ship as the Boss was taking the parade, and we had a couple of spare jets borrowed from 19 Squadron.

The first practice saw us floating around to the south, near to Aachen. OCA had briefed that he wanted to get a feel of how much he could manoeuvre the formation so was planning to wind the turns up a little. I was Number 3 so formating on his left wing. As soon as we formed up and the Whip got us into position, OCA called that he was going to start manoeuvring. Rather than wind it up gently, he seemed to snap on 60 degrees of bank (I'm sure it wasn't as much as that, but that's what it felt like) and there was a bomb burst of Phantoms all over the North German Plain.

By the time OCA rolled out, there was only me and Harry (who was in the Number 2 position on OCA's right wing) left in formation. Those positions were the easiest to fly so we should have been able to hang in there, but it was touch and go I can tell you! OCA called everyone back into Diamond 9 and the clipped replies of 'two', 'three', 'four', 'five', 'six', 'seven', 'eight', and 'nine' spoke volumes about the profanities that were no doubt being thrown around in the eight aircraft behind him.

The rest of the trip saw us manoeuvring more gently and then raging through the German low-level system as a big ten-ship fighter sweep. We did the same thing the next day, but included a dummy flypast at Wildenrath to check timings (all done visually with a stopwatch, map, and compass as there was no GPS in those days).

Two days later, 5 July 1991, was the last day the Phantom flew on 92 Squadron—the final Diamond 9 flypast over the disbandment parade. The flypast was an amazing experience, but tinged horribly with great sadness. After we flew over the parade ground, about seven or eight of the formation flew on to Wattisham to deliver the jets to 56 Squadron, and I and a couple of other jets landed back on at Wildenrath, and taxied into Delta Dispersal for the very last time. I was absolutely gutted as I shut down and shook hands with the ground crew. The dispersal and squadron buildings were practically deserted, and spoke of what was to come when the whole station would close in a year's time.

Apparently, the guys who arrived at Wattisham beat the crap out of the place before jumping onto a Herc that brought them back for the disbandment party. We had a few days' grace before we went our separate ways to pastures new. The Boss had been posted to be the personal staff officer to the commander in chief RAF Germany. It was a huge step up on his career ladder, but the CinC had a bad reputation for being as mad as a box of frogs and not a particularly nice guy. He had called the Boss in for an interview on day one, and asked him how he saw his career progressing. When the Boss explained he was planning to leave the RAF and fly for the airlines at the end of this PSO tour, the CinC told him to clear his desk immediately and get out. We all thought the Boss was awesome anyway, but this sent his credibility supersonic as far as we were concerned. His reasoning was that being the Boss of a fighter squadron couldn't be topped, so it was time to leave and try something else.

4

56 Squadron, RAF Wattisham

Permission to Join Your Squadron, Sir?

I was the first of the 92 boys to make it across the channel to Blighty. I arrived at Wattisham in leafy Suffolk somewhere in the middle of July 1991. My brand-new car was full of all my worldly possessions, which didn't really amount to much beyond uniforms, flying kit, and my stereo stack. I had deliberately arrived on a Friday in the hope that I could check-in with my new Boss, attend one-liners at the end of flying, and then share a drink or two with my new squadron mates at happy hour. I checked into my room in the mess, which was a little depressing. I had been a front-line fighter pilot for two years at this point, living in my own rented house in a German village (apart from the odd night in the back of Van Morrison), yet here I was, in a small single room in an old mess, with none of my mates around me. I unpacked a flying suit, found a plain-coloured wings name badge to put on, and headed off for 56.

No. 56 was a typical UK fighter squadron HAS site—large 'tunnel' style HASs dispersed around a central PBF (the 'hard') exactly like the one they were building at 92 Squadron, and next to that, the 'soft' set of offices and crew room. I knocked on the Boss's door, which was open, and walked in. I lobbed up my smartest salute and said, 'Hello, Sir. My name is Tug Wilson. Permission to join your squadron.' I figured a bit of old-fashioned Battle of Britain-style manners would go down well, and I was right.

The Boss broke into a big grin and replied, 'Permission granted, Tug,' and that began a lifelong friendship there and then. He was incredibly cool and laid back, and I would later find out that he was sharp as shit in the air too. After a quick chat, I got up to leave and bumped into my new flight commander. Klaxon was OCA Flight—a shortish, bullet-headed man with an outrageous moustache. Oh, and he was completely mad. He seemed pretty pleasant, so my spirits were recovering as I entered the hard to see who was around. The place was quiet for a big squadron, but I met a few faces I knew vaguely, plus Lifford from 92 and Fat Billy, who was now the QWI nav since the OCU had folded. There were also a couple of guys I had gone through officer training with.

I was quite happy at this stage until two of the other guys I didn't know asked me when Bobby was pitching up. He had to move into a married quarter, so it was going to be a week or so after me. 'Tell him he needn't bother, as he is going to get chopped as soon as he gets here.' To start with, I thought that, as a joke, it was in pretty poor taste. When I saw that they were serious, it really put my back up. I started to defend Bobby, but these bastards dug in and the whole thing got a bit ugly. I asked how they planned to chop someone who had been operational for years and was an eight-ship leader, especially when one of these idiots had just made pairs lead.

This was the first time (but by no means the last) that I was told, 'You're not in 2 ATAF now.' My initial euphoria at meeting the Boss and Klaxon was fading a bit as these dickheads showed they resented us moving back *en masse*. Suffice it to say, they were the two who didn't show their faces at happy hour, but the good bunch of lads that did initiated me into the Firebirds with the arrival drink—the Green Lemonade. As I have already said, I think it was half a pint of all of the white spirits with a shot of crème de menthe to add the colour. Anyway, down it went, and then down I went about an hour later as the booze did its thing and knocked me out. I had the weekend to recover and a couple of days of admin and officially arriving on Station, before my first trip on 17 July. By this time, Lurch had arrived from Germany, and Bobby was in transit. A couple of the guys going to 74 had also arrived.

LAAAAHHHDS!

My arrival dual check ride was with Sniper, the squadron QFI. Sniper was an ironic nickname as he was supposedly a bit of a tactical desert and had a few detractors on the squadron. I loved flying with him though. He couldn't tell me enough about operating in the UK and it was almost like the trip wasn't long enough for him to impart all the knowledge he wanted to. Even though it was a dual check and therefore an assessed ride, it was a joy to fly with him. We bashed the circuit a few times at the end and then I plonked it down and taxied back to the HAS site.

Even things as simple as shutdown were complicated by my unfamiliarity with the 56 Squadron procedures, but I was still only twenty-six and would be able to pick it up quickly enough. Later that day, I had a quick blast up to RAF Leeming in North Yorkshire with Stanley in the boot (a young nav I had never heard of up to that point; I don't think he had heard of me either) for an overnight to make a jet swap with a mini detachment up there. Once we got back the next day, it was an early stack for a long weekend. Come happy hour on the next day, Bobby and all of the other remaining 92 Squadron guys who were joining 74 had arrived and the bar went mental.

There seemed to be a real split among the established Wattisham guys with most looking pleased to see us, but a few from across both squadrons were somewhat hostile towards us. Unfortunately, human nature being what it is on a fighter squadron, we tended to concentrate on the hostile and try to sort it out. We did this by buying rounds of some sort of red and white shots and passing them around the bar before shouting, 'Is there a Firebird in the house?!' Our mates who had joined 74 did the same with a black and yellow concoction ('Is there a Tiger in the house?!'). It mostly went down well, especially with both bosses.

We thought we had broken down a few barriers until just after Bobby's round when Tikit, one of our new colleagues on 56 walked up to him and said, in all seriousness, 'You're not making any friends here tonight with that behaviour you know,' and walked away. We were speechless—for a couple of seconds—and then all of us ex-92 boys got together and swapped a couple of stories of some of the animosity we had witnessed in only a few days at Wattisham. All of the good experiences were forgotten in a heartbeat, and we drunkenly moaned about our fate as that was the easiest thing to do.

Our perceived slights took on an unnatural form, and we loosely agreed to stick together and kick against them whenever we could. After all, we were Cobras—rah rah rah and rally round the flag boys! It was all immensely childish and mostly without good reason, but these are the things that drunk people find important. At some point in the evening, one of us, and I can't remember who, shouted from the bar, 'Lads! What do you want to drink?' He couldn't get our attention so shouted again, 'LAAAHHHDS!'

We all stopped and mimicked 'LAAAAHHHDS!' back to him, and it seemed to stick. So began our ex-92 rallying cry whenever we were in the bar. As soon as one of us walked into the bar in the future, the assembled group (even if it was just one of us) would shout 'LAAAAHHHDS!' and would get an immediate reply. It certainly wasn't helping to get the few tossers from both squadrons who resented us on board, but we didn't give a shit. Those few guys were rarely in the bar anyway. My next two trips showed the dichotomy we faced in those early days at Wattisham.

You Do Your Job, and I'll Do Mine, Okay?

I had a night dual check with Sniper first. I hadn't flown at night for four months so was woefully out of currency and practice. I was still a little bit out of my comfort zone flying out of a new dispersal with slightly different procedures, and this was exacerbated by the dark. We blasted airborne, and Sniper put me through my paces with single-engine approaches and lots of instrument flying before asking me to join the circuit for some circuits. I broke downwind for the first one and carried out the pre-landers. End of downwind, I seemed to be set up nicely to tip into finals, take full flap, and pull to the doughnut. Then, everything disappeared in the dark.

I was trying to fly it visually but had no idea what I was looking for as I had never seen Wattisham in the dark. My best bet would have been to trust the procedure and keep nineteen units on, but my confusion led to me easing off the alpha and flying through the centreline. I called, 'Going around,' and overshot. 'Sorry about that, Sir,' I said to Sniper, but he was ultra-cool about it. He remained ultra-cool when I did exactly the same thing next time around as well. I was really pissed with myself now and my anger must have translated onto the controls as I overshot.

'I'd just make your circuit a bit wider if I was you, Tug,' said Sniper, so that was what I did. The next three circuits were good and I landed off the last one. I was furious with myself. I was an operational fighter pilot yet I couldn't fly a night circuit or so it seemed. Sniper was brilliant in the debrief. He went through the whole mission patting me on the back and then said, 'I tell you what though, Tug. There was a moment when I thought you weren't going to get it in there.' It was just the right amount of criticism but delivered with a small smile to add a touch of banter. He knew I was beating myself up already.

'Me too, Sir,' I sighed.

'Ah well. You haven't been up at night for ages so that's what that was all about.' Sniper's kudos went through the roof with me right then.

A couple of days later came the counterpoint to that trip with Sniper. I was due to fly a work-up intercept trip with Fat Billy. He had been put in charge of our work-ups to get us UK operational and had gone mad with it, giving the three of us a thirty-trip convex as if we were just starting our first tour. We felt this was a major snub to our previous experience and were building up for a robust discussion (fight) with him about it.

In the meantime, though, I was flying with him on a 1 *v.* 1 medium and low-level intercept sortie. I had not flown with Fat Billy on the OCU, so this was a new experience for both of us. I led a pairs take-off and we transited out to the play area off the Suffolk coast, doing all the usual radar and weapons checks on the way. This stuff was definitely routine these days, but I always had it in the back of my mind that Harry probably thought that in Cyprus just a few months ago. We set up for the first intercept with us CAPing at about 15,000 feet and our target running in slightly below us. I ran through the weapons checks and turned hot. Neatishead radar called our target, and Billy picked him up in PD at about 10,000 feet. Billy called the contact followed by 'Judy, Judy,' to Neatishead. All looked good until he then said, 'Right Tug. It's your intercept.'

I did a bit of a double take in the front and said, 'What do you mean, Billy?'

'You do the intercept,' he said. He hadn't briefed this at all. It was an old OCU instructor's trick to put young student pilots under pressure, and it really got my back up. I put a bit of left bank on and shouted, 'Come hard right, Billy!'

'What?'

'Come hard right now!'

'I don't have a stick in the back—it's not a twin sticker!'

'Ok, I have control. Tell you what, Billy. You do your job, and I'll do mine, okay? You're not an OCU instructor anymore and I am definitely not a student. Shall we start again?'

The rest of the trip went okay, I think. Fat Billy was a little quiet, but that suited me. He didn't bring it up in the debrief and neither did I. However, it was the trigger for Lurch, Bobby, and I to tackle him about our work-ups. It wasn't a long conversation and consisted mainly of us saying, 'Not doing that,' and crossing out trips with a felt pen on the board.

I think the key moment was when we asked him what 1 *v.* 1 LLOLPIs meant. '1 *v.* 1 low-level overland practice intercepts,' he said. We just laughed and crossed all those trips out. We had spent the last two years (three in Bobby's case) leading four- and eight-ships doing LLOLPIs against anywhere up to sixteen–twenty targets at times, so we were buggered if we were going to a 1 *v.* 1 for Billy. We had no more issues with him after that.

In fact, I flew my next two trips with him and he was great. Both of these trips had us tanking from a Tristar. I hadn't tanked from a Tristar before, and it looked massive when I was directly line astern. The basket was rock solid in the airflow and easy to get in (even for me) with Billy's commentary talking me straight in first time and every time. An eventful week ended with me flying once again with Odo, the German exchange nav. The last time I had flown with him was our last trip on the OCU. He was just as good as ever, but I hoped he had seen an improvement in me over the years since our last flight together.

What If Heaven Should Fall?

The next month was taken up with me getting all of my QRA qualifications up to date, so lots of tanking, a phase three VID check (which I did with Lifford again), and an IRT with Sniper. For the first time in my life, I had enough hours to be green rated on my IRT, meaning I could now fly right down to the published decision heights on instrument approaches without having to add on an extra allowance for being inexperienced or shit.

About this time, our new name badges arrived so it was great to be wearing the squadron colours. Joining a squadron meant buying name badges, squadron patches, op badges (once the op check ride was passed), and a squadron mug with your name on it. As Disney (the pilot who ran the squadron fund) handed out our stuff, he noticed that the squadron patches had been sewn incorrectly. The 56 Squadron patch was a shield shape in red with a white border and a white phoenix rising out of some colourful flames. At the top of it were a big '5' and '6', also in white. The badge company had produced them in the wrong colour and all of the white piping, numbers, and phoenix were in yellow.

Disney was going to send them all back, but I asked if I could have one anyway while the replacements were being made. For the whole of my time on 56, I wore a red and yellow patch rather than the classic red and white. At first, I thought it would be a subtle joke as an homage to 92 Squadron, but once we faced the little bit of animosity, I was damned if I was going to replace it. In the big scheme of things, I doubt anyone noticed, but it made me feel better.

Wearing the uniform and badges is a big thing for me, and 56's badges and motto were very cool indeed. Previously on 92, we used to banter the 56 boys that the phoenix rising out of the flames looked like a chicken in a basket, so that's what they became known as. Well, here I was—a Firebird now. The squadron motto was *'quid si caelum ruat'* (What if Heaven should fall?). This is the second-best motto ever (after 'fight or die' of course). If things get so bad that even Heaven falls, the Firebirds will still be here to pull your sorry arses out of the fire—that's how I interpreted it anyway.

Our crew room was chock full of memorabilia, and for a squadron history nerd like me, it was a treasure trove. Pride of place went to a glass cabinet that had Albert Ball's RFC uniform in it. Albert was a very famous First World War fighter pilot who not only qualified as an ace, but also won the Victoria Cross for bravery. Right there in front of my eyes was his very uniform. It was gobsmacking and very humbling. All of this brought back to earth every time I went around to Bungle's house for dinner, when his six-year-old daughter would taunt me constantly by saying, 'Tug! Is there a chicken in a basket?'

Grim

Looking back, there were some absolute standout moments during my time on 56, and all of them were down to the navs that I flew with.

September 1991 saw me back in Deci and hitting the jackpot by being crewed with Grim. I had met Grim down in the Falklands so already knew he was a quality guy. However, when you fly with someone, you really get to see how special they are.

Grim was an older and much more experienced guy, and like Bungle, he really seemed to get the very best out of me. I absolutely loved flying with him, and he was also bloody amazing in the bar. The other residents at that Deci were a German F4F squadron and a Belgique F16 unit. The first couple of days were looseners to get used to flying clean aeroplanes again. We each got a 1 *v.* 1 doggers trip against someone else off the squadron, and also a 2 *v.* 1 to get comfortable with coordinated fighting as a pair.

Grim and I settled into an easy relationship. He revelled in every shot we took and got just as pissed off as me each time we got shot down. He had an amazing skill of getting my eyes on to the bandits prior to us merging. In those days, my eyesight was shit hot, but I wasn't going to see any other aircraft if I was looking in the wrong piece of airspace. Grim was a master at calling the radar picture to me in such a way that it glued my eyes onto the small specks in the distance. German F4Fs were smoky as hell so that helped too. Actually, Blind Pew could have got tally on them at 10 miles, let alone an experienced fighter crew.

As I wasn't on any work-up for ACM this time, our first big mission came almost straight away—a 4 *v.* 4 against the F16s. The F16 was a world ahead of us in terms of power and turning performance and could pull a 9-G turn but didn't have a long-range shot like our Skyflash. However, this was Deci, and as such, we weren't interested in taking long-range kills. We wanted to get into a turning, burning fight, and see if we could get some kills with the Sidewinder and the gun. The only way we could achieve this would be through some sort of deception manoeuvre and getting in unseen—just like against the F15 and the F14. We would be coordinating as a four-ship and doing all the standard professional stuff we did every day, but deep down, we all knew it would be a knife fight in a telephone box, with eight aeroplanes all fighting hard with the horns out—and hell's bells was it!

There were aeroplanes all over the sky—big lumps of metal flashing past the canopy and all the time, Grim and I handing off responsibility to each other for keeping tally on them. Tons of shots were called over the radio and the range controller calling kills and removing jets from the fight with 'bug out' calls. The whole thing was a high-G sweat fest, and despite it being manic, there was always that underlying professionalism of formations trying to work together and support each other. Somehow, we managed to survive late into the fight (and by late, I mean about two minutes from the initial merge) when an F16 floated in front of my nose. I rocked them outboard, pulled hard with a boot full of left rudder, and switched to Sidewinder. A couple more seconds and I would get the growl, SEAM lock it into a tone, and squeeze off the rocket for a certain kill.

'Break right, Tug!' shouted Grim, and with no argument whatsoever, I kicked in a right boot load of rudder as Grim pumped out chaff and flares. There was another F16 on our tail and he called my eyes on for the tally. We were now 1 *v.* 2 against the 9-G monsters, and despite a valiant effort, we had no chance. I soon heard, 'Tug, you're dead. Bug out east.' That was it for that trip.

The fight hadn't lasted long, as the burner had used the gas in a heartbeat and it was time to go home. We pressed down to Alpha North as an eight-ship, and then split into two four-ship echelons for the flat turn onto finals. The F16s looked awesome ahead of us, and I guessed we looked just as good breaking into the circuit. Making sense of the debrief was almost as hard as flying the trip, as we watched aeroplanes and missiles flashing around on screen and lots of shots being called on the radio. They pulled up the cockpit view of the F16 that had gunned us and we were bang to rights. It wasn't particularly pleasant seeing ourselves in the gunsight. The gun is a very personal weapon, but I suppose the fact that we were up against an F16 that could turn itself inside out compared to us lessened the humiliation a little—nothing that a few beers in the Pig and Tape couldn't rectify. It was Friday after all.

'Dunno, Mate. Fridge Went on Fire'

As with my last visit to Deci, there was a GR1 squadron in residence at the same time. This time, it was 2 Squadron or 14. I forget which, but to be honest, I didn't really care anyway. So, we were hoping for a bit of banter with them and maybe a sing off/drink off. To our horror, they turned up in the Pig and Tape with their smart gear on and were heading out to the local restaurant for a squadron meal on a Friday in Deci!

This did not go over well with us at all and we jeered them as they climbed into the minibuses. A couple of beers later, Lurch called Bobby and I into the bar area, showing us an even more shocking sight. On top of the bomber's fridge was a sign-up sheet for beers and softies. On a deployment like this, if you were on a fighter squadron, you paid about £30 in lira to the ents guy and he stacked the freezer with drinks. It was so stinking hot in Deci that a fridge just wouldn't cut it so we had huge chest freezers to keep the drinks cool. So, you paid your money and then you drank the beer, or you didn't—it was your choice. Everyone was in on the deal like a band of brothers.

Signing up and just paying for what you drank was such an individual and alien concept for us that we couldn't fathom it. So Lurch burned their sign-up sheet, but we didn't think that was enough, so the three of us happened upon the idea that if we filled their freezer up with water, all of their beer would be encased in a block of ice by the time they returned from their romantic meal. Okay, so we didn't really think through the physics of it (we were drunk); or the fact that up to now the freezers hadn't frozen any of the drinks so far (we were drunk); or that the freezers were old and Italian and probably not up to the job (we were drunk). We filled their freezer to the brim and turned it to full cold, patting ourselves on the back at a job well done.

A couple of hours later, there seemed to be a lot of black smoke belching out of the bar area onto the patio and then a couple of shouts of alarm. The GR1 freezer was on fire at the bottom and all the plastic was melting. The next thing we knew, the fire had burnt right through, and gallons of water flooded out onto the tile floor. Someone was smart enough to unplug it, and the escaping water doused the flames so all good in the end.

When 2 Squadron (or 14) arrived back for a beer or two, they were horrified to see the state of their freezer. A small inquest of what happened produced only one response—'Dunno, mate. Fridge went on fire.' Magnanimously, we beered them up from our stocks (free of charge, of course—band of brothers and all that), and it all got a bit out of hand from there. The poor bastards were playing catch up all night against a fighter squadron with some serious speed on, and once the singing started, we had them beat.

No. 56 Squadron had a brilliant bar choir and actually sang some proper songs as well as the usual bar and flying songs. The centrepiece was a harmony version of the Sloop John B that I loved. We opened up with that, and they had no response other than to applaud. Then a few flying songs, mostly ridiculing the Jaguar and the Tornado F3. Finally, we got into the dodgy areas of rude and disgusting, and the song that the Hornet guys had taught us in Cyprus almost cleared the bar. It was the best night of singing I had ever experienced. Grim was hilarious. He sang songs I had never heard of, and I will remember his solo rendition of 'My Father was a Lepidopterist' (no, me neither) forever.

Stop Stop Stop!

Saturday was a bit of a clean-up day. The freezer was replaced immediately as it was 'essential equipment', and the GR1 boys attached another sign-up sheet to it. We let them get away with it the second time. That afternoon, we piled into the minibuses and drove out to the coast for a BBQ at the squadron leader liaison officer's place. Bogs had been posted and his replacement was Jock from the F4 sim at Bruggen. It was his last tour before leaving the RAF, and I suppose they wanted to give him a nice, warm, quiet posting to see him out. If anyone deserved a posting like that, it was Jock. He was a lovely guy and used to invite every visiting fighter squadron round while they were on det.

Jock and his wife hosted us brilliantly, breaking out the local red wine known as Monica. By God, it was lethal stuff, almost rivalling Kokinelli with its ability to strip the enamel from your teeth. As the night wore on, we found out that Jock's wing commander Boss was a bit of a dick and had refused the invitation to attend the BBQ again and again. When we found out he lived a few doors down, the Boss decided that the Firebirds should serenade him before heading back to base. We stood in his front garden and gave our best rendition of the Sloop John B. Halfway through, he came to the door with a face like thunder and said something like, 'You will hear of this on Monday morning'. As we filed away to the minibuses, I saw the Boss have a quiet word with him through what can only be described as an 'assassin's smile'. We didn't hear anything on Monday morning about it.

Even if we had, it would have been small beer to me as something much more frightening happened on that Monday. Grim and I were leading a 4 *v*. 4 against the F16s again, and this time we were looking at taking medium-range shots to even up the visual fight a bit. We managed to thin one of them out pre-merge, and then it was split into two separate fights. We were leading a 2 *v*. 1 and the other pair had the difficult job of fighting a 2 *v*. 2. We managed to kill our guy (as we should have done given that we outnumbered him), but the other two were in a spot of bother. The range controller called that we were now under threat as one of the F16s faced up to us. I led our pair up to the north out of the melee.

We were in full burner and unloading down to the base height, when we got a threat call from the north. The guy we had killed pre-merge had 'regenerated' after two minutes of being out of the fight and was heading towards us. Grim called the contact on the radar, but we were out of Skyflash. With the two F16s on our tail, we had no choice but to blow through the northerly guy and run away bravely to sanctuary. My Number 2 was the Boss, and he was in a perfect battle formation about 2–3 miles line abreast and below us to our right. Grim continued the commentary on the bandit ahead of us. We were doing about 1.3 Mach so had mostly negated the threat from behind when I saw a planform F16 in my left 10 o'clock slightly high, but not by much. By the time I processed that he was turning hard towards us, and called the tally, he was on us.

Adrenalin tends to give the impression that time slows down. In this case, it did not happen in slow motion. By the way, speaking of motion, I can confirm that adrenaline is brown and runny and smells of shit. I pushed forwards on the stick as hard as I could, just as the F16 flashed over our canopy. There was a bit of a bang and I immediately called 'stop stop stop!' to end the fight. I was mental in the cockpit. 'Fucking hell! He hit us!' I then calmly called on the radio that I thought we had had a mid-air collision and then continued to rage in the cockpit.

Poor Grim managed to calm me down as the Boss came over to give us a visual inspection. We got word from the range controller that the F16 hadn't felt a thing, so it was unlikely that it had been a mid-air. We had no external damage so Grim and I were able to analyse that the bang may have been a bit of jetwash from the F16 or even Grim's head banging against the top of the canopy as I had pushed the stick hard forwards. I must have lost thousands of heartbeats in those few seconds and was thoroughly relieved to get back on the ground.

The debrief showed that our bandit had my wingman on radar and he never once had contact on us. He was fixated on our Number 2 once he got tally and was blind to us throughout. The telemetry pods that we carried were only accurate in range measurement down to about 30–50 feet. When it stopped recording the range, the cockpit view showed him closing even more on us for at least another full second. The best guess from the kit was 15 feet; the best guess from me looking at him might as well have been 15 inches.

This kind of thing is a natural operating hazard in the fighter world, and although I was shocked and angry and shitting myself, it was a genuine mistake and could have happened to any of us. There is only so much sky, and we had tried to fill all of it with eight aeroplanes. Grim and I were pretty sanguine about it once I had calmed down, until the F16 leader pointed out that his man was in his safety height block and we weren't. Safety blocks were essential in pre-merge and bad weather conditions, but once in a visual fight, they were meaningless. It was everybody's responsibility to clear their own flightpath into the fight, and this guy had failed to do so. We were running away down to base height so were transiting through all of the height blocks and clearing our path as we went, both visually and on radar. Shit happens. By trying to pin the blame on us somehow, when we had deliberately avoided blaming them was petty and unbecoming, so I just called the debrief to a halt and we left it at that.

Grim and I stacked after that and had an early beer to calm our nerves and celebrate not being dead. I stress to this day that the only thing that saved our lives was Grim's skill in talking my eyes on to that F16, while running the radar and checking our Number 2's 6 o'clock. I already thought he was awesome, but this put him in a different league—one of the best navs I have ever flown with, and the son of a lepidopterist to boot!

The Day We Shot Our Leader Down

I had seen enough of the F16s for a while so it was a refreshing change the next day to be flying against the German F4Fs. We had two GAF exchange guys on 56—Odo and a pilot called Drumm. They knew most of the F4F guys, so we had good social times with them at the bar. Whenever we flew against them, it was a much more even fight. The F4F did not have a medium-range missile at the time, and as I have already said, they smoked like the devil. In theory, we should have had an advantage in both weapon system and getting tally. They were canny operators though and needed treating with respect, otherwise they could catch us out.

The first trip against them was a 4 *v.* 4 hooley. The thought of seeing eight Phantoms turning and burning around each other gave me goose bumps. Bobby was leading the whole shebang and was crewed with

Horner, who had taken a dislike to Bobby. Just before the brief, Lurch and I found Bobby moping in the crew room. Horner had frozen him out and was planning the tactics himself. He was also going to brief it all himself with no input at all from Bobby—so much for the crew concept. We didn't think it was a massive deal, but it was obvious that Bobby was stung, and then the brief started.

We did the full coordination brief with the GAF crews and then separated into two four-ship briefs, and this is where it got a bit chippy. Horner was generally a mellow guy, but that morning, he had a real bug up his arse and was aggressive in the brief. He was briefing up some sort of tactic, and it was obvious to the other seven of us that it wasn't going to work. When Bobby raised a point, Horner slapped him down immediately. This sort of thing never went over well with me. If there is one person you do not humiliate, it is the one you are flying with; you do that in private if it is necessary, but never in front of the rest of the guys (unless they are being a total dickhead of course).

As the leader of the second pair, I felt it was my duty to bring up the fact that the tactics were going to get us all shot to shit (Horner's Number 2 was a very junior pilot who was one of the last to graduate from the OCU). Rather than challenge him openly, I just tried to confirm what he wanted us to do and then pointed out the consequences of those actions. He cut me dead with a kind of 'yes, now which bit of the brief don't you understand?' type of response. I was happy to leave it there and let everyone get shot down just to prove a point, but Lurch thought differently.

I think he saw it as some kind of anti-92 Squadron crusade that Horner was on and spoke up much more forcibly than I had. 'Just shut up and do as you're told, Lurch,' was the response. There was almost a collective gasp in the briefing room, and the three of us were left seething. I didn't listen to the rest of the brief as I was too busy plotting what we were going to do to rectify this slight.

Lurch was fuming as we got kitted up and suggested another small briefing in just our pair. It only took two minutes, but we agreed to shoot Horner down ourselves at the start of the first fight to teach him a lesson. Grim was in agreement, as was Klaxon, who was flying with Lurch. We set up in the north of the play area, with our pair about 1–2 miles behind Horner and waited for the 'fight's on' call.

It seemed to take ages, but as soon as the call came, both Lurch and I fired a Sidewinder up Horner's jet pipes. The comm was a hoot to listen to afterwards, as it went, 'Fight's on,'—pause—'Horner, you're dead. Bug out north.' There was a bit of an argument from Horner, but dead he was, and as briefed, I assumed the lead, re-briefed the entry to the fight, and off we went. There then followed a full ten-minute furball fight with the F4Fs. I parked the throttles in the loud section and turned myself inside out. Shots were called, and then flared off. Break calls came thick and fast, and finally kill calls, leaving just one RAF Phantom standing (I forget who, but probably not me), and Horner holding up to the north the whole time.

All of us were out of fuel, so I led our three-ship back to Deci while Horner stayed in the range to burn off his gas. We were buzzing walking back in, especially when we saw Horner breaking into the circuit. The debrief was going to be interesting, for sure. I managed to tell Bobby what happened before we got to the debrief cabin, and he pissed himself laughing. Horner led the debrief with no idea what had happened until they showed the reconstruction of the fight. 'Fight's on' was called, and a missile from each of our aircraft tracked towards Horner before hitting him and producing the coffin around his jet. 'Horner, you're dead. Bug out north.' Horner stopped the tape and looked at us with his purple face ablaze. Lurch and I just high-fived each other while the Germans hooted with laughter. One of them leaned forward from the row behind and whispered, 'What happened?'

'He was a prick in the brief,' I whispered back, and got an appreciative nod. The subsequent 3 *v.* 4 fight was a mess to debrief, so we all agreed that it was a hoot of a fight and let's do it again sometime. We stayed on for an internal four-ship debrief where a bit of blood-letting went on and a few home truths were spoken. After that, it was all forgotten—apart from in the bar, where our new favourite saying was 'Fight's on. Horner, you're dead. Bug out north.'

If He Hadn't Been Naked, I Would Have Kissed Him

Deci this time around was a full three weeks, so we had another weekend in the sun. Friday night saw us at the Pig and Tape sharing takeout pizza and Bratwursts with the German F4F crews. It didn't matter where in the world you met the German Air Force, they always had an endless supply of sausages and strong German beer. Their beer was a bit stronger than our normal tipples so had an instant effect on us. We ended up with guys on the roof serenading everyone on the patio, and somehow Torchy (OCB Flight) was naked in a storm drain. This was rapidly turning into the most bizarre det I had ever been on, and also one of the most enjoyable. I seriously considered that another night like this was going to kill me though.

On Saturday, it was time to strike out and see a bit more of Sardinia rather than just Cagliari and the Pig and Tape. The plan was a road trip north to Alghero. About half a dozen of us booked into a hotel for Saturday night and piled into the minibus for the trip. Alghero was a bit of a millionaire's playground and the hotel was spectacular. I was sharing a room with Bobby again and after checking in, we all gathered on the beach and swam out to a rocky outcrop. We were not the kind of people to just sunbathe, so a competition was devised where we would each dive full length off the rocks and try to catch a frisbee thrown roughly towards us before hitting the water. After a number of inelegant and possibly damaging belly flops, we took the game back to the hotel pool and impressed absolutely no one with our complete lack of athleticism.

The evening saw us in a beautiful piazza sharing a beer and mulling over where to eat. Bobby has an uncanny knack of talking to strangers, whether they want to or not. While we were discussing dinner options, he had cornered an old Italian guy who looked to be out with his twenty-odd-year-old daughter, and they were laughing and chatting away. 'Hey guys. Paola knows a great place to eat.'

'Who the hell is Paola?' I thought and turned to see Bobby walking off with her. We introduced ourselves to her dad, who couldn't speak a word of English, and followed them down all sorts of back streets until we came to a big, old, solid wooden door in the middle of a wall. Paola knocked using the rapper, and a small grill opened up. Paola fired off some Italian and the big door creaked open to reveal a downwards dark staircase. I was convinced this was a bit mafia, or dodgy at the very least, but found myself heading down regardless.

It opened up into a big cellar with lots of tables crammed full of noisy people. However, as we entered, they bubbled us as foreigners straight away and the whole place went quiet as a graveyard as they stared at us. It was almost like we had shat in the fingerbowl, and what we guessed was the owner slowly walked across. As soon as he saw Paola, he cracked a huge smile and between lots of cheek kissing and rapid Italian, we became the guests of honour. It transpired that Paola was an

Italian heiress (or mafia) and was extremely well connected in Sardinia. Her 'dad' was actually a chaperone (or mafia bodyguard) appointed by her real father to watch over her while away on holiday.

I'm not sure if one of her family owned the restaurant, but we were not offered a menu. They were going to serve us the house speciality—spaghetti al Nero covered in squid ink and some sort of red wine to accompany it. It may well have been the best red wine on the planet, but even at twenty-six years old, my taste buds were shot through after abusing them with Kokinelli and Monica, and I could have been drinking paint thinner for all I knew. The dinner was very pleasant and we enjoyed a bit of celebrity status in the cellar once everyone saw we were friends with the mafia princess. The bill was eye-watering compared to our usual Deci fayre, but all round it was worth it for the experience.

Just when I thought the evening was done, Paola invited us all to an exclusive nightclub up in the hills. I have never really been a nightclub person, but it would have been rude to say no. Also, one of our number was convinced he had a shot with Paola, and we probably needed to keep an eye on him lest he screw up and ended up 'sleeping with the fishes'. It's a good job Harry wasn't with us as we might never have seen him again.

Paola had an enormous black saloon with an enormous driver and she took half the guys with her. That left me, Bobby, and Lurch in her chaperone's car. We were expecting the same type of gangster car, but he climbed into an old Fiat 127 and then proceeded to rally his way up the narrow steep hill to the club. I was holding on for grim death as he skidded around the corners and Bobby called out, 'Slow down, Patrese!' on one particular bend.

'Ah! Patrese!' he shouted back and floored it once more. The club was exclusive, full of pretty young girls and boys in designer clothes sipping cocktails. Paola was greeted like royalty, but there were lots of odd looks at the plain-looking ragtag crew she had in tow. The price of drinks was off the charts, and it was obvious this was the cream of Italian youth, come up the hill to be away from the common people, where they could be themselves and do what they wanted. We were definitely the square pegs with no holes to fit into up here in this rarefied atmosphere.

Speaking of atmosphere, there was the distinct smell of wacky-baccy, and once we cottoned on to that, it was time to leave. It turned out that our colleague didn't have a shot with Paola after all, and we clambered into a couple of cabs and made our way back down the hill. We had had our taste of Olympus and found we didn't fit in with the great and the good. What a weird night!

It got a bit weirder when we got back to the hotel at about 3 a.m. I have no idea who suggested we go skinny-dipping in the sea, but that's what we did. As soon as we hit the water, we heard some shouting and turned to see two guys stealing our clothes. I was gutted as they ran off, feeling totally stupid and helpless. While I was wallowing in this misery, Corpse took off and sprinted across the beach with Lurch not far behind. They disappeared out of sight, and Bobby and I plonked ourselves down on the sand. I was drunk and distraught—my wallet, ID, and Baysa-Passa all gone just like everyone else, and I would need to cross the road and get into the hotel completely bollock naked.

A couple of minutes later, Corpse came back into sight casually carrying all our clothes draped over his arms. He had managed to retrieve it all and brought it back to us. If he hadn't have been naked, I would have kissed him. Apparently, the sight of Corpse, who was a big, scary-looking guy, sprinting towards them with his knob swinging freely was enough to freak the thieves out and they dropped our clothes and ran away. It was a huge relief and I hit the sack that morning a very happy man indeed.

Later that day, Lurch and I wandered down the seafront in search of breakfast before our drive back to Deci. As we drank our coffee outside a small café, three of our ground crew walked up to say hello. They had done the same as us and spent the night in Alghero. We shared a coffee with them and as we got up to leave, one of them said, 'Glad you got your clothes back, Sir?'

We stopped dead in our tracks and the realisation slowly dawned on our faces. 'You bastards! It was you, wasn't it?' They laughed their heads off as we shared the story from both sides. They had been walking back from a bar and had seen us climbing out of the cabs and onto the beach. It was too good an opportunity to pass up, so they took our clothes. They also confirmed that the sight of Corpse speeding towards them naked was a picture they will never be able to burn from their minds. Either way, we were going to be the subject of some serious banter from the ground crew the next week.

Il Buono, Il Brutto, Il Cattivo

The Monday after the weird weekend was a brilliant flying day. The afternoon trip was an internal 2 *v*. 2 guns-only trip and lasted a mere thirty-five minutes. It was an old school punch-up with Phantoms almost scraping off each other to get kills. No one gave an inch and no one got a single kill—lots of sweat, lots of G, and lots of afterburner. What's not to like?

The trip in the morning was even better though. Grim and I were leading a 1 *v*. 1 *v*. 1 and we tried to come up with something a bit unusual to spice things up. We did the usual secret draw for weapons, which gave us a small advantage as we knew what was out there. We had fixed it so that no one had more than one missile and everyone had the gun. Allied with that, there was only a thirty-second regen before you were allowed back in the fight after being killed. All told, this would ensure a continuous fight as it would be near-impossible to get two kills in thirty seconds and finish the fight.

It also meant we would need to keep a close eye on any dead fighter as they would only need to extend from the fight for about twenty seconds before turning back and becoming live again just before re-entering. In order to set the scene, I had written the brief the night before in the form of an epic poem. It had a spaghetti western theme, and each crew was based on either *Il Buono, Il Brutto* or *Il Cattivo* (*The Good, the Bad and the Ugly*). Each time I said the phrase, I would whistle the first five notes of the film's theme tune, and Grim would put on a cowboy hat and sing, 'Wah wah waaah!' into his cupped hands.

Crews would be awarded points for kills, bravery, and such, but would lose them for being killed or avoiding the fight by skulking around (all at my discretion of course). The losers would have to wear 'Mare Man' name badges for the rest of the day. 'Having a mare' was a standard phrase for us through training whenever we screwed up, so Mare Man was not something you wanted on your flying suit in the Pig and Tape. Everyone seemed to take it in their stride, and we blasted off into the range for a Mercedes split.

My God, what a trip! I called us to outwards turn, and from the 'fight's on', it was only about five minutes before I had to knock it off as we were all out of gas. Everyone merged together as no one was going to wuss out, and I reckon the only time any of us was outside of the required 1,000-foot safety bubble was when we were kill removed. It was outrageous with none of us yielding or giving anything away, canopy to canopy, flashing past each other. Twenty-five minutes after take-off, we were touching down again. What a spectacular use of three jet's worth of gas. I ran the debrief in rhyme as well and gave the Mare Man badges to Drumm and Lifford for no other reason than I certainly wasn't going to give it to myself and Grim, and the other pilot was Lurch, so Drumm didn't stand a chance, even before we got airborne!

I flew once more in Deci on another 1 *v.* 1 *v.* 1, and then we were into a long weekend stand down before the transit home on the Monday. It was a long old night with plenty of farewell drinks shared with the Germans and the Belgians. As the night drew on, a big group of navs set up a poker school and disappeared into a room together like a bunch of Mafia high-rollers. I was about to call it a night around 3.30 a.m. when the duty admin officer on the RAF permanent staff arrived looking for me.

It is rarely good news when someone in uniform comes to find you in the middle of the night, and this was no exception. My father had suffered a massive heart attack that night and it was touch-and-go whether he was going to make it or not. The Boss and Klaxon came over as I looked as white as a sheet and was sobering up fast. The quickest way to get me home was to fly a Phantom back the next day, as long as I could find a nav that would fly with me.

As Klaxon made the arrangements to get me out of Deci on a Saturday, I wandered into the poker school to be confronted by a wall of cigar smoke and lots of beady, whiskey-fuelled eyes. I told them the situation and asked if anyone was up for flying back with me. They all knew it was 3.30 a.m. and that I was drunk, yet every one of them volunteered on the spot. It did my heart good, once again reinforcing my belief in the special brotherhood I had joined the moment I first climbed into that Phantom cockpit.

The Boss came in and told us he had done a deal with the airfield, and that they could get us out at 7.30 a.m. Shit, I was expecting an afternoon trip, but scurried off to my room to pack and grab a couple of hours of kip. It was a bleary-eyed Tug and Trent who crewed in at about 7 a.m., I can tell you. I profusely thanked our ground crew who had been roused even earlier than us to prep the jet. They looked as rough as us and I am sure that as soon as they saw us off, they spent the rest of the day in bed. Trent and I knew what state we were in, and as such, we double- and triple-checked our way up through Italy and France, landing back at

Wattisham without incident. I told Trent I owed him and then went to the mess to crash out after calling home to see how things were.

Dad had stabilised a bit, which gave me a chance to rest and sober up enough to get in the car and drive to North Yorkshire. I can't say I am proud of the fact that I flew for two hours still technically drunk (so much so I was not fit to drive for some hours afterwards), but I am eternally grateful to the Boss, Klaxon, Trent, our ground crew, and anyone else involved in getting me home that day. I am also grateful to my beautiful jet for ferrying me through Europe when it damn well knew I wasn't at my best, so it gave me an easy ride. Dad made an amazing recovery, and I was able to spend a few days with my parents before heading back to 56.

Trappers

As soon as I got back, 56 was gearing up for its annual Trappers visit. Each year, Central Flying School (CFS) would send some of its agents to front-line squadrons to make sure everyone was flying and operating to the correct standards and following the correct procedures. In Germany, a couple of guys from the OCU had come out and flown with us as Trappers, but they were so maxed out just flying in the low-level system that they found it difficult to criticise anyone anyway. However, we wouldn't have that advantage on 56. The OCU had closed, so it was a couple of pilots and navs in standards flight at Wattisham who were coming over to check us out. This meant two weeks of weapons and tech lectures beforehand as well as some work-up trips.

I flew twice on this work-up with Luke, our QWIL. He was a very capable operator, and because of that, I really felt like I upped my game when flying with him. He was also very funny and a cool guy. Being the QWIL, he delivered a lot of the weapons lectures, and they were a thing of beauty. He was a brilliant cartoonist and drew caricature pictures on the whiteboard of the Skyflash, Sidewinder, and gun. The way he explained the inner workings and tactics of using them was amazing, and I still remember his awesome opening line to the gun lecture. 'Ok, so we have studied the Skyflash, which I like to think is a navigator's weapon. The navs run the intercept to get into the best position to use the Skyflash. Then we looked at the Sidewinder, which I think of as a pilot's weapon. We use it mostly in visual fighting, which is a pilot thing.

Today, we are going to look at the gun. Now the gun, that's a fighter pilot's weapon. Because, if you can't gun anything? You ain't worth shit!'

My oral exam with the two pilot Trappers was a bit chippy. Both of them had previously flown in a couple of the formations I had led since joining 56 and had come in for some criticism in the briefings and debriefings for not knowing their stuff and for their tactical prowess, particularly their use of chaff and flares. They were obviously out to redress the balance a bit so put me through the wringer. I think I came out of it okay, and later that day, I kitted up for my dual check.

I forgot to mention that one of the Trapper pilots was Snitcher, and of course, he was the one I was flying with. I have a real gift for holding a grudge, and I still remembered that bollocking we got off Nemo in the Falklands when Snitcher had snitched on us, so I was determined not to give him anything to criticise on this trip.

The big event on a Phantom dual check was high AOA manoeuvring. I have mentioned it before as it caught out Harry in Cyprus. It was a fine balance between speed, G, and AOA using rudder to turn the aircraft rather than aileron. Snitcher had a special way of doing it, and rather than just briefing me to go into a high AOA turn and then reverse, unload, and pull on his calls, he tried to make it more realistic. His idea was to call a bandit in our 6 o'clock and then call me to break right to start it all off. As soon as he called, 'Break right! Bandit 6 o'clock!' I pulled hard and called 'Flares!' I figured I would play him at his own game. 'Keep talking! Where is he?' I shouted as the G came on and the speed washed off. 'I am no joy, Snitcher. Where is he?' I had the doughnut nailed and kicked a boot full of left rudder as he said, 'Er, er reverse, er, he's er.'

'Come on, Snitcher. Talk to me! Is he nose on?' So on it went, with me driving the exercise until Snitcher got fed up. We set up for another one with him getting a bit more involved, but I had made the point that I could do the manoeuvres whilst also communicating with my nav, looking out, and popping flares. We headed back to Wattisham where there was only enough gas for two circuits and that was the end of Trappers for me.

Where Did You Get That Hat?

That Friday, Bobby and I were allowed a jet to go back to Wildenrath for the weekend, where we partied hard with the 19 Squadron boys. The trip over was a hoot as we initially headed north for graduation flypasts at both Cranwell and Linton. Cranwell was horrible with low cloud and poor visibility. ATC told us everyone else had cancelled, but we asked if we could do a PAR to get in and have a look.

We had a hazy view of the ground at about 400 feet, so overshot and switched to tower to join the circuit. Normal circuit height at 1,000 feet would have put us back in the cloud, so I called for a low-level circuit to put us at 500 feet. We were skirting with the cloud base at 400–450 feet, so I kept it down at 400 and dirtied up the aircraft downwind including putting the probe out and the hook down. I have no idea if the grad students saw us downwind as we could barely see the squadron buildings ourselves. I glued my eyes onto the threshold of the runway around finals as it was very murky indeed. After short finals, I cleaned everything up just as the afterburner bit and we scorched down the runway at about 50 feet. I switched to departures and zoomed up into the cloud, laying all the noise down behind us.

Linton had much better weather, so we were able to do a couple of fast and low flypasts before zooming up and away for Wildenrath. It was a little odd being back at Wildenrath in that as we arrived, we instantly felt at home. After an amazing weekend, we headed back to Wattisham, knowing that we were beyond the beginning of the end of our fabulous aeroplane. What made things worse was that Phantoms were being towed to a scrapyard on the airfield that we had to drive past every day on the way to 56. Aircraft I had flown were parked up on a shitty piece of spare hard standing, ready to be broken up for scrap.

Life went on, and the very next day I passed my op check with Luke. I was only leading a pair against a few targets over the North Sea—a far cry from my eight-ship CAP on my first op check in Germany. The next trip was a four-ship lead check where I took us across to the low-flying area in Wales. So that was me fully operational again, with no more work-up or test rides required until the Phantom went out of service.

I also passed a major milestone of 1,000 hours total flight time in my logbook. It happened on a trip with Grim and went completely unnoticed until I filled in my logbook at the end of the month. For once, I could relax and just enjoy my flying. Timing is everything, and after a long week of varied trips (ECM, 6 *v*. 3 against GR1s, and 2 *v*. 3 Harriers), I had the perfect opportunity to celebrate my newfound qualifications.

I had downed the 56 Squadron op pot the day of my op check, but the Friday that week saw us boarding a coach after a quick couple of beers in happy hour and heading across to the Jag base at RAF Coltishall. We were taking part in an East Anglian happy hour. These happened every few months and were hosted on an unofficial rota. There was an open invite to every squadron in the East Anglian area to turn up and make merry. We arrived at about 6 p.m. so had maybe four hours to go mad before the bus came back for us. There were a lot of GR guys there from the five or six squadrons at Honington, Marham and Cottesmore, the resident Jag mates from Coltishall, a smattering of Americans from Lakenheath and Mildenhall, and us and the boys from 74.

Most of the 74 boys were wearing brand new op badges as a couple of weeks earlier we had defaced the ones on their flying jackets one night in the bar. No. 74's motto was 'I fear no man'. It was a pretty cool motto, but we popped another 'R' in between the last two words in black felt tip, so that it read 'I fear Norman'. This had happened on a regular basis for years, until the guys realised that they couldn't leave their flying jackets on the pegs in the cloakroom during happy hour.

It didn't take us long to get some speed on, especially as we were on the clock as it were. It was cool to catch up with guys on other aircraft that I had not seen since flying training. All too soon, the singing started and the mess cannons came out. Nothing could match the size and power of the 56 Squadron cannon. Out of nowhere came a loud boom, and the bar was showered with shredded paper. The boys had brought two big bin-liners of the stuff and after a few nerve-shredding explosions, we were ankle deep in it.

The station commander at Coltishall was taking it all in his stride up until the final boom, where he saw his nice hat with all the scrambled egg on the peak arc majestically across the room with a trail of shredded paper behind it. We began a chorus of 'Where did you get that hat?' It petered out very quickly as the group captain lost his sense of humour (probably due to the black scorch mark on his hat), and we were ordered to leave the station early. When he found out about it afterwards, as our own station commander, Barry Smallcock (remember him?), was most unimpressed and he charged us all £5 on our mess bills to buy a new hat for the Staish at Coltishall. Suffice it to say, our station commander was not in attendance on the night in Coltishall—thank goodness.

Fatal Accident

On 30 October 1991, I was the station duty officer at Wattisham. This generally meant saluting the raising of the ensign at 8 a.m., and the lowering of it at 4 p.m. (6 p.m. in summertime). It also meant I was on duty overnight for any admin, compassionate, or security issues. I was flying in the afternoon and had arranged for someone else to lower the flag for me. Just after we had finished debriefing the sortie, there was a station-wide tannoy asking for the SDO to meet OC Admin Wing in the officers' mess.

Well, this couldn't be good news was my initial thought, and I was preparing myself for some sort of bollocking, probably because the guy I had arranged to salute the flag must have forgotten. It was much worse though. I met him in the anteroom, and there was only the two of us in there. 'There's been a fatal crash in the Falklands,' he said. My blood turned to ice and I'm sure he saw the colour drain from my face.

'Oh shit,' I replied.

'It's okay,' he said, 'It's a Germany crew'. I almost punched him in the face there and then. He knew he had dropped a bollock. I will give him the benefit of the doubt and say I knew what he was trying to say, but how does anyone get to that rank and position and not have any awareness of what they are saying? He instantly went to the top of my 'dickheads I have met in the air force' list. He then gave me the names. It was Animal and Sansom. I knew Animal really well from training and the OCU, and Sansom was one of the staff navigators at the Tac Weapons school at Chivenor. He was a brilliant guy and always the students' friend. They had crashed in the sea somewhere to the north of the islands and were missing, presumed dead. Earliest reports showed no sign of wreckage.

My whole body went numb and I have no idea what else he said. As soon as I got my faculties back, I tried to call Bungle over at 74 as I knew he and Sansom were best mates. I was too late though as news had already spread and guys were making their way over to the bar. Following a fatal accident, the squadron in question (in this case, 19) would go to the bar *en masse* and drink themselves stupid on the dead crew's bar books. Although this sounds a little macabre, those bar books would then be written off by the mess. I think this is one of the most beautiful traditions of military aircrew.

Even though we weren't in Germany with 19, we still knew the guys who were missing and so we would have a similar wake at Wattisham. I imagine the same thing happened at the other fighter bases of Coningsby and Leuchars. I was SDO so not able to drink, but as soon as I entered the bar, a young admin officer, who I barely knew, came up to me and took the SDO's bag from me saying, 'I'll take the duty off you for tonight, Tug.' I couldn't thank him enough (nor Trent, who had arranged it for me) and joined the rest of the guys at the bar.

A fighter squadron wake is pretty much a closed-door affair, and once in the bar, you can do whatever you like (in reason) and it is forgotten the next day. I don't mind admitting that I and a lot of the guys cried our eyes out and got steaming drunk telling stories of our two comrades in arms. Animal was a legendary party monster, and we tried our best to emulate his drinking prowess (badly). It was announced that night that Bungle had been selected to sit on the board of inquiry accident investigation and would be flying to the Falklands in the next day or so. Given that Sansom was his best friend and very close to the family, I thought this was a crass and callous decision, and with only a minor bit of thought, the RAF could have chosen someone else.

In those days, we were pretty good at the short, sharp shock of getting shitfaced whenever someone died in an accident, and particularly bad at dealing with the longer-term aftermath. Basically, 'you've had your night of moping, now get on with it'. That was how I found myself back in the air only two days later leading a four-ship sweep through North Yorkshire and the Borders. The accident and the fate of our buddies was put aside. Word filtered back from the Falklands that Animal and Sansom had just filled to full off the C130 tanker and gone straight into a hard-manoeuvring fight. The belief was that the heavy aircraft must have departed and gone out of control. The cloud tops were down at only 2,000 feet or so and it was thought there might have been a visual illusion. When they went into cloud out of control, they should have ejected, but maybe they thought they had more height to play with and try to recover?

In the big scheme of things, we investigate accidents to get to the root causes so that we don't make the same mistakes in the future, but Animal and Sansom were gone, and any speculation on how and why was not going to change that. Some weeks later, Wildenrath held a memorial service for the crew and the RAF laid on a C130 for anyone from Wattisham that wanted to attend. It was a weird sight, seeing us all in our Number 1 dress uniforms piling up the rear ramp of a Herc, all of the married guys with their wives in smart dresses, and sitting down on the dirty fabric and metal seats usually reserved for paras.

We landed at Wildenrath on a bitterly cold day and were bussed to the church for the ceremony. There were no coffins as the wreckage was never found, and when Animal's pregnant wife walked up to the front, I cried my eyes out all over again. My most favourite hymn is 'I Vow to Thee, My Country'. I tried my best to sing it through, but the line of 'that lays upon the altar, the dearest and the best' destroyed me. It is the one line I still can't sing. The wake in the mess afterwards was brutal, and we were all the worse for wear as we staggered up the ramp of the Herc later on. Lifford was absolutely shitfaced and playing up a bit despite his wife and the rest of us trying to calm him down. The final straw was when he gobbed off to the C130 Loadmaster and the captain tossed him from the flight. A less drunk 'adult' got off with him to look after him and the ramp closed, leaving them on the apron. His wife was not happy, and I imagine his sober trip back the next day and arrival at home were somewhat uncomfortable.

I'm 200 Miles North of Scotland!

As we marched inexorably towards the final demise of the Phantom, I was picked to go on a joint maritime course (JMC) exercise. This would turn out to be the worst det I have ever been on, and by that, I mean in my whole RAF career. We deployed six jets to Leuchars, and as the exercise was taking place way north of Scotland, we had very early starts and long transits to even get to the play area. This needed tanker support from the VC10 fleet, so each trip was scheduled to be long and tedious. Both Bobby and Lurch were on the team, but we were also bundled up with a couple of the guys who had been openly hostile towards us in the early days. Two of them had been the arseholes who said they were out to chop Bobby.

I was flying with Thumper who I barely knew and had never flown with. We did a low-level intercept 3 *v.* 3 on the way up to Leuchars, and that was a good shakedown for us to get to know each other's styles. No. 43 and Treble-One Squadrons were now Tornado F3 outfits so it was shaping up to be a decent time in the bar each night. Sniper was the det commander so happy days.

Things went sour from the off. The very early starts didn't help, and the JMC had a sort of 'just thrown together' feel about it, with us having to constantly reset as 'the navy aren't quite ready' excuses came across the radio. There was a squadron of Buccaneers flying ultra-low to attack the ships (no one flew low level like the Buccs), and we were supposed to sweep for them. It was all a bit chaotic and we mostly got separated into singletons after defending against the enemy fighters and ship defences. It was apparent, both at the time and in the debrief, that none of us had much of a clue what was going on.

There was a classic bit of comm on the first mission from Sniper. He called up London mil radar and asked for a steer back to Leuchars as he was short of gas. When they asked him his position, he shouted, 'I'm 200 miles north of Scotland!' We would have chuckled in the cockpit if we weren't so shocked and angry about the lack of professionalism and organisation of the JMC as a whole. More worrying though was the sniping that crept into our debriefing. Guys who I didn't rate on the squadron at all (two pilots and one nav in particular) were all out criticising other much sharper people in the formation. This got steadily worse as the det went on.

The bar was buzzing, and Corpse had brought the cannon and was doing his party piece of peppering the bar with shredded paper. Then two young lads from the F3s, who had followed me through training, brought out their mess cannon. This thing was enormous. They had test-fired it only once, and it had shot a speed tape ball the size of a basketball right over the roof of a HAS. It had been immediately banned by their Boss for being far too dangerous. Lurch and I were fascinated by this and asked what would happen if they fired it at someone. 'Probably kill them,' they replied.

I looked at Lurch and he looked at me. Next thing, we had talked Corpse into standing on a table at one end of the bar to catch the ball from the cannon. He was drunk enough to give it a go, so the F3 boys fuelled it up. There was a nuclear-style explosion that sucked the air out of the atmosphere, and the speed tape ball shredded on its way to Corpse, who leapt off the table just in time to see the ball shatter a picture frame on the wall behind him. He damn near shat himself! That was the end of the cannons for that Det.

The following day was a nightmare—two trips with a total of over five hours airborne, with the first trip taking off in the dark and the second trip landing in the dark. It was made worse by shit weather all round and the usual JMC 'navy not quite ready' kerfuffle. We were bomb-bursting jets all over the place, and after the first presentation, Thumper's radar gave up so we were reduced to being a visual fighter only. I stuck to my element lead like glue and Thumper's head was on a swivel, but we eventually got spat out of the fight and ended up alone and unafraid.

Gas was getting tight, so we asked for vectors to the tanker. The medium and upper levels of airspace were full of thick cloud layers, so we asked for full control to find the VC10. Of course, the controller's radar went dark with a technical hitch, followed by an intermittent comms failure. As a last resort, we tried an intercept on air-to-air TACAN alone (impossible really) in the hope we would get a visual on the tanker, but eventually had to call it a day and make the long trip back to Leuchars. God that was hard work—three and a half hours of achieving bugger all.

The other five jets had similar stories to tell, and once again the debrief was tetchy. During the debrief of the second sortie, I noticed that Bobby's pilot, Tikit, was openly slagging off Bobby, and this induced the other two idiots of his clique to jump on the bandwagon. I stewed for a little on it and then let it pass as it was late and dark and I was knackered. Tikit and Bobby were leading the next day, so they needed to get planning. Tikit walked out with the rest of us, saying that Bobby was going to plan and brief it and off he went to the bar. Bobby's brief the next day was a bloodbath.

To provide some balance, Bobby had screwed up the initial part of the plan by having us transit through a temporary airway at the 'fight's on', which wasn't as temporary as he thought. Even I thought, 'For God's sake, Bobby,' as it was a real schoolboy error, but the three hyenas jumped on him, including Tikit. This is unforgiveable. Tikit had taken no part in the plan or brief, not even sanity-checking things for Bobby, yet here he was, sticking the knife in. Thumper thought he would get in on the act until I nudged him and told him quietly to 'shut it'.

It got more brutal to watch and, in the end, I told everyone to button it so we could hear the rest of the brief, and we could sort out the start point at the end. They were like a dog with a bone though, and it was the most distasteful thing I have ever seen in a brief. Lurch and I gave Tikit and his buddies the cold shoulder and flew off into yet another shit exercise sortie. I let Thumper know my thoughts on what had happened, and he had the good grace to keep quiet about it.

We knew the debrief was going to be horrid, and Lurch and I stood up for Bobby as much as we could. Yes, he had screwed up the start of the plan, but the rest of it was sound. Tikit and his cronies systematically took Bobby apart. I could only interject so much and was elated when Sniper finally stepped in and moved things along. Bobby looked like he had been machine-gunned at the end of it, so it was time for a bit of 92 Squadron bonding in the bar. I just couldn't believe that squadron mates could act like that towards each other. Believe me, debriefing in Germany was hard, sometimes brutal, but was always fair and never personal. Also, what the hell was Tikit thinking, railing on his crew mate like that?

The more beer I threw down, the more annoyed I got. There was an uneasiness in the detachment and everyone could sense the rift, but I didn't give a shit, I was so angry. A little while later as I returned from the loo, I bumped into Tikit at the door to the bar. He was obviously trying to break the ice and said to me, 'Hey, Tug. Wow. Bobby had a bit of a mare today, didn't he?'

I was amazed at how calm I was. 'Let's not chat about it in front of him mate. Let's go through to the Scruff's bar,' I said as I propelled him to the door. As he turned around in the Scruff's, I forced him to back up against the wall by getting right in his face and unleashing on him. 'Don't you ever do that again to any nav you fly with! How dare you talk to him like that? Where the hell were you during the planning, you lazy bastard!? You just let him hang, didn't you? Then you and those other two wankers sat there and threw darts. Well, let me tell you this, Tikit. Bobby is sharper than you, those two dullards, and most of the other stale bastards on this squadron. If you had been any good, you would have been in Germany mate. I suggest you go and apologise to your crew mate. And tell the other two, if they have a problem with it, then they know where I am'.

I'm not sure if that was the exact speech, but all the main points are correct. There was probably a bit more swearing in there if I am being honest. I left Tikit and headed back to my mates at the bar, as if nothing had happened. I didn't tell Bobby about this until twenty-seven years later at a reunion in London. He had tears in his eyes when I told him, and so did I. He always said that 56 was the worst of times because of days like that, but also the best of times as he, Lurch, and I were tighter than any band of brothers could be.

Another Posting and Almost a Missile

The last two JMC trips were somewhat quiet all told. Debriefs were professional, yet stilted, and not surprisingly Tikit went out of his way to be obsequious about Bobby's performance. It was all a little false, but there we are. I was glad to get back to Wattisham at the end of the week. Everyone on the fleet was looking to the future, and once again, the poster was due in town with his manning plan. It was expected that most guys would move across to the F3, but there were plenty of rumours that younger guys would probably have to take a couple of years as a sim instructor before eventually getting an OCU course. I didn't fancy this in the slightest as I wanted to keep flying, so I went for a chat with the Boss beforehand.

I really fancied being a tactics instructor on the Hawk at the TWU (either Brawdy or Chivenor). The job looked awesome, and because the RAF was shrinking after the Defence Review, the AFT and TWU courses were amalgamating, so eventually, it would all happen at Valley. As a TI, I would also get the chance to get a QFI qualification, and that could prove very useful in the future. Most of the fast jet exchange tours were going to TWU instructors at that time, so I figured it was my best chance to get my hands on an F15, F16, or F18. The Boss was very helpful and completely onside, saying he thought I would make a great instructor and would write me up as such.

By the time I had my interview with the poster (I noticed his horrific zit had healed up nicely), it was a done deal. I was given the very last TI slot out of Brawdy before it was closed. Timing meant that I would be leaving 56 about three–four months before the end of the Phantom. I would miss all of the huge parties and various flypasts, but this TI slot was a great deal and was the next logical step in me maturing as a military aviator.

The next two months were December 1991 into January 1992, and the sorties could not have been more varied or intricate—2 *v*. 2s, 4 *v*. 4s, 8 *v*. 10 against F18s and Sea Harriers as well as lots of F3s and GR1s. There was lots of tanking, and by this stage, I had every nav on the squadron in my logbook with me.

No. 56 were conducting a missile shoot over at Valley, but I was not on the detail. However, one of the jets went unserviceable over there with radar problems so Lea and I took a spare aircraft over at the end of January. We were just expecting to jump straight in the jet we were replacing and bring it home, but it developed a hydraulic problem so we were delayed. Luke thought we might as well fly on the next missile shoot that afternoon, and he put us down as secondary shooter. I was willing the primary to go unserviceable, but unfortunately not, and they got their shot away no problem.

Our return jet was still down so we had to overnight at Valley. We had no spare kit or wash kit so just hung out in the bar all night. Our jet was a bust the next morning, but the main issue was that both Lea and I were heading off to the Falklands (me in a day or so, and him a week after) and had to get back to Wattisham pronto. Our only option was to get a driver to take us to Bangor railway station and for us to use a travel warrant to make our way across country.

What a journey. We set off at around 7.30 a.m., and our torturous trip took us through Crewe, into and across London, to get a train to Ipswich where an RAF driver met us and delivered us back to Wattisham at about 10.30 p.m. Remember that neither of us had any civilian clothes so we did the whole journey in flying suits. We removed all of our badges and rank as there was a huge IRA terrorist threat and carried our helmets, life jackets and g-pants in big bin liners. We felt very exposed on Crewe station waiting for our connection, and even more so trying to get across London. Our helpful London cabbie asked, 'You two astronauts then?'

'Something like that, mate.'

Falklands Again—Orange Llamas Again

The very next day, I loaded my bags into the minibus that would take me and Sly to Brize Norton to overnight before our trip to the Falklands. Fatty and Bungle from 74 were heading down south at the same time so there were four of us sharing the pain. It would be weird being on det with Bungle again, but not flying with him and I was a bit jealous of Fatty. However, Sly was a really nice bloke and I was sure he would be a good partner down there. At this point though, I had no idea just how good he was, and how much fun we would have together.

I had none of the apprehension of my first trip to the Falklands so was much more relaxed about the trip. On the way down, we were sitting beside Martin Hanrahan of the BBC. His news reports from the Falklands conflict were the soundtrack to the war, and he was heading back to film a special report commemorating the ten-year anniversary.

Quite by chance, the four of us would take a not so starring role in his report, but more of that later.

It was a really good bunch of lads this time on 1435 Flight. The fleet was shrinking as guys were posted to various places, so we all knew each other really well. Sniper was the Boss and he was absolutely superb. I arrived just as he was about to start his mad period, but he held it together throughout and turned out to be a brilliant, loyal, and supportive Boss. I had only flown with Sly twice beforehand, and one of those trips was cut well short with a stuck AoA gauge, so we had very little idea what it was going to be like together in the air.

There was no need to worry on my part because from trip one together, he was fantastic. We slotted straight into operating as a crew, and his pure enthusiasm and joy for flying were infectious. We did all the usual things on a first Falklands sortie, such as a PD to Stanley, lots of circuits at MPA, and outrageous low-flying all over the islands. As the F4 was going out of service, Sniper didn't give a shit about aircraft fatigue, so we pulled the wings off.

Just as we were heading back to MPA, we got a request to do a simulated attack on the resident RN frigate, which we duly did. The plan was to simulate an Exocet missile attack, so it was a case of scraping our bellies across the surface of the sea to see if the frigate's on-board defences could track and kill us. At the end of a couple of attacks, they asked us for a supersonic flypast, which we politely declined. Our shock wave would do too much damage unless they buttoned absolutely everything down tight. Back on deck, I made sure the chute was well clear before I turned around on the runway.

I knew Snitcher was 8,000 miles away, but you never know what lengths these sneaky bastards would go to. Also, I was supposedly a lot more experienced and professional these days and didn't want any more screw-ups in my last couple of months on the jet, especially with the BBC News cameras in town. We reacquainted ourselves with the Goose, but Sly was a bit of a fitness kind of guy, so we spent plenty of time playing squash and table tennis to offset the booze. My game was volleyball, and as officer in charge of the RAF Wattisham Volleyball Club, we had amazing success winning the Suffolk League. I would love to claim the credit, but we had a RAF player and the captain of the WRAF team on the squad, and I was happy to bask in their reflected glory. Anyway, there was a big inter-unit volleyball tournament going on at MPA, so I was well-served to keep my skills up.

Sly and I began our life on Q almost as soon as we had flown our arrival trip. We were Q1 with Fatty and Bungle on Q2 when the BBC arrived to film a Q scramble for their report. We had to clean up the Q shed a bit before their arrival and pretended to be busy reading aircraft manuals and intelligence reports while the BBC took some background fluff footage.

Then came the main event—the scramble. The magic of television is in the editing, so we spent an hour doing a stop/start scramble. First off, they filmed us leaping into action as the hooter went off. We ran past the camera to the pegs with our kit on. Then we stopped and filmed it all again from a different angle. Then we stopped again, and so on. We must have kitted up four times until they were happy with it.

Then they waited outside the Q shed for us to burst out of the door. Sly and I would break left and run up the tube, and Fatty and Bungle would be straight up the ramp to Q2. Of course, it was blowing a bloody gale and the tube was flaming horrible as usual. The thrill of possibly appearing on TV was wearing away as we ran halfway up the tube for the fourth time in full kit. We were hot, sweaty, completely out of breath, and still had to film the start-up and take-off before going flying.

The film crew asked for one more go to finally get it in the can, so we set up once again. I burst out of the shed and powered up the tube into the teeth of the wind. It took me a couple of seconds to realise that Sly was ahead of me and yet there was someone running alongside of me. I turned to see Fatty puffing along beside me looking right back at me. We both stopped and stared, and in between heaving breaths, I spluttered, 'What the hell are you doing?!' He pushed me in the chest and we had a bit of handbags until he realised that he was running for the wrong jet, and then just sat down in the tube taking huge gulps of air and laughing his head off. That was the end of the filming and not surprisingly, we didn't make the final cut of the BBC report.

After all the messing about, we finally blasted airborne as a singleton. With no one to fight against and no tanker, we just raged around the islands doing a NAVEX and generally dicking about, enjoying ourselves. There was a moment of reflection as we deliberately flew out to the rough coordinates of where they thought Animal and Sansom had gone down. Once we were there, or thereabouts, I rocked the throttles outboard and dumped some noise in a vertical climb, which hopefully they heard in some sense. We got to chatting as we crossed over the Sound into West Falkland, and I brought up the myth of the orange llamas that people had tried to spoof me with last time I was down south. 'Did you not see them then, Tug?'

'Don't you start, Sly. I wasn't born yesterday'.

Sly was adamant that I fly us over to Beaver Island to take a look, and I humoured him to keep the peace. Bugger me—there they were: a whole herd of orange llamas just ambling around with not a care in the world. If Sly was smug, he was gracious enough not to show it, and I admitted defeat with an apology and a pledge to trust everything he said on det.

The next two trips were brilliant. We were fly crew and had the full Falklands experience of low-flying, flypasts, fiery crosses, escorting the Tristar, intercepts with visual fights, and tons of tanking from the C130. I was having so much fun flying with Sly that it hardly felt like work. He was great on Q during the tedious down times and a brilliant mate to go to the bar with, or on a trip to Stanley. Our crew and personal relationships were cemented forever on our next flight together.

What Is the Nature of Your Emergency?

Everything was going swimmingly to start with. A nice pairs take-off saw us split away from each other at about 50 feet and we sped off for a coordinated fiery cross from two different attack directions. Having blasted the airfield into submission just below the Mach, we joined up as a fighting pair to run some intercepts against the low-flying Herc. The idea was to tie up the Herc, so the free fighter could get in unseen, which was tricky to do at low altitude. The Herc could manoeuvre at really low speeds, which would give us a problem being fully loaded up with the weapons and tanks.

As the trip progressed, a thickish layer of cloud moved in at around 2,000 feet. After a couple of fights, we joined on the C130 to tank and then start the exercise all over again. I loved tanking off the C130. The basket was stable, and Sly talked me in off the first prod, so we filled to bursting. Once fat with gas, we reset to 50 miles from the target and turned in. The GCI controller at Mount Kent began his patter, and I rocked them outboard to get some height on. As soon as the burners bit, there was an almighty bang and the right-hand engine seized solid with a mechanical failure. I called, 'Stop Stop Stop!' and pulled both throttles out of burner, identified the problem, and stop-cocked the right.

Looking back, I am amazed at how automatic the drill had come out. Kent was still talking so I called that we had an engine failure and asked him to 'standby'. He kept on talking though. While normally this would have been an irritation, right then, I had bigger fish to fry. My very heavy Phantom was not able to maintain its height on dry power, and we were descending a bit too fast for comfort. I told Sly I was in burner now on the left, but we were still heading down quickly towards the cloud tops. While I struggled with the aircraft, Sly called, 'mayday' just to shut the guy at Kent up.

He didn't take the hint though and kept transmitting asking the standard questions. 'What is the nature of your emergency? What are your intentions?' The one that finally got to me was 'how many POB? [persons on board]'. He knew we were a Phantom so the answer was obviously two for God's sake! As we got closer to the cloud, I lost it and transmitted, 'Just shut the fuck up!' He went quiet after that.

Number 2 had joined up and offered help, and the C130 was standing by as on-scene commander, just in case we needed to eject. We were really close to the cloud tops, and my hand was hovering over the emergency jettison button. This was our last option before ejecting and would punch off our tanks and weapons to reduce the drag, but there were a couple of issues with that. First, I had no idea if they would drop on the public as we were above cloud. Secondly, there would be a whole world of hurt afterwards in the Board of Inquiry. Short of ejecting though, it was turning into our only option.

All the way through, Sly was updating me on his best guess of what was below us and I was letting him know how confident I was that we were turning the corner on drag and how quickly we were approaching the cloud. Number 2 was shadowing us all the way through and had called back to MPA to prep them for a possible ejection. Like some cheap action movie, our aircraft stopped descending just as our belly kissed the cloud tops (yes, that is actually true), and we ever so slowly started climbing away.

A couple of minutes later, we had burned enough fuel to control the aeroplane with just dry power, and were able to turn back for MPA. I was relatively happy now, so cleared Number 2 off ahead of us to land and get the jet back on Q to replace ours. The Herc did the same, and we limped back to set up for a long straight in approach. I can't tell you how happy I was when the tyres met the tarmac.

Fatty and Bungle Hit Trouble

Timing was perfect in that we handed over Q and went into two days of stand down. Our first night was lost to us as we drank away the stress of the emergency. Late the next day, we took a drive into Stanley for a break, then it was back in time to take over Q again and continue the cycle. A couple of us had arranged for a memorial to Animal and Sansom. Lurch had kicked it off and arranged a large rock to be helicoptered in from a quarry by the Chinook flight, and Grim and I had sorted a plaque with the guy's names on it and 'larger than life' as the inscription. I think Animal's wife made the trip down to see the *Padre* dedicate it, and it still stands in front of the Q shed.

The next time we were up as airborne Q, we got vectored out to the south to check out some unknown shipping. We found a smallish vessel steaming through a part of the south Atlantic that was way too close to the Falklands for comfort. We buzzed it a couple of times, and Sly took some photos with the Q camera. We thought no more about it until later in the day when the intel officer brought the prints back. What few markings the ship had identified it as a Russian trawler, and by trawler, he meant a spy ship.

That was a first for both of us and another photo in my logbook. That evening, we were sharing Q with Sniper and his nav, Slug, when the phone rang. It was Bungle, who sounded a bit drunk and very cross and wanted to speak to Sniper. For fifteen minutes, we only heard one side of the conversation, which ended with Sniper calmly telling Bungle he understood and would sort it out tomorrow, and to just go to bed for now. With a big sigh, he put the phone down and told us the story.

Apparently, there had been a private dinner in the mess for the great and the good (squadron leaders and above, mostly blunties), and they had decamped to some sort of private bar a bit like the Goose. Bungle and Fatty had got wind of it and gone along to the after-party and had been there quite a while chatting to all and sundry. This kind of genteel gate-crashing went on all the time down south, and the Goose always seemed to be full of random people drinking free beer (free to them as the Phantom crews had paid for it).

Out of nowhere, wing commander something or other had snatched their drinks from them, opening up with 'who the hell are you?' and telling them to piss off. Bungle is a very proper individual and had been around a while, so he took umbrage to this approach. 'Who the hell am

I? Who the hell are you to talk to us like that?'—maybe not so proper when drunk, but Bungle didn't know this guy from Adam and was incensed by how he had been treated. The mistake he made was in not backing down when the guy replied, 'Wing Commander [insert random name of dickhead here]. I am OC FIADGE [Falkland Islands air defence ground environment].'

Bungle was still cross about the way he had been talked to and an argument ensued. To cut a long story short, they were thrown out of the party, called Sniper, and went to bed. We figured it would all blow over in the morning. We figured wrong. Sniper was summoned from Q and told to be in OC Ops's office with Bungle and Fatty. OC Ops was a wing commander Phantom nav that we all knew, so we were expecting he would smooth it over, especially as he had seen the whole thing first hand, including the initial challenge by OC FIADGE.

In the meantime, I got an extra flight with Slug while Sniper was indisposed so all good for me. When we got back down on the ground, all hell had broken loose. OC Ops had thrown our boys under the bus. They were banned from all of the public rooms in the mess and had to eat all their meals over on Q. The pettiness of it was astounding. It got even worse when OC Ops announced that Bungle and Fatty would be on the next Tristar home. So, we were down to a four-crew programme, which basically meant day on-day off Q.

Even More Trouble

Sniper had been torn a new arsehole too, but to his credit, he took it in his stride. He tried his best to protect the guys, but the wing commanders closed ranks and were busy sticking up for each other. OC FIADGE and OC Ops went straight to the top of our shit list and were ring-fenced there for the rest of the det. Throughout my career, I have always been amazed at how the wing commander rank had the ability to disconnect the weaker-willed individuals who got to that rank from the reality they are living in.

Within a couple of days, OC Ops was calling Sniper, demanding to go flying. Did he not realise we all hated him? None of the remaining pilots wanted to fly with him, so Sniper took him airborne himself. Good job I wasn't dicked to do the trip—I would have made the bastard puke his ring up, and then done it all over again and again.

Another outcome of this social faux pas was that the senior Blunties called for the Goose to be closed yet again. It was always those that never got invited that were the most vocal. Word came down from on high—Goose closed. We held a sort of wake for Bungle and Fatty the night before they left. We held it in the Goose, sod the consequences. They couldn't send all of QRA home. The only reason the RAF was down south was to support QRA in the first instance anyway. For a week afterwards, we boycotted the bar and just drank on our own in the Goose. I think the bar sales must have hit a cataclysmic low, but at least OC FIADGE and OC Ops had somewhere quiet to drink and pat themselves on the back that they had showed 1435 Flight who was the boss. I am sure OC FIADGE, wherever he is now, is still dining out on that one.

The next Tristar I escorted in had Horner and Lea on board plus the hastily formed replacement crew for Bungle and Fatty, so we were back to full strength on the programme. We had missed a stand-down period, but I was a QRA geek so was happy to keep going. Sly was the same and I think Sniper was grateful that we had all knuckled down and made it work with our siege mentality. The resident RN frigate was back on the scene, much closer to shore, so we spent a few days giving them more training with ship attacks. We would try and throw them all sorts of scenarios with coordinated pairs and singleton attacks from all angles and heights.

Their defensive manoeuvres were gobsmacking to watch. To see that amount of metal steep-turning so hard it was almost right over on its side was a sight to behold, and we loved working with them. They kept asking for supersonic flypasts, and we kept declining. I was duty auth up in the tower one day and watched Lola and Horner get airborne as normal. I had just been made up to authoriser status prior to this det, and it was a nice acknowledgement of my newfound experience and professionalism. It also meant Sly and I could share the auth duties.

About five minutes later, the two jets came back over the airfield in an outrageous fiery cross that had my phone ringing and OC Ops baying for their blood. I calmly told him that from my vantage point, both aircraft appeared to be above 250 feet and below 500 knots. He was not happy and it was obvious that relations had broken down so much that we were going to have to behave like nuns over the airfield. The knock-on effect was that the RAF regiment rapiers were not going to get any meaningful training.

I still wonder if OC Ops thinks he did a good job around that time. I mean, whenever he was a flight lieutenant deployed to the Falklands, was he trying to tell us he and his pilot never broke the low-flying rules or added a few knots to a flypast? The hypocrisy was off the charts. I thought no more about it and waited around until the pair were safely back on deck and shut down. I bid farewell to the ATC folks and went back to QRA for a cuppa. We were just shooting the shit on Q when Sniper came in with a piece of paper in his hand and asked Horner and Lola what their attacks on the boat had been like.

'Nothing out of the ordinary, Sir. Why do you ask?' Sniper held up the paper and said we had received a flash safety signal from the frigate, suggesting we check the underside of our jets, as the boat had lost a 40-feet whip aerial from the HF radio on the last flyover. The guys were adamant that they were nowhere near low enough to have hit anything, and Sniper believed them but said the jets were being checked anyway for belt and braces. The problem though was the signal itself.

Unfortunately, the captain of the frigate had sent the signal to a worldwide list of addressees, including the Admiralty. News travels fast, and Sniper had already been leant on by the great and the good in the RAF, and they wanted to know what the hell was going on with 1435 Flight. There was a bit more discussion about the trip, and another call from the UK came through for Sniper. Things took on a bit of a pace, starting with JENGO coming over and saying there was no damage or witness marks on either jet. Obviously, the aerial had come off in the jetwash of the flyover. They were not quite in the clear though.

Sniper walked back in, looking like every piece of shit in the western world had hit his fan. Whoever had called him had ripped him a new one (again) and ordered him to ground the two crews involved. We had only just got back to five crews for Q and were instantly slashed back to three. Sniper's next comment was not a surprise. 'Sorry, Tug, Sly. Looks like you are back on Q as of now'.

Command were going to send a pilot out from standards at Wattisham to run a unit inquiry investigation, but that would take a few days, so it looked like we were going to be on perma-Q for about a week before they would hopefully clear the guys to fly again. We were all bloody furious that some idiot on a boat had caused the grounding of two of our crews by not being selective with his distribution. The worst thing was that we didn't know if he was trying to be helpful getting us to check our jets and just made a mistake sending it to all and sundry, or he was just being a dick and did it on purpose. With Bungle and Fatty, and now this, we took the easy option and accepted that everybody outside 1435 had it in for us, so bugger them. We only had a week left on our det and barely made it back to the mess other than for a shower and the odd meal. We were the bad boys of MPA, and everyone knew what had happened. So, we scowled a lot and went back to Q.

Come On Down

Flying still continued and we got a lot more of it than we should have with the two grounded crews still in the shit. Then, my final trip of the det sent my irony reading right off the scale. The frigate had docked and was hosting a 'families' day' event for the more permanent personnel down south. People like OC FIADGE and OC Ops were stationed there for twelve months. The ship would take the families out for a few hours and host them with food and drink while giving a guided tour of the various sections of the boat and do some demonstrations.

Part of the festivities would be a flypast or two by 1435 Flight. As OC 1435, Sniper was invited on board, so I slotted into his cockpit and led the pair with Slug. I briefed up the sortie (our wingman was Will Phillips), but when we got to the part about the families' day, I said I wouldn't be going below 500 feet or above 350 knots. These flypasts would look pretty tame, but we were still in a bad mood with the captain of the frigate and didn't think his big event deserved our input. Also, if OC Ops was on board, why would we give him anything to bollock us about? Will agreed and Sniper knew what our plan was before he departed for the harbour. The last thing we were going to do was put on a show and get dobbed in again. It was the usual trip with intercepts and tanking, then it was time to head to the boat.

We switched frequency to the frigate's fighter controllers and checked in, asking for their latest weather conditions and a steer so we could find them. They already had contact on us as we were up around 10,000 feet, so gave us a vector in. It was all very professional until the idiot on the radio said, 'We're looking forwards to a great show from you so come on down!'

I was almost speechless. 'Did he really say that, Slug? After all the bloody trouble they have caused us?' Will and I floated over in close formation, took a lazy turn, and repeated it a couple of times. According to Sniper, the families on board 'oohed' and 'aahed' a bit, but all of the uniforms were a bit thin-lipped that we were just going through the motions and not doing anything remotely exciting. We changed things up a bit and split into two singletons for a couple of coordinated runs from different directions.

The radio came to life again with the controller asking if we could spice things up a bit to make it more exciting. I responded with a curt 'copied' and just continued with the plan. I felt as though we had made our point and called for the final run. I had briefed that the final run would be 250 feet and 500 knots to show the navy what they were missing and how good the demo could have been, and then we would bugger off home. I dropped us down and scorched over the boat, rocking the throttles into burner just as I pulled up. There was a huge bang on the left-hand side, and the turbine temperature went off the scale. Locked in surge, I pulled the throttle off and turned off the LP fuel cock. This was getting to be a bit too often for my liking.

Slug switched us back to MPA approach, and we warned them that we would need the approach end cable rigged once Number 2 was down. I told Will we were okay and he blasted back to get on the ground. My final Phantom trip in the Falklands ended with a graunch as the hook took the cable and we lurched forwards in our seats surrounded by the flashing lights of the fire trucks and the ambulance. Hours later, Sniper got back and told us what it looked like from the boat. The families thought we had saved the best for last. As the engine let go, there was a huge bang, and loads of sparks and flames shot out of the left jet pipe. As everyone cheered, thinking it was part of the show, Sniper just sighed and made his way quietly to the bridge to listen in to the radio gabble about the engine failure.

The Shortest Man in NATO

As we waited to board the Tristar home, I told Sly what a blast he had been, and even though this was my last time down south in a Phantom, I knew I was leaving, having cemented a friendship and partnership I would remember forever. I was almost sorry to go home. Then the movers called everyone forwards in alphabetical order and the moment turned to shit again. Returning from det always starts off a little strange with a feeling of disconnection, but it was good to catch up with everyone on the squadron again and especially the 'Laaahddss!'

I was on the last lap of my Phantom adventure, but there was still a lot to cram in, even in two months. The first event was a group bollocking from the station commander, who was incensed that his glorious career was being tainted by the bad behaviour of his aircrew. The two incidents down south (Bungle and Fatty being sent home in disgrace and the whip aerial incident that wasn't) were the final straws for him, so he ordered us all to the station briefing room for a collective telling-off.

Barry Smallcock had zero credibility with us, so not a single person from either squadron seemed to give a shit about the upcoming bollocking. 'Gentlemen! The station commander!' shouted the station warrant officer, and we all rose and snapped to attention. Then the shortest man in NATO bustled up to the front and turned to face us. We stayed at attention while he delivered the bolly, which meant most of us couldn't actually see him. There were a few sniggers as he took three attempts to pronounce the word 'disrepute' (to this day I still say 'distinsnute'), and I vaguely remember being told how unprofessional we all were, but little else.

Standard procedure during a bollocking is to tune out and stare at a piece of space 2 feet above the person's head, which in Barry's case was not very high at all. Punishments to Bungle and Fatty were mentioned for poor officer qualities, and they were dobbed to be SDO every night for a month each, and that should have been that. Had he stormed out there and then, it might have had some impact, but as before at the dining-in night in Wildenrath, he took the opportunity to deliver a state-of-the-nation brief. He told us these were exciting times as the UK government was in discussion with Greece to possibly sell some of our Phantoms to them—like we gave a damn! We weren't going to be flying them anymore so why should we care?

He lost us almost straight away, but insisted on talking for another twenty minutes before dismissing us. I drove past the Phantom graveyard on my way back to 56. Two cranes were destroying the jets in the most violent way possible—huge metallic grab hands crushing the cockpits and fuselages while angle grinders took off the wings and tailplanes. The Greeks needed to get their cash together sharpish, otherwise all they would be getting was a bag of scrap.

Did I Really See That?

That Friday was my final big booze-up on the Phantom. It was Wattisham's turn to host the East Anglian happy hour, and knowing this would be our last opportunity, it was going to be a big one. It began in a HAS at the squadron, where we had loads of chairs set out in front of a big briefing board. All told, there must have been 200 of the region's aircrew sitting there getting some serious speed on as we kept them beered up. Luke then got up in front of everyone and welcomed them to Wattisham's TDPU.

To make sure we got something useful out of the event, before just getting hammered, he wanted to give a short tactics brief. Everyone looked a little confused, but he explained that as fighters, we were able to deal with any enemy tactics that we were faced with—a bold challenge to all the bomber guys in the HAS. However, there was one tactic that we found impossible to handle, and he wanted to give all the bomber crews the secret.

Luke then proceeded to brief, while drawing out one of his brilliant cartoons, an amazingly funny tactic called 'whistling line astern'. I won't bore you with the premise, but it is enough to say it is the funniest brief I have ever seen, and he carried it off brilliantly. All of the Brit Tornado and Jag guys saw it for the spoof it was straight away and settled in to enjoy it. The American A10 drivers and F111 crews were not so sharp and were totally sucked in by what Luke was briefing. We sat back and enjoyed the show as they kept jumping up and shouting, 'This is bullshit!' It went on for a good fifteen minutes before they twigged what was going on.

For the last couple who still thought it was real, there was a big reveal at the end as Luke introduced three 'ladies' who started to dance on the makeshift stage out front. Their dancing ability was not the only thing somewhat lacking, but the Americans lapped it up. Did I really see that? Did that actually happen? Luckily, a few of us had some arrangements to take care of for the party in the mess, so made our excuses and left (to quote every dodgy reporter from the *News of the World*).

We were shoulder to shoulder in the bar for most of the night and things got a bit outrageous. Barry Smallcock and his hat were conspicuous by their welcome absence. Perhaps he had been warned off by the station commander at Coltishall? As always, the evening ended in flames. A few guys had bought properly engineered rockets that they set off. These things went all the way up to 2,000 feet or so and were pretty impressive. There was lots of cheering and singing outside in the dark.

Then came the *pièce de résistance*. On cue, from each end of the mess, an old car drew slowly into sight. Both cars had their roof chopped off and sitting on top was a piano, which was being played, and which were on fire. I know Harry was playing one of them, and looking back, I wonder if his parents envisaged this future for him when they paid for his piano lessons as a child? It looked spectacular and very funny. It certainly blew a bit of mess cannon action out of the water, even more so when the two cars crashed into each other in front of the mess.

Someone, somewhere, dumped a load of fireworks into each piano and we all stood back to watch as the cars caught fire too. A couple of minutes later, the pianos exploded in showers of pretty sparks. Again, did I really see that? Did that actually happen? It wasn't long until the fire section, who had been pre-warned, shooed us all back into the mess and put the big fire out. A couple of guys rode their motorbikes into the bar à *la* Animal House, and shortly afterwards, a load of very drunk aircrew piled into their buses and went home. I have never understood why the Russians didn't launch their big offensive on a Friday evening— they could have marched all over us!

In my last month on the jet, I seemed to fly a lot with all the navs I loved. The only one missing was Bungle, who was over on 74. We were supporting all sorts of exercises, so the trips were pretty big—8 *v*. 10s against lots of different types. In the middle of all that, Wattisham was tasked to provide a Diamond 16 formation over Buckingham Palace as part of a flypast for the queen's birthday, and AOC 11 Group came down to lead it himself.

The AOC was a popular guy (for once) and an experienced Phantom driver who kept current on type. Luke and I took part in the first practice leading the airborne spares. Neither of us were available for the flypast itself so would just slot in to any position during the practice if someone broke. The station commander introduced the AOC at the start of the brief and then handed over. The AOC gave a good brief, but then someone asked what the breakout plan was just in case another aeroplane came close aboard the formation. 'Well really, it's every man for himself,' the AOC said with a shrug. Now we all knew roughly what he meant, but it came across as a bit gash.

There was a fair amount of consternation in the crowd, but Smallcock leapt up and blustered about how they would come up with a plan and get back to us. He had planned it all out for the AOC and had forgotten to include the breakout plan so had unwittingly embarrassed the AOC—career going down in flames, Sir? As no one went unserviceable during the trip, Luke and I had a very pleasant time floating around the Suffolk countryside watching a beautiful Diamond 16 made up of the best jet in the world. It was made even better by knowing that all sixteen pilots were sweating and hyperventilating while being told by the Whip to 'move forwards 2 feet'.

Last Trip

On 1 May 1992, it finally arrived—my last F4 trip. I was leading an eight-ship and was escorting a load of Tornado GR1s on some sort of attack mission on exercise. What made the trip extra special was the fact that I was flying with Bobby—one of the first navs I had flown with on the front-line was sharing the important and emotional event of my final flight on the Phantom. It's an odd thing, but I barely remember the trip. Despite it being a big mission, it was so automatic operating with Bobby that there was nothing out of the ordinary to report. I could not have felt more comfortable, in stark contrast to my first Phantom trip exactly three years and one month before. Flying with one of my best mates made it a little less upsetting that I wouldn't get to rage around in my mean looking jet again.

It was cool bringing the eight-ship back to Wattisham, and we broke into the circuit as two four-ships. I overshot on finals to let the other seven land and then scooted out to initials. We blasted back into the circuit in afterburner, very fast and not very high, and I broke us over the HAS site as everyone was taxiing back in. Then it was all professional again as Bobby called out the pre-landers and I set up for finals. I like to think the old rusty girl knew it was our last date together and she put herself right on the doughnut for my final finals. I was hoping the chute would fail so we would have to bolt airborne again, but it didn't, and with a heavy heart, I put the brakes on. That was that.

It was a chilly and grey day, but once the pins were in, we popped the canopies up to taxi in (of course we did). All of the guys from the mission were waiting by our HAS, and as we came around the apron in front of the shelter, the fire engine nosed into sight. This was my own personal fire engine. The one that would completely soak me as it was my last trip. I shut down and climbed down the ladder, knowing I would never climb it again. I thanked Bobby with a hug for sharing my last trip.

The Boss shook my hand and handed over a glass of champagne, and we had our photo taken by the station photographer. To this day, that photo is one of my most prized possessions. The Boss was an exceptionally cool and laid-back man and had my complete respect both as an aviator and a human being. Almost ten years on from that handshake, I would work for him again, and even though he would be an air commodore at that point, he would still be that mellow and friendly character that was squeezing my hand and wishing me luck. All too soon, the toast was over and I was sent on my lonely walk to the centre of the apron.

Gallons of high-pressure water hit me all over as I was doused by the fire engine. Luke and Slug then struck on the idea of putting a small hose inside the neck seal of my immersion suit and began to fill me with ice-cold water. The cold was bad enough, but after a minute or so, I was carrying an extra few stones of water and could barely lift my feet to walk. All I could do was lie down and unzip my immersion suit to let the water drain out. I shivered all the way back to the mess, where I had a long, hot shower and changed into fresh flying kit for my final night in a front-line fighter bar for who knew how long? I have no idea what happened that night, but at a guess, I got drunk, sang some songs, fell over, and was put to bed—pretty standard really.

The End

So, my Phantom odyssey was finally at an end. The jet would continue without me, but only for a few months before it lay down and called it a day. It would be trite to say I joined the Phantom as a boy and left it as a man, but if you looked at my growth as an aviator, then it is not too far from the truth. The aeroplane gave me such confidence in myself that it changed me forever. I am the man I am today because of the Phantom. Time and again, I have said how much I loved the Phantom and flying it.

Looking back, I know that I was actually in love with it and I miss it so much even to this day that it aches inside of me. Together, we achieved a lifetime's worth of experiences in just a little over three years—first time supersonic; first use of afterburner; first time being responsible for someone else's life in the cockpit; first time tanking (ouch); shooting

F14s, F15s, F16s, and F18s; gunning MiG-29s; Battle Flight and QRA scrambles; leading eight- and sixteen-ships; Diamond 9 and 16 flypasts; engine failures; and the beautiful blue jet.

It also gave me pure life experiences on top of that. It tried to kill me; took me to the Falklands, Cyprus, Deci, and Iceland; gave me my op badges; inducted me into the fighter brotherhood; made me believe in myself; gave me some of the most outrageous nights in the bar and on det; gave me my best friends; and took some of them away. Then, my glorious, wonderful Phantom was taken away from me by a changing world, and a disinterested government that had never flown it and could never see the unmatched beautiful ugliness that only its pilot or nav could love. So, when the end came and it rolled over and breathed its last in a filthy damp graveyard, it truly broke my heart.

All told, I amassed just under 700 hours on the Phantom. I was desperate for another year that might well have taken me to the coveted 1,000-hour badge, but alas no. However, I treasure every minute of those 700 hours (even the shitty trips on the OCU). Every minute was spent in the company of high-quality people with the same fighter squadron mentality.

Of course, some navs and pilots stand out more than others due to the frequency of flying with them and the shared experiences. Those few, in my case, helped to make me who I am today, and for that, I will always be eternally grateful to Bouncer, Jimbo, Grim, Sly, Bungle, and Bobby— they are all friends for life.

Each year, on the Friday before Remembrance Sunday, Spencer organises a Phantom reunion in a pub just off Trafalgar Square in London. Somewhere in the region of 200 people turn up, and we reminisce while getting drunk and pretending we are still young fighter squadron legends. I catch up with lots of old friends and colleagues, and we tell each other the same stories every year. It is our mutual love for the Phantom, and for each other, that keeps bringing us back. It does my soul good.

Also by TUG WILSON

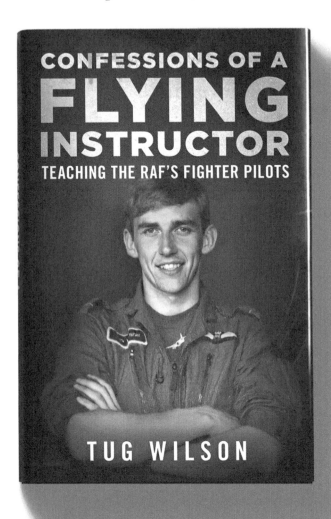

CONFESSIONS OF A FLYING INSTRUCTOR
TEACHING THE RAF'S FIGHTER PILOTS